Decoding the
U.S. Corporate Tax

Also of interest from the Urban Institute Press:

Contemporary U.S. Tax Policy, second edition, by C. Eugene Steuerle

War and Taxes, by Steven A. Bank, Kirk J. Stark, and Joseph J. Thorndike

Encyclopedia of Taxation and Tax Policy, edited by Joseph J. Cordes, Robert D. Ebel, and Jane G. Gravelle

Tax Justice: The Ongoing Debate, edited by Joseph J. Thorndike and Dennis J. Ventry Jr.

Decoding the U.S. Corporate Tax

Daniel N. Shaviro

THE URBAN INSTITUTE PRESS
WASHINGTON, DC

THE URBAN INSTITUTE PRESS
2100 M Street, N.W.
Washington, D.C. 20037

Library of Congress Cataloging-in-Publication Data

Shaviro, Daniel N.
  Decoding the U.S. corporate tax / Daniel N. Shaviro.
    p. cm.
  Includes bibliographical references and index.
  ISBN 978-0-87766-757-5
  1. Corporations—Taxation—Law and legislation—United States. I. Title. II. Title: Decoding the US corporate tax. III. Title: Decoding the United States corporate tax.
  KF6455.S53 2008
  336.2'070973—dc22

                                                                              2008051686

Printed in the United States of America

11 10 09   1 2 3 4 5

THE URBAN INSTITUTE is a nonprofit, nonpartisan policy research and educational organization established in Washington, D.C., in 1968. Its staff investigates the social, economic, and governance problems confronting the nation and evaluates the public and private means to alleviate them. The Institute disseminates its research findings through publications, its web site, the media, seminars, and forums.

Through work that ranges from broad conceptual studies to administrative and technical assistance, Institute researchers contribute to the stock of knowledge available to guide decisionmaking in the public interest.

Conclusions or opinions expressed in Institute publications are those of the authors and do not necessarily reflect the views of officers or trustees of the Institute, advisory groups, or any organizations that provide financial support to the Institute.

To my late father,
Sol Shaviro,
one of the kindest individuals
I have ever known.

Contents

Acknowledgments

I am grateful to Yoram Margalioth and two anonymous reviewers for their comments on an early draft of the manuscript.

Introduction

As Mark Twain once said, people always talk about the weather, but they never do anything about it. Among policymakers and experts on taxation, the same has frequently been true of corporate taxation. The U.S. corporate tax has been around since 1909—longer than the current individual income tax—and continues to be an important institution, raising well over $300 billion per year. Continually studied by lawyers and economists alike, and frequently singled out as urgently needing reform or even abolition, it has nonetheless trundled along through the decades, only rarely changing significantly.

But just as human activity may finally be affecting the weather in an era of global warming, so the corporate tax could soon be headed in new directions. Here the main precipitating forces, in lieu of rising carbon dioxide levels, are globalization and rising worldwide capital mobility, along with financial innovation in designing the instruments that are traded in capital markets. These trends have the potential to transform such fundamental elements in the functioning of the corporate tax as how much revenue it raises, whom it burdens, and to what extent it burdens anyone at all. They therefore do not merely invite, but may end up necessitating, a major rethinking of how (and if) the U.S. corporate tax operates.

Even if something needs to be done, however, just what should be done remains keenly disputed. As much as the corporate tax has been studied, in many respects both experts and the public still poorly understand how it truly operates on the ground.

The following observations illustrate the public and expert confusion and dissensus, along with the political pressures that may make corporate tax law changes hard to avoid:

(1) Corporate integration, a tax reform idea that would eliminate the existing double tax on corporate income at both the entity and shareholder levels, is widely supported by academics across the ideological spectrum. Yet it has so little public support that President George W. Bush, at his political high-water mark in 2003, working with a generally complaisant Republican Congress, could not get it fully enacted. Not only did Congress merely reduce, not eliminate, the shareholder-level tax on dividends received, but it provided that this tax reduction for shareholders would expire after 2010, potentially bringing the old system back in full force, and in the interim creating substantial uncertainty among investors and corporate actors regarding what to expect in 2011 and beyond.

(2) The scheduled 2011 "sunset" of the rate cut for dividends guarantees continued active political consideration in Congress of what the corporate tax regime should look like. However, political equipoise is unlikely to be reached any time soon, even if the rate cut is either extended or allowed to expire. Republicans tend to be committed to some form of permanent corporate tax relief (relative to the full double tax), while Democrats tend to oppose it, and neither side appears interested in reaching a stable compromise. Thus, continued instability seems highly likely even once the sunset problem is resolved.

(3) There has recently been movement on both sides of the aisle in Congress to lower U.S. corporate tax rates, and thus to make them significantly lower than the top individual tax rate. Corporate tax rates have generally been declining across the world, reflecting international tax competition that the United States may increasingly have to heed. Top individual rates face considerably less competitive pressure, so long as wealthy people are reluctant to leave the United States just for tax reasons. However, a large gap between corporate and individual rates is a potential tax-planning bonanza for taxpayers who can shift their income into a corporate entity and avoid the second level of tax. It also raises serious questions about fitting a lower corporate rate into

an overall system that may still be intended to distribute tax burdens progressively.

(4) Proponents of double taxation of corporate income and tougher corporate tax enforcement often think of the corporate tax system as a way of increasing the tax system's progressivity by burdening shareholders (or investors generally) that are relatively wealthy. Those on the other side of political debates concerning the corporate tax often appear to agree that it does this, and to merely have a different policy preference regarding whether progressivity is good or bad. However, there are serious and unresolved empirical questions about how the corporate tax affects progressivity. Increased worldwide capital mobility suggests that workers, rather than investors, may principally bear the burden of the corporate tax, but this remains empirically uncertain (although supported by several recent studies).

(5) When not focused on progressivity, political arguments about the corporate tax often center on the question of how tax burdens should be divided between the individual and corporate sectors. On its face, this is nonsense (unless it is shorthand for something else, such as progressivity or different sectors of the economy), given that only flesh and blood individuals, as opposed to legal entities that exist only on paper, can actually bear tax burdens. The main reason why, at least at present, the United States actually needs a corporate-level tax has nothing directly to do either with progressivity or with the proper division of burdens between the supposed individual and corporate sectors. Rather, it is because the U.S. system employs an income tax, rather than a consumption tax. The former involves taxing savings (most conveniently, on a current basis), whereas the latter waits until people actually spend the money they have earned. Thus, in an income-tax environment, failing to impose taxes at the corporate level would turn all corporations (as defined for tax purposes) into special tax-free savings accounts. In a consumption-tax environment, by contrast, we could simply wait for corporate earnings to be withdrawn by investors and consumed, without effectively turning corporations into tax shelters.

(6) Economists seeking to model the corporate tax, so that they can understand its distributional or other effects, face the challenge that it offers them an ill-posed problem. What the corporate tax system actually does is unclear, since its true content depends on how a set of highly formalistic line-drawing exercises—for

example, defining corporate versus noncorporate entities for tax purposes, or distinguishing between debt and equity—end up being resolved in practice. I call the various legal distinctions on which corporate taxation is built "pillars of sand," because they continually threaten to crumble unless reinforced.

A common solution to the economists' modeling problem is to make a simplifying assumption that everyone knows is not entirely true. An example would be assuming either (1) that the debt and equity labels for financial instruments are purely elective without regard to investors' actual economic relationships, or (2) that the labels embody a clean binary division between two radically different flavors with distinct constituencies, like chocolate and vanilla ice cream. Neither assumption is entirely true, but which one the models adopt as the superior proxy for the truth can radically affect conclusions. For example, if the debt-equity choice is purely elective, the perceived double tax problem can flip over into a concern about whether the corporate tax unduly benefits, rather than unduly burdens, the choice to do business through a corporate entity.

(7) Actual corporate behavior is not well understood. So simple a question as why companies pay dividends, rather than retain the funds or repurchase shares of their own stock, continues to be hard to answer. And much observed managerial behavior, such as the obsession with boosting reported financial earnings even if investors can still get the bad news by reading the financial reports' footnotes, is difficult to square with the assumptions of rational behavior and market efficiency that often are so powerful in economic analysis.

(8) Business interests argue, with increasing support from recent economic research, that globalization makes it ever more important, as a matter of U.S. national welfare, to increase U.S. multinational firms' competitiveness in overseas markets. But advocates disagree about whether U.S. national self-interest is better served by making sure that these firms, when considering outbound investment, face tax rates that are (1) no higher than those of their foreign competitors, or (2) no lower than those that they would face upon investing at home. One cannot do both at the same time when countries' tax rates differ.

*   *   *   *   *

Against this background of complexity and confusion, this book has the following aims. First, it lays out the main policy issues raised by the corporate tax and shows how their analysis is affected by adopting different assumptions about the underlying mysteries concerning what the system really is and does. As we will see, while virtually no reasonable assumptions could lead to the conclusion that the current system actually makes sense, it is hard to say which of its distortionary rules most needs addressing. The harm caused by double taxation, for example, might be either great or small, depending on which assumptions one adopts about how the tax operates. In the international realm, while there is widespread consensus that the current rules for taxing U.S. multinationals on their outbound investment are extremely inefficient, the contours of an optimal regime (even among politically feasible alternatives) remain disputed due to the lack of a properly comprehensive framework for analyzing the issues.

Second, this book considers where corporate taxation is headed given three important trends. The first of these is ongoing financial innovation, which makes the system's building blocks, such as the debt-equity distinction, ever more fragile and manipulable. The second trend is rising worldwide capital mobility. The third trend is rising political instability in U.S. tax policy, resulting from the sharp partisan divide and from long-term budgetary shortfalls that will eventually require significant tax increases. Expectations about future tax policy turn out to be very important in shaping the incentive effects of corporate taxation today.

Finally, this book analyzes the implications of the underlying analysis and trends for corporate tax reform. In particular, it argues that corporate integration may not be worth doing, unless, contrary to the design choice in the 2003 Bush administration effort, the distinction between debt and equity is eliminated. Keeping the distinction would increasingly permit investors, as predicted 30 years ago by economist Merton Miller, to effectively elect to pay tax either at the corporate rate (by holding equity) or at their own individual rates (by holding debt), whichever is lower. With substantial tax-exempt players from around the world participating in the marketplace, taxing U.S. corporate income even once may increasingly become problematic unless this effective election is eliminated by treating debt and equity the same.

Given the difficulty of proper corporate integration and the risk that it would fail to become a stable regime, this book argues that corporate tax-reform efforts might fruitfully emphasize taking other directions. Three possibilities in particular are (1) lowering the U.S. corporate tax rate for reasons of international competitiveness, (2) radically simplifying the U.S. international tax rules without greatly changing the level of taxation, and (3) addressing corporate executives' well-known proclivity for simultaneously understating corporate income to the Internal Revenue Service in their tax returns and overstating it to investors in published financial statements.

The remainder of this book proceeds as follows. Part one, "Basics," reviews what the corporate tax is, why each of its key elements exists, and what economic distortions these elements, working in tandem, create. Part two, "Economic Theory Meets the Corporate Tax," reviews several dueling pairs of economic models that support radically divergent views of how the corporate tax affects the creation and distribution of national economic wealth. Part three explores the international dimension in U.S. corporate tax policy which, if anything, involves greater disagreement and confusion than the domestic dimension. Finally, part four, "Where Is the Corporate Tax Headed?" examines possible directions for legal change. It starts by examining leading approaches to corporate integration and their desirability given underlying economic and political trends and the pillars of sand. It then turns to the alternative reform directions described above, and concludes by asking what is likely to happen—a question that depends as much on whether the U.S. political system can still function effectively, in an era of pervasive partisanship and sound-bite-driven policymaking, as it does on anything lying within the current parameters of the corporate tax.

PART I
Basics

There is no Platonic ideal of the corporate tax. If there were, it might have a discernible abstract core of meaning and content, like that one might associate with such Platonic concepts as a triangle, the color red, or a dog. Many tax concepts, such as income, have this sort of character. But the corporate tax is different. Rather than having a coherent core, it resembles a ramshackle mansion erected by multiple builders whose work was crudely joined together once the pieces were almost complete. And this turns out to have crucial effects on how, and how well, the corporate tax functions.

Before analyzing the corporate tax, we need to review its basic features and rationales. To this end, chapter 1 examines why we have all the components that, taken together, comprise the present U.S. corporate tax. Chapter 2 then examines the main economic distortions that result from the individual and combined operations of these parts, while chapter 3 examines the "pillars of sand" that make its structure so manipulable and hard to understand.

1

Why Have a Corporate Tax?

Before asking why we have a corporate tax, one must define what the corporate tax is. The term can be defined narrowly or broadly. On the narrow side of the spectrum, it might mean only the tax levied directly on corporations. Broadening the definition a bit, it might additionally refer to the taxation of those owning financial interests in corporations, such as stock or debt. One can further expand the term to include anything distinctive in the tax treatment of anyone engaged in transactions with corporations—for example, corporate employees who receive compensation.

Only the broadest definition does justice to the tax system's impact on people and activities in or near the corporate sector of the economy. Look at one piece without the others, and it is easy to draw myopic and inaccurate conclusions about the overall landscape. At the same time, however, each separate piece has its own particular logic. This chapter, therefore, first describes the overall system, then addresses the rationales for the different components, and finally addresses the rationales for how the components presently interact with each other to create at least theoretical double taxation of corporate income.

The Components of the U.S. Corporate Tax System

Corporations, as defined for U.S. federal income-tax purposes, are legal entities that either (1) are literally incorporated under the law of a U.S. state (or under any foreign equivalent of U.S. corporate law), (2) have ownership interests that are publicly traded,[1] or (3) in certain circumstances elect to be classified as corporations. Thus defined, corporations are subject to U.S. taxation if they either are classified as U.S. residents or have U.S.-source income (two concepts discussed in chapter 7). U.S. entities meeting the tax definition of a corporation often are called C corporations, because many of the special rules applying to them are in subchapter C of the Internal Revenue Code.[2]

The tax rate on U.S. corporations starts low (15 percent on the first $50,000 of annual income and 25 percent on the next $25,000) but then rises to 34 percent and finally peaks (for income above $10 million) at 35 percent. While the tax rates for individuals escalate at much lower income levels than they do for corporations, 35 percent is also the top rate for individuals, under law that is currently scheduled to remain on the books through 2010. After 2010, when tax cuts enacted during the presidency of George W. Bush will expire unless Congress passes a new law extending them, the top rate for individuals is scheduled to revert to its pre-2001 level of 39.6 percent.

Historically, the top marginal tax rate for corporations has usually been below that for individuals, and at times substantially below. This informally adjusts for the fact that corporate income may end up being taxed a second time when it is distributed to shareholders (as discussed below). A further tax disadvantage of incorporating a business, however, is that if the corporation has losses, its owners will not be able to deduct them against their other income, as might otherwise have been possible. Moreover, even if C corporation status is tax advantageous in the current year, its long-term desirability depends on the subsequent tax treatment of the company's owners.

Before turning to the owner level, several further aspects of the corporate-level tax are worth describing briefly. For the most part, corporations and individuals use the same or similar rules in computing taxable income and tax liability. The aforementioned subchapter C, however, contains a host of special rules related to the corporate "life cycle"—that is, incorporation, various corporate acquisitions of new assets or other companies, asset distributions to shareholders, and liquidation.

Often, these rules permit the avoidance of current tax consequences, even when assets are changing hands in what the system might otherwise deem a taxable sale or exchange, so long as assets are moving into corporate solution from the noncorporate world, or else are moving around sufficiently innocuously within corporate solution, as in certain cases where one corporation acquires or disgorges another. When assets move out of corporate solution, however, there typically is a tax of some kind on the recipients, and possibly on the corporation as well. Subchapter C is so complicated that it takes up many well-paid tax lawyers' entire careers, and makes it a rule of ordinary prudence that no major corporate deal should ever take place without tax lawyers sitting in the room.

This brings us to the tax treatment of payments by a corporation to the holders of financial claims against it, such as a right to repayment of cash advances or to a share of corporate profits. Although many different instruments that create financial claims against a corporation have their own distinctive rules—for example, options and notional principal contracts—a fundamental tax divide exists between instruments classified as debt and those classified as equity.

Debt (or a bond) is conceptualized as creating an arm's-length relationship between the corporation and a third-party provider of capital (the bondholder or lender) that requires compensation. Consistent with this view, interest on debt is generally deductible by the corporation (subject to various interest disallowance rules that respond to suspected tax-planning opportunities) in addition to being generally includable in income by the recipient.

By contrast, equity (or stock) is conceptualized as giving the holder an inside or ownership interest in the corporation, rather than the interest of a third party that is negotiated at arm's length. Accordingly, dividend payments to the shareholder are thought of as something that the corporation "wants" to do, rather than as an outlay demanded by a third-party provider of capital. Dividend payments accordingly have always been nondeductible. From the standpoint of the shareholder, however, they are deemed income, suggesting that they should be taxable.

If dividends are nondeductible but includable and earnings are distributed to shareholders, equity-financed corporate income ends up being doubly taxed. Thus, suppose that both the corporate and shareholder rates (including for dividends received) are 35 percent. A corporation that earns $100 will retain $65 after tax. Once this money is distributed to shareholders as a dividend, the shareholder will retain only $42.25 after tax. By contrast, the shareholder could have kept $65 after tax by either (1) not doing business through a corporate entity or (2) using debt financing, thus permitting the corporation to distribute $100 as deductible interest and eliminate the corporate-level liability.

Concern about the double tax has, at times, prompted exceptions to treating dividends as fully taxable income. Thus, upon the 1913 inception of the modern U.S. federal income tax, dividends were exempted from the normal 1 percent tax on individuals, although subject to a progressive surtax that reached 6 percent. Since the corporate rate, like the normal individual rate, was 1 percent, this guaranteed that corporate income would in effect be taxed only once (at the normal-plus-surtax rate that applied to noncorporate income). This approach basically remained in place until true double taxation was implemented in 1936 (Bank 2003, 489–516).

Double taxation was significantly scaled back in 2003, when dividends were made taxable at no more than 15 percent, rather than at the full individual rate. Under the original Bush administration version of this rule, dividends would have been entirely exempted from individual-level taxation, so long as the underlying earnings had been fully taxed at the corporate level. Congress eliminated any such requirement from the final legislation, in addition to merely lowering the dividend rate rather than exempting dividends.

When one corporation holds stock in another corporation, taxation of the intercorporate dividends can lead to three, rather than two, levels of tax. In practice, multiple taxation of tiered corporate structures is alleviated by dividends-received deductions for shareholders that are corporations. However, the deduction is less than 100 percent unless the shareholder corporation owns (including through affiliates) at least 80 percent of the stock of the dividend-paying corporation. Thus, with bad planning, multiple levels of taxation can indeed accumulate as earnings make their way up the corporate-ownership chain.

One last important tax difference between debt and equity is that annual interest payments on the former are effectively presumed, for tax purposes, whether or not they actually are made. Thus, suppose you pay $100 for a corporate bond that will lead to your being paid $121 upon its maturity in two years, but nothing before that time. This implies an interest rate of 10 percent, with interest accruing (though unpaid) in the amount of $10 in the first year and $11 in the second. Under the original issue discount (OID) rules, both you and the corporate issuer must annually take these interest accruals into account, giving the issuer deductions and you inclusions, even before anything is actually paid. Annual interest accrual for tax purposes is therefore involuntary.

Dividends, by contrast, are not taken into account for tax purposes until they are actually declared and paid. This means that the second level of tax on equity income is at least formally voluntary. Avoid ever paying dividends, and you never face the second level of tax. There is, however, a penalty tax, called the accumulated earnings tax, on companies that keep such earnings on hand and use them to fund an investment portfolio, rather than distributing them or using them in a business, with the forbidden purpose of avoiding the shareholder-level tax.

Shareholder-level taxation can arise even without any corporate distributions to shareholders, through the application of capital gains taxation to sales of stock. Thus, suppose I invest $100 in a new corporation that earns a further $100, reduced to $65 by a 35 percent corporate tax. If I now sell my stock for $165 (the money I put in plus the after-tax profit), I have $65 of capital gains (the excess of the amount realized over my $100 cost basis).[3] Thus, I effectively face a second, shareholder-level tax even though no dividends have been paid out. At present, the top U.S. long-term capital gains rate, like the dividend rate, is only 15 percent, but taxpayers may face both of these taxes if a shareholder sells her stock for a gain and then the replacement shareholder receives a dividend.

A little patience can eliminate the capital gains tax as well, however. Under U.S. tax law, when you die and leave property to your heirs, they generally inherit it with a basis equal to its fair market value at the time of the bequest, even if this exceeds the decedent's cost basis (i.e., the amount he originally paid for the stock). Thus, if the stock value simply remained at $165, my children, after inheriting the stock, would be able to sell it for that price without paying any tax on the built-in gain.

The treatment of stock sales as capital gains has important implications for corporation distributions. If you sell your stock back to the issuing corporation, the result is a capital gain, no less than when you sell it to a true third party. The ability thus to effectively distribute corporate earnings via share repurchases or redemptions, rather than via dividends, was especially beneficial in the years before 2003, when the tax rate on dividends often was much higher than that on capital gains. Even today, however, the share repurchase route can be appealing because capital gain is measured as merely the excess of the amount realized over your basis for the surrendered stock, whereas a dividend distribution is taxable in full.

Thus, suppose a corporation has two shareholders, each owning 10 shares of stock with a cost basis of $10 each. If the corporation gives each shareholder a $15 dividend distribution, then each has $15 of dividend income. By contrast, if the corporation buys 1 share of stock from each shareholder for $15—assuming for the moment (counterfactually) that the form of the transaction as a share repurchase is respected—then each shareholder has capital gains income of only $5 (the excess of the $15 amount realized over the shares' $10 cost basis).

While the U.S. corporate tax system accepts that share repurchases are distinct from dividends, it does not automatically accept the taxpayer's characterization of a given transaction. Even if a taxpayer uses the form of a share repurchase, it will be taxed as a dividend unless it meets any one of four specific statutory tests contained in section 302 of the U.S. Internal Revenue Code. These tests examine the degree of proportionality of the overall share repurchase, and thus whether it has sufficiently changed the shareholders' proportionate interests to be treated as a "true" repurchase. In the above example, where both shareholders surrendered 1 out of 10 shares for $15, the tax-planning scheme would fail and they would be treated as having received a $15 dividend. By contrast, if one of them sold 2 shares for $30 while the other sold none, changing the ratio of outstanding shares to 10-8, they would likely avoid dividend treatment.

While a transaction formally constituting a share repurchase is taxed as a dividend if it is overly symmetric as between the tendering shareholders, there also is a circumstance in which what looks like a dividend is treated like a share repurchase. Dividends are only taxed as such if they are deemed to be made out of the corporation's earnings and profits (henceforth, its "E & P"). Otherwise they are treated as a return of capital, reducing the shareholder's basis in the stock and creating capital gain once the basis has been reduced to zero.

The basic idea here can be explained intuitively as follows. Suppose that on day one you establish a new corporation by paying $100 for all its stock. On day two, before the company actually does anything, you decide that it really only needs $80 to fulfill its business plan. So you take $20 back. Conceptually, this might best be thought of as a mere return of some of the capital you invested, rather than as an extraction of corporate profits (which do not yet exist), and thus it is treated simply as reducing your stock basis to $80, rather than as a taxable dividend.

In practice, however, the E & P prerequisite for dividend treatment is usually unimportant, at least with respect to large, publicly traded corporations. These entities have been around for long enough, and have generated sufficient E & P over the years, that they are unlikely to run out any time soon. And as long as the company has any remaining E & P, whether historical since the U.S. federal income tax was created in 1913 or arising in the current taxable year, distributions to shareholders (including through overly symmetric share repurchases) are treated as made out of it, and thus considered dividends.

A further distinctive element of corporate taxation concerns the payment of compensation to employees, in particular those who are also major shareholders or high-ranking executives. Owner-employees, if they want to take money out of the company, may be eager to claim that a distribution is salary rather than a dividend, so that the company can deduct it.[4] For this reason, only "reasonable compensation" can be deducted as such by the corporation, and any "unreasonable" excess received by a shareholder-employee may be treated as a dividend.

However, there is no generally enforced symmetric rule addressing "unreasonable" underpayment of compensation by C corporations. Thus, suppose you charge your wholly owned C corporation nothing for your highly valuable services. This might be good tax planning if you have a higher marginal tax rate than the corporation does, since then your tax on the inclusion would exceed its tax saving on the deduction. Tax law sometimes imputes transactions that one infers "really" occurred even though they have not been observed. In this case, the imputed transaction might involve the deemed payment of an arm's-length salary followed by its reinvestment in the company as a fresh contribution to capital. But this generally is not done, helping to make corporate taxation potentially beneficial to people whose tax rates exceed the applicable corporate rate.[5]

Another special executive compensation rule of note applies to high-ranking corporate executives in publicly traded corporations. Since the early 1990s, when stories about the immense salaries being paid to U.S. corporate executives first began to attract widespread attention, publicly traded companies' deductions for salary paid to a top executive have been limited to $1 million per year. In effect, the shareholders are punished, through an increase in the company's tax bill, in response to the apparent fear that the chief executive is taking advantage of them by arranging to be paid too much. However, the deduction limit does not apply to performance-based compensation, such as where the executive's salary depends on reported earnings or the stock price. The million-dollar limit is therefore widely regarded as absurdly easy to circumvent.

Moreover, its enactment apparently prompted some companies to increase executives' cash salaries to $1 million, on the view that this was now the established benchmark level, and to make greater use of stock options that arguably contributed to the corporate governance scandals of the Enron era.

Why Levy a Tax on Corporations?

A corporation is simultaneously two distinct things. The first is a legal entity, recognized in the law as a separate juridical person from its owners for various purposes. A given corporation may actually be hard for any owner to control as fully as her own personal business affairs, given that control may at least formally be vested in a board of directors (and through it, corporate officers) whom the owners only periodically get to select through the exercise of voting rights. Second, a corporation is also properly viewed as a mere aggregate of its owners, whose creature it entirely is.

The Entity and Aggregate Views

From a certain point of view, only the aggregate really exists. Legal person or not, a corporation cannot itself (like actual people) have feelings such as pleasure or pain, and can only act or decide through human agents such as employees or owners. Yet its legal character as a separate entity may have practical importance, including the possible creation of a state of affairs in which it, like various other social institutions, has a kind of internal character and arc of continuously unfolding historical development that no individual can easily alter. Thus, viewing corporations' separate-entity status as meaningful, and as indicating that they often are more than just aggregates, is not entirely a fallacy or myth unless interpreted to support a false conclusion, such as that a corporation can itself bear the burden of a tax, which would require the capacity for feeling pleasure and pain.

In the daily workings of the corporate tax, both entity and aggregate views are deployed in different contexts, depending on which seems locally more convenient. For example, the tax on shareholder dividends applies an entity view, since shareholders would not be freshly taxed on simply withdrawing cash from their own bank accounts. But testing share repurchases for disproportionality reflects an aggregate view, by showing a realistic appreciation of the importance of who owns what percentage of the company.

As it happens, when the modern U.S. corporate income tax was first adopted in 1909—initially as an excise tax on the privilege of doing business as a corporation, since federal income taxation would be unconstitutional until 1913—both the entity view and the aggregate view appear to have influenced the enactment decision (Avi-Yonah 2004), although the latter apparently more so. That is, more of the motivation seems to have been to tax shareholders indirectly on their shares of corporate income, given that they could not yet be taxed directly, than to create a new regulatory lever in response to the rise in preceding decades of huge corporations as powerful social and economic actors (Bank 2007). To this day, both entity and aggregate views continue to underlie important reasons—some persuasive and others spurious—for retaining a corporate-level tax.

Entity-Based Reasons for a Corporate-Level Tax

Levying a tax at the corporate level is so logical administratively that in any reasonable, generally applicable tax system, it would at least be seriously considered. Income taxation inevitably is based mainly on observable economic transactions, such as sales of goods and services. Against this background, it is hard to keep from noticing corporations' prominent role in both interbusiness and consumer transactions. Corporations regularly handle large cash flows, have internal recordkeeping systems, and are accustomed to dealing with government authorities. As Richard Bird (1996, 10) notes, the rationale that bank robber Willie Sutton offered for robbing banks—"because that's where the money is"—clearly applies to corporations. So it is natural (if not entirely inevitable) that they should be large players in the mechanics of operating a tax system. They are regularly made taxpayers not only in income-tax systems like that in the United States, but in value-added, sales, and property taxes around the world.

Administrative convenience is not necessarily the only reason for levying tax at the corporate entity level, however. Two further reasons, one logical and one fallacious though widespread, indicate doing so as well. The logical reason relates to the well-known separation of ownership and control in many large corporations (Berle and Means 1932). If corporate managers have considerable autonomy to do what they like with assets that are in corporate solution, and can avoid close scrutiny and control by the shareholders, then it may make sense to levy a tax at the level that they control. For example, if one wants to influence business behavior through the tax system, it may be vital to influence the actual actors, even if they are ostensibly just stewards for someone else.

Second, but spuriously, when we see prominent corporations doing lots of important things (albeit through human agents), it is natural to start personifying them, and to imagine that they actually are people who can bear the burden of a tax, as opposed to merely legal persons. The tendency to think this way is not limited to unusually ignorant or thoughtless observers. Thus, the New York Times periodically runs front-page articles with titles like "Corporations' Taxes Are Falling Even as Individuals' Burden Rises"—as if there could really be a tax borne by inanimate legal constructs.[6] To similar effect, the economist Alan Auerbach tells a story, from his days as deputy chief of staff of the U.S. Congress's Joint Committee on Taxation, in which the House Ways and Means Committee was meeting behind closed doors to consider a corporate tax increase, opposed by Republicans but potentially more congenial to Democrats.

"Come on," one of the Republicans objected. "We all know that corporate taxes are really borne by individuals."

"Ah," replied one of the Democrats—a prominent member of the committee, who was generally considered savvy and well informed— "but as we all learned in economics class, back in college, that is only true in the long run."[7]

The Democratic congressman had evidently confused two basic economic ideas. The relevant one was that a tax has a burden if it affects someone's welfare, which means that it can only be borne (in the short run as well as the long run) by people or other sentient beings. The other idea, which I examine with regard to the corporate tax in chapter 4, was that the incidence of a tax that nominally is placed on one set of individuals may shift and end up being borne instead by some other set of individuals. That potentially takes time, but the passage of incidence from inanimate things to sentient beings is necessarily instantaneous. We would not say that my bank account bears a tax burden before gradually transmitting the burden to me.

Given the tendency to personify corporations, many people might view failing to tax them directly as a great wrong, even if the true incidence of tax burdens between individuals was exactly correct. And even insofar as voters understand that a corporate tax necessarily hits some set of people, the ambiguity of exactly whom it is taxing may be politically advantageous. For example, when the United States in 1986 surprised many people by adopting a version of fundamental tax reform, one key to the legislation's political feasibility was that it combined overall revenue neutrality with a tax cut for every income cohort of individuals from the top to the bottom of the scale. How could this possibly be? The answer was that it shifted nominal or direct tax burdens from individuals to corporations, thereby inviting its portrayal as a revenue-neutral universal tax cut, since the corporate tax increase was not being attributed to anyone in the official tables.

This ambiguity of a corporate-level tax's incidence, given that it is not directly being paid by any individual, can be politically important even outside the fraught circumstances of trying to enact fundamental reform (which risks creating angry losers by taking away their tax breaks). Senator Russell Long used to state, as Rule Number One of tax legislation: "Don't tax you, don't tax me, tax the fellow behind the tree," meaning that it was best to avoid making anyone feel that the burden was actually theirs. A corporate-level tax, whether good policy or bad, is hard to over-look as a political option when the alternative is to levy more taxes directly and explicitly on some group of voters.

Aggregate-Based Reasons for a Corporate-Level Tax

Taking an aggregate view of corporations and viewing them merely as agents of their shareholders suggests that the only reason for a corporate-level tax is to reach the shareholders indirectly. Even just from this stand-point, however, a corporate-level tax is potentially appealing. By using the entity as a collection vehicle, one centralizes administration of the tax and needs only a single reporting taxpayer. One also avoids needing to determine how the corporate income ought to be divided among the shareholders. These advantages may well be worth the downside, which is that use of a corporate-level tax impedes taxing each shareholder at the correct marginal rate for that person. Instead, all of the corporation's income presumably must be taxed (at least in the first instance) under its particular rate structure.

In an income tax, as opposed to a consumption tax, there is a further reason for imposing a corporate-level tax on income as it is earned. "Income" has famously been defined as the taxpayer's consumption plus her change in net worth (Simons 1938, 50). All else being equal, your net worth increases if companies in which you own stock make money and therefore see their share prices rise. In a consumption tax, which leaves changes in net worth outside the tax-base equation, you can wait to levy the tax until you have withdrawn your share of the profits and consumed them. However, in a properly functioning income tax, the tax on your increase in net worth should not be deferred. Exempt the income while it remains in corporate solution, and from the income-tax standpoint one has created a tax shelter—in effect, an unlimited tax-free savings account via the use of corporate entities.

What's more, *Eisner v. Macomber,* a famous U.S. Supreme Court tax case from 1920, held that until shareholders concretely realize a corporation's earnings, such as through receipt of a cash dividend, they cannot constitutionally be taxed on those earnings. Whether *Eisner v. Macomber* remains good constitutional law on this point is unclear, but in any event the political and administrative obstacles to taxing shareholders on undistributed corporate earnings might be formidable. If properly designed income taxation requires taxing corporate earnings on a current basis, and an entity-level tax is the best or even the only way of doing this, then the case for an entity-level tax may be compelling.

Even if one favors collecting corporate tax at the entity level, the progressive marginal rate structure for corporate income (involving 15 percent and then 25 percent rates on the first $75,000 of income) makes no sense whatsoever. Graduated marginal rates for individuals respond to genuine differences between them, such as how the burden or deprivation that results from paying a given dollar of tax may be much higher for a poor individual than for one who is rich. However, graduated rates at the entity level bear little if any relationship to this, since they depend on the entity's net income rather than that of its owners. Further, corporate rate graduation creates a need for rules to determine whether taxpayers are unduly exploiting it by dividing what is in principle a single enterprise into multiple identically owned sibling corporations.

Why Levy a Tax on Shareholders?

The two distinct taxes that shareholders face, on dividends and on capital gains from selling the stock, obviously are conceptually linked. After all, the market value of stock, determining what you can sell it for, should generally depend on the present value of the cash flows that it is expected to generate, which can only come from receiving dividends, from selling the stock to someone else who would then get the dividends, or from receiving a share of corporate assets at liquidation. Nonetheless, the dividend and capital gain issues are worth considering separately due to certain distinct problems, both practical and conceptual, that are closely associated with the tax treatment of shareholder capital gains.

Dividend Tax

There are three main reasons for taxing shareholders on the dividends they receive. A bad but politically important reason is that people may simply be inclined to forget about the corporate-level tax. If I receive a dividend from a big company like General Electric in which I own a few shares, it could not possibly look more like income than it does. A large and remote organization that I do not control or even influence has sent me a check that I deposit in my bank account, apparently enriching me. Even if the stock price goes down—as one would expect at the moment when the dividend is actually paid and therefore no longer attaches to owning the stock—we are accustomed to ignoring, for current income-tax purposes, fluctuations in the value of unsold assets such as stock. And the tax that General Electric may have paid on the underlying earnings is out of sight and perhaps all too readily out of mind.

A second, more defensible rationale for taxing dividends relates to the corporate-level tax that we actually have. Shot through with tax preferences and tax-shelter-planning opportunities as everyone knows it is, to what degree can we count on it to have levied an adequate tax at the corporate level? As an illustration, if you look at General Electric's published income statements, you will observe that, year after year, it reports federal income-tax payments that are less than 20 percent of its stated financial accounting income. Book-tax gaps, which arise when the company reports more income to shareholders than it does to the Internal Revenue Service, are endemic, providing strong evidence of tax sheltering, albeit also of financial accounting manipulation (Shaviro 2007b). If the entity-level tax has gaping holes, then, while one's first choice might be to fix that tax, keeping the shareholder-level tax until one does so (or even permanently, if the entity-level tax is politically or administratively too hard to fix) may be a plausible fallback position.

Finally, one may actually support double taxation of equity-financed corporate income, as I further discuss below. If, for some reason, one wants a double tax, then by definition the dividend tax is needed if one cannot tax shareholders on mere stock appreciation.

Capital Gains Tax

As evidence that taxing shareholder capital gains is conceptually distinct from taxing dividends, the 2003 Bush administration proposal would only have exempted the latter. To prevent companies from needing to pay dividends just to keep the stock value from rising above the shareholders' basis in their shares as corporate earnings accumulated, the proposal would have permitted companies to make deemed dividend payments—that is, to report fictional transactions in which a tax-free dividend was paid but then reinvested by the shareholder in the stock. But this coordinating device would not have prevented shareholders from having taxable capital gains whenever the stock price rose for any other reason—for example, because optimism about a company's future earnings had risen. So, by design, the corporate integration proposal did not wholly eliminate shareholder-level taxation.

The reasons for being leery of eliminating the tax on shareholder capital gains, even if one is eliminating the dividend tax, are twofold. First, one would risk blasting a hole in the taxation of *any* capital gain upon the sale of appreciated assets. Thus, suppose one was planning to sell a building that had recently doubled in value. Incorporate the building, sell the shares in this newly created corporation rather than the building itself, and presto—one has avoided any current tax on the building sale, if sales of corporate stock are generally tax exempt. Clearly, Congress could try to address such maneuvers by drafting antiavoidance rules, but these are inevitably complicated and imperfect. So continuing to tax shareholder capital gains is potentially a plausible solution.

Second, an underlying conceptual problem suggests taxing shareholder capital gain in some instances even if the underlying stock is in "true" corporate businesses that are being fully taxed at the entity level. To see this, it is useful to step back for a moment and ask why an investor might hold stock even where not anticipating current cash flow from dividends. Microsoft, for example, until recently had an announced policy of not paying dividends, yet its stock was, entirely reasonably, considered a perfectly good investment. One reason for holding Microsoft stock, even when it was not paying dividends, could be that one was thinking about the very long term, when Microsoft might be liquidated and throw off lots of cash. One could also, however, reasonably anticipate selling the stock in the interim to another investor who would herself know that she could always sell it to another investor who would count on being able to sell it yet again (at least, so long as Microsoft continued to do well).

Generalize this beyond the stock of genuinely profitable companies, such as Microsoft, and you get the Greater Fool Theory. This theory holds that you are not a fool to buy high-priced stock in a company that may eventually tank, as long as you can find a greater fool first who will pay more for the stock than you did. And that person, in turn, may rationally count on finding a still greater fool, who in turn is counting on exactly the same thing.

All these people need not actually be fools, of course, especially if there is no particular reason to think that the company's business model is unsound. Economist John Maynard Keynes (1964, 156) famously offered the following description of the individually rational (if socially bizarre) practice of trading in corporate stock:

> Professional investment may be likened to those newspaper competitions in which the competitors have to pick out the six prettiest faces from a hundred photographs, the prize being awarded to the competitor whose choice most nearly corresponds to the average preferences of the competitors as a whole; so that each competitor has to pick, not those faces which he himself finds prettiest, but those which he thinks likeliest to catch the fancy of the other competitors, all of whom are looking at the problem from the same point of view. It is not a case of choosing those which, to the best of one's judgment, are really the prettiest, nor even those which average opinion genuinely thinks the prettiest. We have reached the third degree where we devote our intelligences to anticipating what average opinion expects the average opinion to be.

In the stock price "beauty contest," while it is rational to think about what others think others will think, it may often be quite irrational to think that you can systematically make money by playing this game. Thousands of day traders learned this lesson the hard way when the U.S. stock-market stopped rising through the roof in the early 2000s. There is, however, potentially a way to make money systematically by trading stocks, thereby regularly generating shareholder-level capital gains above the normal rate of return. The trick, for those who can manage it, is to invest time and effort in gaining and analyzing information about fundamental value (or even transient value) before it disseminates widely enough to be fully incorporated in stock prices.

Insider trading offers one potentially lucrative, albeit illegal, way of generating stock-trading profits through personal effort. However, it may be possible to do the same thing using only publicly available information, depending on how swiftly and efficiently market prices move to incorporate such information. If your analytic skills permit you to realize, five minutes before anyone else, that Microsoft stock is badly over- or undervalued, you can make a killing if you are able to trade fast enough on this temporarily unique understanding. It is hard to know whether anyone can actually consistently do this. Certainly, however, various hedge fund managers have persuaded wealthy investors to give them millions of dollars in compensation on the premise that they can do it.

The capital gains that such a hedge fund manager generates reflect a reward for economic activity that is not being taxed at the corporate level, even assuming a well-functioning corporate tax. The corporate tax base reaches actual corporate profitability, as distinct from success in predicting such profitability or other causes of shifting stock prices.[8] If this type of activity is significant enough, it creates a genuine policy reason for not exempting all shareholder capital gains from tax, even if one favors just one tax on corporate profits and the entity-level tax is fully doing the job on that score.[9]

Why Treat Debt Differently than Equity?

As we saw earlier, interest and dividends are treated differently with respect to (1) corporate-level deductibility, (2) the tax rate applied to the recipient, and (3) whether payments are imputed if no cash changes hands. It would be nice to report that there are good tax-policy reasons for treating debt and equity differently; however, there is little direct defense for the resulting creation of tax biases in corporate financial structures. The differential treatment of debt and equity is less a deliberate aim of tax policymakers than a byproduct of administrative concerns plus the blind application of certain tax concepts' apparent internal logic.

As noted earlier, shareholders are conceptualized as corporate alter egos, payments to whom would not logically be deductible, whereas bondholders are conceptualized as true third parties, demanding compensation at arm's length. Chapter 3 will show how poorly, even on its own terms, this story sometimes tracks the modern world of corporate high finance. But if accepted, it provides a seeming formal tax logic, as distinct from any economic or policy logic, for treating the two instruments differently at the corporate level.

Why not, then, limit the difference in treatment to that in corporate deductibility, along with, perhaps, the imprecise offset of more favorable treatment at the shareholder level? In other words, why not impute dividend payments even when not made, no less than interest payments? The fact that we do not do this may in part be further imprecise compensation for equity's worse treatment at the entity level. It also, however, responds to a fundamental, administratively motivated distinction that the tax law makes more generally between fixed-return and contingent-return assets (Warren 1993). Often, relatively fixed returns are taxed each year on a yield-to-maturity basis, as per the treatment of OID bonds, while taxation of contingent returns is on a wait-and-see basis, thus permitting tax-favorable deferral of the gain until it is observably realized.

A bond with a fixed interest rate has a definite value at maturity, and thus a definitely known value each year if we ignore two important considerations: changes in the issuer's default risk and changes in interest rates. (A bond with a fixed interest rate tends to lose value if interest rates rise, and to gain value if they fall.) Stock returns, by contrast, may be relatively unpredictable. It therefore is unsurprising that the tax law has developed in such a manner as to impute unpaid interest but not unpaid dividends.

Once this distinction between predictable interest and unpredictable dividends was made law, it proved resilient enough to extend beyond the reach of its original rationale. Recent years have seen the rising use of ever fancier contingent-debt instruments, the payments on which depend on as-yet-unknown events. Faced with the question of whether contingent debt should be treated like fixed debt or like analogously unpredictable stock, the Treasury decided, in effect, that debt is always debt, and thus provided rules for accruing contingent interest deductions and inclusions despite the admitted uncertainty as to their ultimate amount. This simultaneously reinforced the existing debt-equity distinction in the law and undermined one of its apparent rationales.

Why Impose Double Taxation?

On its face—if not always in reality—the tax law singles out equity-financed corporate income to face a double tax. What might be the reason for disfavoring such income? The analysis so far has emphasized the reasons (both good and bad) for each piece of the package that potentially adds up to double taxation, but this is different from actually wanting all the pieces to add up that way. However, that they do so add up is hardly a mystery and has attracted extensive discussion over many decades. Thus, even if one sees elements of happenstance in the genesis of the double tax, its retention can only be deliberate.

In fact, the political origin of the double tax is clear, although not especially edifying. Again, prior to 1936, dividends were subject only to the surtax on individuals' income, not the regular tax, which had the effect of ensuring that the underlying corporate income would only be taxed once. If you know a little American history, it is easy to surmise what must have happened in 1936. Falling amid the Great Depression, 1936 was near the high-water mark of populist hostility to the rich and calls for increased redistribution of wealth. So perhaps adoption of the full double tax reflected the era's "soak the rich" stand in politics.

As it happens, the seeming logic of this surmise only goes to show that a little knowledge can be a dangerous thing. Corporate managers were the ones who pushed for the switch to a full double tax (Bank 2003, 514–515). Eager to avoid pressure to distribute dividends to their shareholders, which would have reduced the free cash subject to their discretion, they successfully pressured Congress in 1936 to make dividends fully taxable in lieu of imposing an extra tax on undistributed earnings. Corporate managers have ever since remained decidedly unenthusiastic about corporate integration, and prefer lobbying for corporate tax preferences, such as accelerated depreciation (Arlen and Weiss 1995). Even in 2003, their support for the Bush administration's corporate integration proposal was less than deafening.

As Steven Bank (2005, 153) notes, "few commentators suggest that we would consciously adopt it if we were working from a blank slate, and most openly recommend double taxation's demise." However, the following arguments have been deployed in favor of retaining the existing system, either because it is already in place or on the view that improvements would be hard to implement.

Revenue loss. Despite tax-planning opportunities to avoid the double tax, the current system still raises revenue. Thus, in 2003, the Bush administration's initial dividend-exemption proposal had an estimated 10-year revenue cost of $383 billion (Burman 2003, 753). The United States, like many other nations, faces a long-term fiscal gap, reflecting inadequate revenues to pay for projected spending (Shaviro 2007a, 7). If double taxation were simply repealed without financing (such as an offsetting tax increase or spending cut), the effect on the fiscal gap could conceivably eliminate more than 100 percent of the otherwise projected efficiency gain. And while this is no argument against a fully financed repeal of the double tax, requiring financing inevitably would make repeal of the double tax more controversial and politically difficult.

Progressivity. As chapter 4 will show, the incidence of the double tax— who really bears it in economic terms—is controversial. If, however, repealing it would reduce the progressivity of the fiscal system, then anyone who favors keeping the system at least as progressive as it is today must consider what is politically likely to arise in its place. One thus could argue for retaining the double tax based on either of two time frames. The short-term argument would be that no comparably progressive instrument replacing the double tax is likely to emerge in the near term under current political conditions. A longer-term argument might hold that double taxation increases the politically feasible level of overall progressivity, perhaps due to its hidden incidence and support from corporate executives who want an excuse not to distribute loose cash to their shareholders. These arguments depend, however, on the underlying assumption that the incidence of the double tax is indeed progressive.

Windfall gain to shareholders from repeal. Adam Smith (1976, 457) is commonly credited with the view that the only good tax is an old tax. Some analysts, such as the economist Martin Feldstein (1976), have similarly argued that once a bad tax rule is in place, there are equity grounds for retaining it so that people who have relied on it will not be adversely affected. Thus, even if the deduction for homeowners' mortgage interest payments ought never to have been enacted to begin with, repealing it arguably would be unfair to the owners of existing homes, who might suffer a windfall loss in the value of their homes from unanticipated repeal.[10] Repealing the double tax arguably creates a prospect of windfall gain for existing shareholders, who now might be able to receive dividends tax free after having invested under a contrary assumption. This concern could lead one to oppose elimination of the double tax, absent a sufficiently well-designed method for limiting the transition gain to new equity (American Law Institute 1989, 92).

Indirect response to gaps in the corporate tax base. Less dependent on the transition problem of getting from the double tax to an integrated system is the view that the shareholder level of tax, even if otherwise undesirable, is a useful backstop, making up for the failure of the entity-level tax to tax enough corporate income the first time around. Suppose, for example, that corporate tax shelters, used by profitable companies to avoid paying tax on their earnings, cannot be curtailed effectively due either to administrative problems or a lack of political will. Then the shareholder-level tax, while still distorting companies' financing and distribution decisions, might have appeal for indirectly reducing the overall bias in favor of corporate investment.

The lay version of this argument is that two wrongs can make a right. Economic analysis gives it the more edifying label of the "theory of the second best," under which its merits depend on whether the second wrong's offsetting of old distortions empirically exceeds its creation of new ones.

Taxation of rents. In lay terminology, rents are what you pay your landlord each month. Economists, however, use the term to denote "payments to resource deliverers that exceed those necessary to employ the resource" (Gruber 2007, 205). An example would be Michael Jordan, back in the day, when he could earn $30 million per year playing basketball and no more than, say, $100,000 doing anything else with his time. The existence of this $29.9 million excess of what Jordan could earn by playing basketball over the next best use of his time potentially has an important tax policy implication. If he planned to work in any event, at whatever occupation paid him the most, one could tax away all of the extra return (leaving only, say, an extra cent) and he still would play basketball rather than doing anything else. A very high tax would therefore result in no economic distortion of behavior, contrary to what one normally expects.

Large businesses, which typically are incorporated, often are said to enjoy rents. McDonald's, for example, might be able to sell greasy meat-flavored slop for a decent price, relative to the direct production cost, because consumers feel their stomachs grumble and reach compulsively for their wallets upon seeing the familiar golden arches.[11] Double taxation has an arguable efficiency rationale insofar as it functions as a way of taxing rents that otherwise would not face more than the normal tax rate. However, its design and reach do not seem closely associated with identifying rents, and it distorts various business decisions (as we will see in chapter 2) even if its effect on rents themselves is nondistortionary. Accordingly, the rents-based argument for double taxation, like the preceding ones, requires that one posit the political or administrative unavailability of superior alternatives.

*   *   *   *   *

There are decent rationales for each piece of the corporate tax. For example, both the entity-level and the shareholder-level tax may make sense considered independently, and an ideal system might well have elements of both. The overall system, however, would be extremely hard to defend if one were starting from a blank slate. Only political and administrative constraints on changing it properly in midstream could make retention of the current system seem desirable.

2

Efficiency Problems
with the Corporate Tax

The corporate tax, in cases where it imposes double taxation, is sometimes called unfair. This is a hard case to make, however. Corporate shareholders invest knowing that the system is in place. Presumably, they would not invest as they do unless they expected better after-tax returns than the next best investment choice. So the complaint about the double tax is better posed in terms of its distorting taxpayers' economic incentives and thereby causing inefficiency. Or rather, since all real-world taxes have efficiency costs, the complaint is that the corporate tax creates inefficiencies needlessly by adding arbitrary distortions on top of those that we are stuck with in any event. Before exploring the bill of particulars, however, let's briefly review what inefficiency means in tax policy and why it matters.

If taxation's sole goal were to avoid all inefficiency, we presumably would meet the government's revenue needs by imposing lump-sum taxes, or those in which the taxpayer's decisions do not affect her liability. The classic example of a lump sum tax is a uniform head tax, under which each individual owes the same amount. Thus, suppose the U.S. government, which is spending more than $2.5 trillion per year in a country of slightly over 300 million people, simply charged each individual about $8,000 a year in lieu of all existing federal taxes. Leaving aside the problem of actually collecting the money from people who do not have it, this tax would be an economist's dream— if, counterfactually, economists cared only about efficiency.

Such a tax would be extremely unappealing distributively because it ignores ability to pay. Bill Gates owes the same amount under a uniform head tax as a homeless person does. Its efficiency merits are genuine, however—even if grossly inadequate to make one yearn for its adoption— and thus are worth understanding given that, in evaluating other, more realistic trade-offs, efficiency may often rightly carry the day.

Ignoring the compliance and administrative costs of the uniform head tax (which surely could be low), the great thing about it is that the burden it imposes on each individual—$8,000—exactly equals the government's fiscal benefit. There is no waste, in the sense of taxpayer detriment, that simply represents a personal loss without an offsetting benefit to anyone. Perhaps the government would end up wasting much of the money it collected, but that is a problem of spending policy, not tax policy.

The reason taxpayers don't lose anything, beyond the $8,000 a head that they actually pay, is that the uniform head tax does not affect their marginal incentives or induce changes in behavior aimed at reducing tax liability. Of course, this is not to say that taxpayers would make exactly the same decisions as they would if the head tax did not exist. Suppose you have a spouse and two children, meaning that your family must pay a total of $32,000. It certainly is plausible that you or your spouse would decide to work more than in the case where the family owed no tax. But this would mitigate the burden that the tax imposed on you, rather than increasing it, as otherwise you wouldn't have done it.

Now let's take the case of a tax that requires more money from Bill Gates than from you, and more from you than from a homeless person, by relying on a measure of ability to pay such as income, consumption, or earnings. While this surely is preferable on balance to uniform head taxation, it has the disadvantage of penalizing and thus discouraging productive economic activity. Therefore, in some cases it actually destroys economic value above and beyond the transfer of value to the government.

A simple example might involve hiring a babysitter so one can go out for a walk in the park. Suppose that you would be willing to pay the teenager down the street up to $10 for an hour of his babysitting services. He would be willing to do it so long as you pay him at least $8. Whether the price you agree on is $8, $10, or somewhere in between, the transaction creates $2 of social surplus. As measured by your willingness to pay and his reservation wage, the service's value to you is

$2 greater than its apparent disvalue to him. Thus, socially speaking, the transaction has only winners and no losers (leaving aside what your children may think of it!).

Now, however, suppose the government is imposing a 30 percent income tax (and suppose that the teenager actually reports his income and is subject to the 30 percent rate). Even if you pay $10, the teenager will not end up keeping more than $7, which is below his reservation wage. So the deal does not take place, and social surplus is destroyed without any benefit to the government, which collects no tax on the transaction that never happened. Economists call this lost surplus "deadweight loss," since the detriment to you and/or the teenager[1] is not offset by any revenue gain to the Treasury.

Again, we willingly pay this social price for having an income tax instead of a uniform head tax because it improves the distributional consequences of the tax. Bill Gates presumably pays more tax than the rest of us if we are accurately measuring income. An income tax cannot avoid burdening and discouraging two things that we otherwise might wish to leave alone— decisions to work and decisions to save. We accept the resulting loss of welfare to individuals, in cases like that of the babysitter, because we consider the trade-off socially beneficial on balance.[2] But this is not to say that we should cheerily add other distortions and resulting creations of deadweight loss simply because we have started on the path of doing so. To the contrary, we should try to avoid layering other distortions on top of the two basic ones from income taxation, unless we find those extra distortions likewise justifiable on balance.

The Four Corporate Tax Biases, and Binary Choice versus Effective Electivity

Taking as given that a corporate income tax will discourage working and saving, the issue turns to whether its various design features (discussed in chapter 1) cause other distortions as well. Four main distortions have been identified in the voluminous corporate tax literature (see, e.g., Shaviro 2000b, 159–162). The first pertains to the choice between using a corporate or a noncorporate entity. The second pertains to the choice between debt and equity financing of a corporate investment. The third pertains to the choice between distributing corporate earnings to shareholders and retaining them in corporate solution. The fourth pertains to the choice between the forms of such distribution that are taxed as dividends and those that are taxed as capital gains.

The remainder of this chapter explores two issues with respect to each tax bias. The first issue is how tax bias arises from the interplay of tax rules, and when it lies in one direction (such as favoring the use of debt over equity) instead of the other. The second issue is how each of the four potential sources of tax bias may create needless inefficiency. For purposes of this inquiry, I will rely for now on an intentionally naïve simplifying assumption that I will revisit and modify in chapter 3. The assumption is that each of the four margins at which there is tax bias involves a simple binary choice between two highly distinct alternatives (such as classic debt versus classic equity) that the tax system can readily identify. In other words, taxpayers can choose option A with one set of characteristics, or option B with a different set, but without the opportunity to mix and match characteristics or otherwise split the difference, and also without the opportunity to hide the true choice made from the IRS.

An opposite, though equally extreme, assumption would be that tax-payers can do whatever they like along each of the four margins, without the tax system's having any effect on what they actually do, because they can do A and say they are doing B, or vice versa, and the tax system will believe them. This view would rest not on a claim that taxpayers are committing fraud, but rather on their having sufficient planning flexibility to marry whatever set of economic arrangements they like to whatever tax characterization of these arrangements they find most advantageous. I call this view *effective electivity*, since it suggests that taxpayers are in virtually the same position as they would be if tax returns expressly permitted them to select the label of their choice no matter what they were actually doing. The only difference between explicit and effective electivity is that, under the latter, formal legal structuring details do the work.

With full effective electivity, a given corporate tax bias would yield no direct inefficiency, since businesses could in fact arrange their affairs however they liked without tax consequences.[3] In the remainder of this chapter, my reason for assuming the accuracy of the first view, which sees biased binary choices rather than effective electivity, is not that this view is necessarily more correct. Indeed, as we will see later on, effective electivity is increasingly gaining relative descriptive accuracy. The biased binary choices view still has some degree of truth, however, and its consequences therefore remain worth understanding.

Corporate versus Noncorporate Entity

Being a corporation for tax purposes has four main implications. First, it causes the entity's income to face the corporate marginal tax rate, rather than the owners' individual marginal tax rates. Second, the owners cannot deduct the entity's losses against their own gains or vice versa if (by reason of the entity's corporate status) they are separate taxpayers. Third, distributions to the owners are taxable, without being deductible at the corporate level, if deemed to be corporate distributions, such as dividends. Fourth, the applicability of any rule in the tax code that applies solely to corporations (or noncorporations) may depend on the entity classification. An example is the statutory $1 million limit on non-performance-based compensation paid by a publicly traded corporation to its top executives. This rule does not apply to legal entities that are instead classified as partnerships.

Where the corporate rate is no lower than the top individual rate (as under present U.S. law), being a corporation for tax purposes will almost always hurt, rather than help, if it makes any difference. (The main exception would be if a favorable rule, such as one allowing particular deductions, applies solely to corporations.) Historically, however, the top corporate rate has often been below the top individual rate. Further, as we will see in part 4, there is an excellent chance that this state of affairs will soon resume. When this is so, corporate status can be tax favored rather than tax discouraged.

Suppose, for example, that the top corporate rate is lowered to 25 percent, the top individual rate is raised to 40 percent, and corporate-level loss disallowance is not a big problem because the corporate taxpayer has many different lines of business activity (permitting losses from one to be deducted against net income from another). Now corporate status is likely to be tax advantageous for prospective owners in the top bracket who are confident that they can generally avoid having taxable corporate distributions.

The result is deadweight loss and inefficiency, wholly on top of that which is implicit in income taxation, if people respond in either of two ways. The first is to conduct the same business that they otherwise would have, but in a suboptimal way via the tax-motivated choice of what would otherwise have been the wrong entity. The second is to choose one activity over another, despite its being less profitable on a pretax basis, where the choices differ in their compatibility with the corporate and noncorporate forms. To make more sense of these possibilities, however, one needs to ask why it might matter whether one used a corporation or not. What real differences between entities does the special treatment of corporations potentially target, and why might these differences matter?

Potential Real Consequences of the Choice

As noted in chapter 1, an entity qualifies as a corporation for U.S. tax purposes if it either is established under any U.S. state's incorporation statute or an identified foreign equivalent, or has public trading of ownership shares. Corporate tax status therefore is associated with (1) the use of any specific incorporation law, (2) the legal features typically associated with such laws, and (3) establishment of the mechanisms for public trading. Let's see why each of these might matter.

Applicability of a Specific Incorporation Statute

All contracts, including those between investors, are inevitably incomplete. People cannot possibly anticipate every contingency, and it would be overly costly to try. Thus, the statutes creating particular legal entities, such as a corporations, provide at a minimum default rules that may prove important. They may also contain mandatory features, such as those for internal governance and dispute resolution.

Thus, suppose one likes Delaware corporate law as administered by Delaware judges, or believes that prospective investors would respond favorably to it. (Delaware is indeed the leading U.S. state for incorporations, reflecting high regard for its well-developed corporate law system.) To have access to this body of law, one must register one's business as a Delaware corporation. This, in turn, may make tax status as a C corporation effectively unavoidable.[4]

Features Typically Associated with Corporate Law

The modern business corporation rose to prominence in the second half of the nineteenth century. Strictly speaking, a corporation was simply a legal entity registered under the incorporation statute of any state. Corporations commonly had the following attributes, however, distinguishing them from at least the garden-variety forms of unincorporated businesses, such as general partnerships and individual proprietorships:

Limited liability. A proprietor or general partner shares in all liabilities of the business unless she has separately used contractual means of limiting her liability. Thus, rather than having her financial downside limited to the amounts that she has chosen to invest in the business, she potentially may be called on to pay not only all unsatisfied debts owed to lenders or other counterparties, such as employees and suppliers, but any tort liabilities that the business ends up incurring. Unless contractually modified, however, limited liability may be a curse rather than a blessing in cases where it makes others less willing to deal with one's business, or induces them to demand more favorable terms in other respects (such as a higher interest rate).

Exchangeability of ownership interests. Shares of corporate stock can typically be sold to any third party, perhaps even through organized public markets such as a stock exchange. General partnership interests, by contrast, usually cannot be sold or purchased. One does not, for example, hear of young lawyers buying interests in major law firms—they must instead pay with "sweat equity" and hope to one day be rewarded.

Exchangeability is a convenience to any owner who is eager for a more liquid investment than she would otherwise have. Other co-owners' capacity to sell their interests is potentially an inconvenience, however. For example, one may care who one works with in the business, or be eager to keep co-owners that have deep financial pockets (especially absent the corporate attribute of limited liability).

Separation of ownership and control. A proprietor obviously can act for herself, and general partners as well have traditionally had the full power to act on behalf of, and indeed to legally bind, their partnerships. A corporate shareholder, by contrast, legally has no direct power, other than voting for directors that appoint employees, along perhaps with the right to vote on a few important matters, such as mergers or liquidations. As with exchangeability, while limiting one's own powers (albeit here in the corporate rather than the partnership setting) may seem disadvantageous, it has the associated virtue of limiting the powers of one's co-owners as well.

Unlimited life. Partnerships typically dissolve and are reconstituted, at least for formal legal purposes, whenever a partner leaves or joins the preexisting group. Corporations, by contrast, keep going until their charters expire (although typically they are perpetual) or they are expressly liquidated. However, while unlimited life commonly appears among the list of defining corporate attributes, its practical significance has often been too limited to require much attention.

Capital lock-in. A further classic distinction between corporations and partnerships pertains to the funds that the co-owners have placed at the business's disposal. Partners may have the right to withdraw their contributed shares at any time, albeit subject to the full terms of their contractual relationships. Shareholders, by contrast, do not get any right to access the amounts they contributed in exchange for their shares (Bank 2006). Dividends typically depend on a voluntary act of declaration by the board of directors, and share repurchases require that the corporation be a willing buyer. Once again, the choice of corporate form (ignoring the potential to modify contractually its practical implications) combines an irksome restriction on oneself with a beneficial restriction on one's fellow owners, yielding net benefit in some cases and net detriment in others.

Public Trading

The rule treating certain publicly traded entities as corporations generally applies if interests in a given entity are either (1) traded on an established securities market or (2) readily tradable on a secondary market or the substantial equivalent thereof. In practice, one can certainly try to make ownership interests easy to buy and sell without meeting either definition. However, entities may find it difficult to tap large capital markets, by offering reasonable liquidity and convenience to prospective buyers and sellers, unless they agree to meet these terms. Corporate tax status may therefore be hard to avoid when prospective investors would value the advantages of access to public capital markets.

*   *   *   *   *

In sum, many factors may affect whether one prefers to do business as a corporation. To a significant extent, however, the attributes have something important in common. The corporate form is well suited for accessing public capital markets, rather than simply using one's own cash or that of lenders that make a fixed interest rate loan based on limiting their assessment to one of solvency. Third-party investors that are looking for good opportunities to make a bundle (going beyond the traditional lender's fixed return) are likely to want limited liability and the ability to sell their shares, while also wanting to let the managers, who presumably know the business, continue to run things. Such investors may also (if they care) be encouraged by the potential application of a well-known and reputable system for resolving internal governance disputes such as that provided under Delaware corporate law.

Accordingly, if the tax system penalizes use of the corporate form, businesses may end up being discouraged from going public, and sectors of the economy in which access to broader capital markets is important may tend to be too small. If corporations are tax favored, the biases are reversed. This potentially will disfavor closely held businesses, and the sectors of the economy where they congregate, if use of the corporate form is affirmatively inconvenient for them rather than merely unnecessary.

Debt versus Equity Financing

Corporations avoid double taxation, even insofar as they promptly pay out their earnings to the suppliers of their funds, when they use debt rather than equity financing. The use of debt therefore is often tax preferred to the use of equity. For the purposes of the corporate-level tax, it is better to get a deduction for payments to investors than not to get one.

There also is a second circumstance in which debt gets more favorable tax treatment than equity. Suppose one wants to retain funds in corporate solution, rather than paying them out currently, and that the corporation's tax rate is higher than that of the investors. (They might, for example, be tax exempt.) For equity, even if incurring the second level of tax would not be a problem, the corporation will continue to pay tax at its high rate on funds that it continues to hold and invest. For debt, even if annual interest payments are not being made, OID rules ensure a notional transaction in which interest is annually deducted at the higher corporate rate and included at the lower individual rate, yielding a net tax savings to the parties.

Equity, by contrast, is tax favored over debt if the corporation's tax rate is lower than that of the investors and the parties can avoid dividend or other distributions, thus eliminating the second level of tax. The analysis here is the same as if one were choosing between a corporate and a noncorporate entity, since all of the income gets taxed once either at the corporate rate (if one uses equity) or the investor rate (if one uses debt and pays out all the earnings as interest).

With a 15 percent tax rate for dividends, equity also is tax favored if current distributions are planned and the tax savings at the investor level—from paying tax at 15 percent rather than, say, 35 percent—exceeds the value of the corporate interest deduction. In illustration, suppose a given company has such large losses from prior years that it will not have a positive income tax liability any time soon. Thus, its marginal tax rate on extra deductions or inclusions is effectively zero. Money that it pays out to investors will not give it tax savings even if characterized as deductible interest rather than as nondeductible dividends. The investors, however, will benefit if their receipts are styled dividends, taxable at 15 percent, rather than interest, taxable at 35 percent.

Potential Real Consequences of the Choice

To see why the choice between debt and equity might matter, taxes aside, consider the starkest forms of each, at opposite sides of the spectrum. Straight or classic debt involves an "unqualified obligation to pay a sum certain at a reasonably close fixed maturity date along with a fixed percentage in interest payable regardless of the debtor's income or the lack thereof."[5] Simple equity, by contrast, "connotes an unlimited claim to the residual benefits of ownership and an unequally unlimited subjection to the burdens thereof" (Bittker and Eustice 2006, 4–12). In such a case, the shareholder presumably intends to "embark upon the corporate adventure, taking the risks of loss attendant upon it, so that he may enjoy the chances of profit."[6]

Further classic characteristics of the two types of financial interest reflect the logic of their starting points. Debt holders generally have priority over equity holders (i.e., they are paid first) to increase the certainty of their getting the promised principal back plus interest. Equity holders get to control the corporation by voting their shares, reflecting that the debt holders have no reason to care how well it does so long as they get their promised return. Debt holders get creditors' rights to enforce their claims in court if necessary, thus providing a backstop given that they otherwise lack control. Default on the company's obligations to them may (under U.S. law) trigger administratively costly bankruptcy proceedings that are designed to protect their collective claims to available corporate assets and to adjudicate who among them gets what.

Why Favor One Set of Characteristics over the Other?

Where investors face a polar choice between using the two instruments in their classic forms, the factors that may induce favoring one or the other include the following:

Investors' risk preferences. If investors are generally risk averse, and thus prefer fixed returns to highly variable returns with the same expected value, then classic equity will have to offer a risk premium, increasing its expected return above that of classic debt, in order for the two to compete in the marketplace on equal terms. In general, one would expect the risk premium to be such that the marginal investor, who is choosing between the two with respect to his last available investment dollar, is indifferent. Even in these circumstances of market balance, however, particular investors that differ in their appetite for risk may be reluctant to disrupt the varying ways in which they have balanced the two in their portfolios. A tax preference for either instrument may induce some investors to accept an inferior risk profile as the price of generating tax savings. This may lead to excess burden or deadweight loss, no less than does the babysitter example from earlier in this chapter.

Insiders versus outsiders. Often, a given business opportunity can accurately be seen as having two types of potential investors. One is the insiders, who may have come up with a given idea and/or expect to be the ones executing it, but who need outside capital either because they don't have enough or to diversify their underlying risks. The other is the outsiders, who furnish capital in hopes of getting a good return but realize that they know less than the insiders about the business's prospects and operations and will be unable or unwilling to exert as much influence on what happens. Classic debt and equity can play a variety of important roles in mediating the relationship between the two groups to mutual long-term advantage.

Suppose a corporate venturer or organizer has a good idea or opportunity, offering him the prospect of an above-average rate of return on investment. The canonical example is Bill Gates founding Microsoft, if we posit that he was highly likely to succeed, not just extremely lucky. When someone in this position needs outside capital, he is not going to want to share the extra return, and will not have to do so if credit is available and he can sufficiently demonstrate that lenders will get their money back. Thus, if 6 percent was the going rate when Bill Gates was founding Microsoft, he would not have needed to pay more, even if lenders would have liked to get more of the upside, since if one prospective lender tried to demand more, Gates could always ask another instead.

Giving oneself the equity, and accepting outside cash only in the form of fixed-rate debt, provides a convenient method for reserving the rents for oneself while giving outsiders only the return they could have expected in any event. Optimal allocation of the expected returns may be impeded, however, if the debt-equity distinction ends up placing a thumb on the scales in a manner that affects the economics of the parties' underlying arrangements.

A second set of insider versus outsider problems that the choice between debt and equity can address is the difficulty that outsiders may have in monitoring what the insiders are up to. One possible advantage of debt is that it relieves the outsiders of needing to monitor anything short of default risk, while also strengthening insiders' incentives to try hard by reserving to them the entire variable upside. In other circumstances, equity may be what the outsiders want. By giving them the same return as stockholding insiders, it eliminates the insiders' incentive to make risky "heads we win, tails you lose" bets in which they will either make a fortune for themselves or default to the detriment of the debt holders. Once again, however, tax considerations may disrupt the optimal balance, yielding reduced pretax returns that the parties offset with tax savings.

Investor remedies if things go badly. That debt holders can foreclose if specific payment obligations or other covenants are not met may give them an advantage in some circumstances over equity holders, who may find it harder to promptly halt managers embarked on a losing economic course. On the other hand, foreclosure in the U.S. legal system sometimes means that administratively costly bankruptcy proceedings will end up consuming a significant fraction of remaining corporate asset value. Even taking the occasional need for such proceedings as given, either as an entrenched feature of the U.S. legal system or (more optimistically) on the view that they actually help to preserve remaining value and adjudicate competing financial claims once things have gotten bad enough, the prospect of triggering them nonetheless may make the debt-equity mix a delicate balancing act. Tax considerations may interfere with the optimal balance, however, if they bias the debt-equity choice.

Distribute versus Retain Earnings

Tax Consequences of the Choice

That the shareholder-level tax does not arise until corporate earnings are distributed (leaving aside stock sales) is commonly viewed as creating a corporate-level "lock-in" with respect to such earnings. That is, current distributions are discouraged. Unlike the corporate law feature of capital lock-in, such discouragement would arise even where all shareholders otherwise would favor the declaration of a dividend.

In fact, however, while the dividend tax can have this effect, the full picture is considerably more complicated, and there are plausible scenarios in which the corporate tax system actually favors immediate distribution of earnings. Under very specialized circumstances (discussed in chapter 5 with respect to the "new view" of dividend taxation), the timing decision may be genuinely tax neutral. But these circumstances do not generally hold today.

Suppose a company's two equal shareholders want the company to distribute a $100 dividend to each, but only if the tax consequences aren't overly adverse. The tax-planning issues that this raises can be divided into two parts: effects on the corporate distributions tax that the shareholders ultimately pay, and effects on the tax rate that would apply to any further income earned on the $200 that they want the company to distribute.

Effect on the Distribution Tax

If a taxable corporate distribution is bound to be made at some point, then the choice the shareholders face is not between paying and avoiding a tax, but between paying one today and paying it later. Ordinarily in income-tax planning, deferral of liabilities is a good thing: it lowers the present value of the tax that you ultimately will have to pay. In the corporate distributions setting, however (as further discussed in chapter 5), things are more complicated because the amount that ultimately will have to be distributed (if the company liquidates someday) is growing by reason of the positive return to the funds that the company is keeping on hand in the interim.

Tax rate changes between now and the future, whether known with certainty or merely expected or even guessed, may also throw off the determination of when it is best, from a tax standpoint, to distribute corporate earnings. One might want to wait for a dividend tax cut or distribute funds in advance of a dividend tax increase. Adding yet another complication, waiting preserves the option to select a low-rate rather than a high-rate year in the future, which could be valuable if tax rates on corporate distributions seem likely to oscillate unpredictably.

In practice, lock-in surely predominates over "push-out," or preferring sooner dividends for tax reasons. This, however, reflects the step-up in basis of capital assets at death (discussed in chapter 1). Thus, if I buy stock for $10 and its value increases to $100, I cannot sell it without realizing $90 worth of capital gain. If, however, I hold it until death and bequeath it to my children, they can sell it for up to $100 without paying any tax.

The step-up in basis applies no less to share repurchases than to third-party sales. Thus, the step-up permits corporate earnings to leave corporate solution without leading to any shareholder-level tax. So the dividend tax is not inevitable: deferring it can often mean eliminating it without having to keep the funds in corporate solution forever, and the assumption of lock-in by reason of the dividend tax is often correct. But all this might change if the stepped-up basis rule for inherited property were to change.

Interim Tax Rate on Retained versus Distributed Earnings

This brings us to the second part of the tax-planning problem: the difference between the corporations' and the shareholders' marginal tax rates on investment returns. If the corporate rate is the lower of the two, then keeping funds there means that the investment return on the funds will be taxed at a lower rate if dividends are not distributed. Under today's law, where the corporate rate equals the top individual rate, this is unlikely to happen unless the corporation is in a loss position, and thus will not have net taxable income in any event. It potentially becomes a big issue, however, when the corporate rate is significantly the lower of the two. Historically, Congress responded to this possibility with the accumulated earnings tax, which subjected corporate income from passive investments to a punitive special rate if funds in excess of those needed by any active corporate business were being retained with tax-avoidance intent. The incentive to defer corporate distributions if the corporate rate is lower applies more generally, however.

Potential Real Consequences of the Choice

Why might it matter, taxes aside, whether corporate earnings are distributed currently or not? In the above example of two equal owners deciding about a $100 distribution to each, it probably does not matter much, since they control the company, unless they are personally cash constrained and, in the absence of a current distribution, would need to borrow the money from third parties at a greater transaction cost.

For large, publicly traded companies, however, who has the money may matter a great deal. For example, managers may simply want to keep the money on hand, so they will have a bigger empire to play with, even if the uses that they plan to make of the money are in fact suboptimal. Tax-deterring corporate distributions may therefore have systematically bad effects, by motivating the shareholders to go along even if they understand that this will reduce the pretax profits derived from using the funds.

While systematic corporate governance problems might conceivably create a case for tax-encouraging distributions, this could be inefficient in many circumstances as well. Suppose that managers with good projects, which they could persuade a lender to back, are forced to substitute additional debt financing for the use of internally generated earnings, thereby increasing transaction costs while their activities remain the same. Or suppose a company's unique business opportunities raise the possibility that it would be able to make better use of the funds than could the shareholders, but that distrust and asymmetric information prevent the managers from persuading either the shareholders or outside lenders that this is so. Once again, tax-encouraging distributions could systematically make the problem worse.

Here as elsewhere, there is an argument that tax neutrality is likely to be the best design solution from an efficiency standpoint. While corporate governance problems might conceivably support tax-encouraging distributions in at least some circumstances, this is far from being a precisely tailored remedy to the underlying problem of managerial motivation. If there is a desirable direction of bias, however, there is good reason to doubt that the current rules, with their tendency to create lock-in, lean the right way.

Form of Distribution

Tax Consequences of the Choice

The tax rules for corporate distributions create three possible advantages for share repurchases over dividend distributions. The first is basis recovery for the former but not the latter, reducing the amount that will be included in income by reason of a share repurchase. This advantage may be particularly significant where shareholders plan to await the basis step-up from inheritance before getting out their cash in exchange for all of their stock.

Second, share repurchases generally yield capital gains rather than ordinary income. While the main historic advantage of capital gains status, a lower tax rate than that for ordinary income, currently does not create a distinction between the two types of distribution given dividends' (at least temporary) 15 percent rate, there remain special circumstances in which capital gains continue to be treated more favorably.[7]

Finally, while dividend distributions must go to everyone, at least among the holders of a given class of stock, share repurchases can be tailored to shareholders' varying tax circumstances. Thus, suppose a company offers to redeem 10 percent of its outstanding stock, based on whoever tenders first. All else being equal, one would expect the offer to be taken disproportionately by those for whom the adverse tax consequences are smallest (or even zero).

Where the shareholder is a corporation, the direction of tax bias may reverse. Dividends-received deductions may result in more favorable treatment of dividends than share repurchases. Of course, if tendering is elective, companies that are shareholders in other, unrelated companies can presumably manage this problem for themselves.

Potential Real Consequences of the Choice

The efficiency cost of generally tax-favoring repurchases over dividends relates to the underlying definitional rule that a repurchase must be sufficiently asymmetric, in its effect on shareholders' relative ownership interests, for its character as such to be respected. For relatively closely held companies that a few large shareholders dominate, the problem is one of potentially disrupting the desired internal balance of power, or at least making its maintenance transactionally more costly (such as through the need to neutralize the effects of a relative ownership change through careful planning).

For public companies in which the shareholders are diffuse and powerless, an additional problem arises. Share repurchases, given that they generally must be asymmetric to avoid dividend treatment, afford managers special opportunities to enrich themselves at public investors' expense whether the inside information they have indicates that the current stock price is too high or too low. If it is too low, share repurchases enable them to increase their stake by buying out tendering shareholders at a bargain price. If it is too high, they can engage in "false signaling . . . [or] announcing repurchases they have no intention of conducting in order to inflate the stock price, enabling them to unload their own shares at a higher price" (Fried 2005, 1328).

*   *   *   *   *

Any tax system that attempts to differentiate tax liabilities based on people's circumstances (such as the difference between being Bill Gates and a homeless person) is bound to cause regrettable deadweight loss. Corporate taxation, however, adds seemingly gratuitous inefficiencies to those that are inevitable given the reasons for heeding ability to pay. It interferes in various business and financial decisions that one might wish the players were simply left to make for themselves. Accordingly, the system will always rightly be controversial whether or not we can decide how best to change it.

Pillars of Sand in the Structure of Corporate Taxation

A core problem with the corporate tax—both having it and under-standing it—is that the underlying concepts on which it relies lack clear meaning. To show how much this matters, consider the income tax. Income's well-defined economic meaning, as the taxpayer's consumption plus her change in net worth (Simons 1938, 50), has important practical implications. Because the concept is relatively clear, income-tax law can rely on it in various settings. For example, the Internal Revenue Code specifies that "gross income includes all income from whatever source derived"—thus capturing anything that the code's drafters failed to list—and authorizes the IRS to modify taxpayers' accounting methods as needed to accomplish a clear reflection of income.[1]

A Tax Built on Pillars of Sand

To the benefit of those who want to study and understand it, it is also clear what (in principle) the income tax does. Reflecting the distributional aims that underlie the current tax system, the income tax burdens work and saving, which again are concepts with relatively clear economic meanings. Thus, when proponents of fundamental tax reform debate whether we should aim for a comprehensive income tax or instead for a broad-based consumption tax, which would burden work but not saving,[2] the intellectual parameters of the debate are clear (see Shaviro 2008a).

Now compare this with the actuating distinctions in the corporate tax, such as corporate versus noncorporate entity and debt versus equity. These concepts have no core. "Corporation" or "debt," for example, simply cannot be put on the same clear theoretical footing as "income." At best, they are clusters of historically observed characteristics that have tended to travel together. Thus, as we saw in chapter 2, corporations have typically had limited liability and a separation between ownership and control, among other key attributes, while debt has typically offered fixed returns, creditors' remedies, and no voting rights. Even any one of these characteristics typically could vary along a continuum. For example, the return on a financial instrument can be almost fixed, subject only to long-shot contingencies (as even classic debt is, given the possibility of default). Or it can be slightly less fixed than that, or again slightly less, continuing indefinitely by tiny degrees until it looks like classic equity.

The possibility of mixing and matching the attributes of supposedly opposite entities or financial instruments makes things more complicated still. Simple binary choice is a myth even if effective electivity does not as yet fully hold either. In practice, therefore, identifying the actuating concepts of the corporate tax is a matter of pure line-drawing—requiring that, right next to the line, things which are almost the same be treated as if they were completely opposite (see Weisbach 1999).

In practice, taxpayers always have reason to push for as much effective electivity as possible. The tax system responds by imposing frictions that burden free choice, making it harder for taxpayers to get their preferred tax classifications unless they accept associated real-world consequences that they may dislike. For example, if one wants to use Delaware corporate law or offer ownership shares that are traded on registered public exchanges, one cannot avoid having one's entity classified as a corporation. Thus, the noncorporate election potentially has a price.

Real world frictions are not constant across time, however. Instead, they constantly change with tax-planning innovation, broader marketplace developments, and evolving legal rules. In effect, the corporate tax is built on pillars of sand that are perpetually crumbling and being reinforced. Understanding this process is one of the keys to understanding the likely future of the corporate tax, and I therefore offer two brief case studies to give a sense of how it operates.

Distinguishing Corporate and Noncorporate Entities

As we saw in the prior two chapters, any legal entity that is literally a corporation under the laws of any state (or the foreign equivalent of U.S. incorporation statutes) is unavoidably a corporation for U.S. federal income tax purposes. This provision immediately has some force because incorporation is popular, reflecting that it offers a well-understood and well-developed legal regime. For example, some founders of companies that either want to go public immediately or anticipate doing so down the road may decide that the ability to use Delaware corporate law is valuable enough to justify the tax price.

Others, however, may only want the characteristics typically associated with corporate law, such as tradable shares and the separation of ownership and control. Such taxpayers learned early on that corporate characteristics can be achieved without the corporate form. An example is using a limited partnership to replicate the corporate-shareholder relationship without actually incorporating.

Limited partners, like corporate shareholders, typically have limited liability, the right to sell their interests, and no right to act as partners on behalf of the partnership. So a limited partnership, which typically must have at least one general partner, is the legal entity equivalent of a centaur. Rather than having the head of a man attached to the body of a horse, it has a general partnership attached to a set of limited partners that, for most purposes, might as well be corporate shareholders. Suppose that, as in some notable early cases, the only general partner is a corporation, itself featuring the separation of ownership and control and having few assets, so that its hypothetical full liability as a general partner is rendered meaningless by its underlying corporate limited liability. Then, it would seem, one truly has a corporation in all but name, as far as the entity's true attributes are concerned.

The IRS recognized this problem early on and developed a "corporate resemblance" test that listed a set of key features and asked which type of "true" entity a given specimen resembled more. This enterprise was bound to invite some taxpayers to figure out how they could be just noncorporate enough for tax purposes. However, it could perhaps have had some success in limiting taxpayers' ability to elect noncorporate tax status while still having substantial corporate attributes, if the U.S. Treasury Department had not shot itself in the foot by guessing wrong about the direction in which it would benefit from slanting the rules.

For many years, professionals, such as lawyers and doctors, were not permitted to incorporate under state law. For tax purposes, however, they wanted to avoid self-employed status, even if in truth they worked for themselves, because at the time only employees of distinct taxpayers could enjoy tax-favored fringe benefits (such as pension plans and excludable health insurance). Being in a partnership was not good enough, since the income is taxed directly to the partners. Thus, creative minds thought of using limited partnerships that they could argue were really corporations for tax purposes (notwithstanding state law bans on literal corporate status).

The Treasury evidently wanted to block this end-run around the rules denying tax-favored fringe benefits to the self-employed (however nonsensical these rules may have been). So it drafted corporate resemblance rules that, while highly formalistic and thus manipulable, were also significantly tilted toward denying corporate status. These rules listed four classic corporate characteristics—limited liability, exchangeability of ownership interests, separation of ownership and control, and unlimited life—and held that an apparent partnership would not be reclassified as a corporation unless the corporate characteristics predominated (i.e., three of the four counted as corporate). This would be evaluated without any weighing of the factors' relative importance or how close to the line they were.

Purely as a matter of form, partnerships technically dissolve whenever an old partner leaves or a new one joins, even if this supposed dissolution has no legal consequences whatsoever. Accordingly, the doctors' and lawyers' partnerships unavoidably lacked the corporate characteristic of unlimited life. Add their legal difficulties, under state laws regulating the professions, in either limiting liability or making ownership interests tradable, and they were dead in the water as far as being corporations for tax purposes was concerned.

Having won this glorious victory, the IRS then doubly lost the fruits by the early 1980s when states enacted special "professional corporation" statutes for the likes of doctors and lawyers, while Congress made the Treasury's regulatory gamesmanship irrelevant by extending various tax-favored fringe benefits to the self-employed. A number of states also passed new statutes inventing a new type of entity, the limited liability company (LLC), that taxpayers could use if they wanted to avoid formal incorporation without being relegated to state partnership law.

Meanwhile, the entity classification winds had shifted direction. Taxpayers now typically wanted to avoid C corporation status, while still having the typical characteristics (such as limited liability) of corporate shareholders, so they could invest in entities that would give them the right to claim a pass-through share of tax-shelter losses. Limited partnerships automatically lacked the meaningless corporate attribute of unlimited life, and thus only needed to add one more to avoid corporate status. Absence of limited liability could easily do the trick without needing to have any practical consequences. For example, one could technically establish it by creating a limited partnership in which the only general partner was a corporation that itself had limited liability and was only thinly capitalized.

While the Treasury, in theory, could have responded by changing its entity classification rules to lean the other way, in practice this would have been politically difficult. Instead, Congress, in the landmark Tax Reform Act of 1986, met the tax-shelter challenge, albeit by creating various loss-limitation rules for individuals rather than by addressing entity classification. The act also, however, gave new impetus to the aim of avoiding the corporate form by making the corporate tax rate higher than that for individuals. Now no second tax was needed for corporate status to be tax disadvantageous. States, meanwhile, began enacting "master limited partnership" statutes that eliminated the need for any general partner at all. So new corporations in all but name could now fairly easily avoid ever having to face corporate taxation.

Congress responded in 1987 by adding the rule under which being publicly traded makes one a corporation for tax purposes. Mutual funds, however, have tradable shares, but no one believed these should be subject to a separate corporate tax. In response, Congress created an exception to the new rule. It provided that entities earning predominantly passive income, such as interest and dividends, would not be classified as corporations by reason of being publicly traded.

Here matters largely rested for the next 20 years. Meanwhile, the Treasury, evidently finding its interests sufficiently protected by the public-trading rule and aware of the corporate resemblance test's porousness and manipulability, withdrew that test in 1997 and ruled that formally noncorporate entities such as LLCs, if not publicly traded, could simply elect either corporate or noncorporate classification as they preferred. This was called the "check-the-box" test, because checking a box on the applicable tax return was literally how one made the election.

Tax-planning innovation to defeat the new rule proved to be just around the corner, however. In 2007, the Blackstone Group, a leading private equity partnership, announced and executed a plan to go public, earning millions of dollars for its prominent principals, without thereby becoming a corporation for tax purposes. The plan involved clever and aggressive, but apparently legally unassailable, regulatory "gamesmanship" that exploited the passive income exception in unexpected ways to achieve legislatively unintended results (Fleischer 2008). Specifically, otherwise pointless "blocker entities" were installed between the active business level and that of the publicly traded entity so that the active business income could magically be transmuted, as it passed up the chain, into capital gains and dividends that qualified as passive.

Leading members of Congress immediately responded by proposing legislation to "save" the publicly traded partnership rules from the end run that Blackstone's tax planners had discovered or invented, but as of early 2009, it remained uncertain whether anything would eventually pass. So the continuing capacity of the corporate tax to reach newly emerging, publicly traded, active business entities remains unclear.

Even if Congress prospectively blocks this route to escaping corporate status for tax purposes, other future challenges might be imagined. The fix might itself prove porous over time. Or taxpayers might develop new ways to offer the liquidity benefits of being publicly traded without qualifying even as readily tradable on the substantial equivalent of a secondary market. Or perhaps the winds will shift again toward taxpayers' wanting corporate status in cases where it is inconvenient to incorporate or arrange for public trading. The "end of history" is unlikely here, especially given the lack of a coherent underlying concept.

Distinguishing Debt from Equity

Distinguishing debt from equity is even harder than distinguishing between corporate and noncorporate entities. Here, one cannot glom onto anything analogous to legal entity-creating statutes, such as incorporation laws, since companies can issue whatever financial instruments they like without having to use a state-provided package. Nor does anything akin to public trading provide a convenient divide, since both debt and equity in public companies are typically tradable. The tax law therefore faces a challenge in defining debt and equity, resembling that which would arise in the entity classification context if the only available tool were making lists of corporate and noncorporate characteristics.

As we saw earlier, classic debt and equity differ in a number of dimensions. Classic debt offers such features as (1) a fixed return, (2) a fixed maturity date on which all still-outstanding principal and interest will be paid, (3) creditors' rights including bankruptcy enforcement, (4) payment priority over equity holders, and (5) no voting rights or other means of exercising control, other than perhaps to protect one's credit position. Classic equity, by contrast, offers such features as (1) a variable return depending on the success of the corporate enterprise, (2) no fixed maturity date, (3) no creditors' rights, (4) subordination to the claims of debt holders, and (5) voting rights.

Presumably, these packages emerged historically because their combinations of features often made sense. For example, they give voting control to the investors that have more reason to care about exactly how well the business is managed (since debt holders need only worry about bankruptcy), and they protect the position of those that are otherwise outside the loop by giving them priority and enforcement powers. Yet mixed packages have proven entirely and indeed increasingly feasible over time.

To get a sense of how daunting classification is in practice, consider that Congress in 1969 enacted a statute instructing and empowering the Treasury to issue regulations comprehensively defining debt and equity for tax purposes. The statute even helpfully offers a nonmandatory and nonexclusive list of the factors that the Treasury may want to treat as important.[3] Yet no such regulations have ever been issued—although the Treasury twice issued proposed regulations that drew widespread criticism—and it is now clear to everyone that none ever will be.

In the absence of clear guidance, law firms frequently write memoranda for their clients opining on whether particular instruments are debt or equity. These memos typically proceed by analyzing extensive laundry lists of factors derived from a leading article by the tax practitioner William T. Plumb (1971). Because so little has changed doctrinally since the article was published and the prospects for any sort of intellectual breakthrough appear too poor to encourage would-be successors, this article, which takes up no fewer than 272 pages of the *Tax Law Review*, remains the gold standard of debt-equity analysis despite its extreme antiquity as secondary legal sources go.[4]

Two problems impede applying the debt-equity line in practice. The first is that instruments with both debt-like and equity-like features are increasingly common and accepted. For example, contingent debt instruments, having classic debt features such as fixed maturity dates but variable returns that depend on objective information such as the movement of interest rates or stock indexes, are so common now that the Treasury has issued regulations specifying how deductions and inclusions for unpaid interest on them should be computed. The second problem is that any given feature on the laundry list of relevant factors may fall in the middle, be hard to observe accurately, or not matter economically to the parties (thus freeing them to structure it purely with an eye to the tax result they prefer).

For example, clear though the distinction may seem between a classic debt holder's fixed return and a classic equity holder's variable return, this distinction was shaky from the start for two reasons. First, even the simplest classic debt instrument has a variable return insofar as there is default risk. Taxpayers early on began exploiting this fact by classifying instruments as debt even where the chance of default was quite high and presumably compensated for by higher interest rates, as in the case of junk bonds.

High default risk, creating significant variability in expected returns, does not necessarily require an unusually speculative business venture. Thin capitalization (i.e., a high debt-equity ratio) can do the trick as well by leaving only a meager cushion to repay all debt holders if the business fares at all below maximum expectations. Courts early on duly identified likelihood of repayment and thin capitalization as pertinent factors in the debt-equity analysis, but generally without catching any but the most extreme cases if taxpayers otherwise planned carefully.

Second, all one needs to make a seemingly fixed debt instrument highly variable in practice is an option to convert it into stock of the issuer. Thus, suppose a corporation issues $100 of debt in the form of a two-year OID bond, paying 10 percent a year and thus to be settled in two years by a $121 payment. Suppose, however, that the bond can be converted at maturity, at the option of the holder, into one share of the issuer's stock (trading at a price of, say, $95 on the day when the OID bond is issued). Now the OID bond has a variable return, because, if the stock is selling in two years for more than $121, the holder will presumably convert. Indeed, the holder may enjoy almost as much upside risk as a current shareholder.

This is only one example of how options can change the risk analysis. Similarly, seeming shareholders may lose the upside if the company has the option to "call" the stock at some point in the future for a previously agreed price, or equivalently the downside if they hold a "put" option entitling them at will to sell the stock to the company (or anyone else) for such a price. It was decided early on, however, that conversion options generally would not change the tax analysis of a given instrument unless exercise was certain. This deliberately blinkered disregard of option features was perhaps inevitable given that, to assess a given bondholder or shareholder's true position, one would need to examine *all* of his or her financial positions as they changed over time and whether they appeared on the face of the instrument at issue or not. Otherwise, taxpayers would be able to elect whatever treatment they liked, through the choice of which options they treated as part of the same instrument.

Once the point about ignoring options is conceded, however, almost nothing is left of the risk analysis. Companies can issue instruments with identical economics to that of issuing stock, yet claim to have created debt that generates deductions for unpaid interest.[5] Shareholders can lock in debt-like fixed returns by holding "collars" that limit both the upside and downside risk through options compelling or permitting them to sell for a prearranged price, and yet continue to be treated as holding stock. [6]

Other factors on Plumb's laundry list can similarly fail to provide meaningful guidance:

- While an overly distant maturity date indicates that a supposed debt instrument is actually equity, numerous cases hold that a term 40 to 50 years in the future, or even in one case 89 years, is not excessive (Plumb 1971, 415–416). Whether repayment of all principal is guaranteed at maturity can be an important factor, but matters little economically (in present value terms) if the maturity date is significantly deferred.
- While the presence or absence of voting rights is important to the legal analysis, shareholders often do not care about them, and their true significance can be affected through the use of special voting classes of stock or supermajority requirements, potentially rendering a particular voting power close to meaningless.
- Since remedies for failing to meet performance standards can be flexibly adjusted in any event, the presence or absence of creditors' rights can be trivial or formalistic.
- If a corporation already has conventional debt and equity, a new issuance with intermediate priority between the two can be called

either subordinated debt or preferred equity. It ranks second out of the three classes either way.

• Among the key evidentiary factors suggested by the case law are the name officially given to an instrument and the ostensible intent of the parties (Plumb 1971, 411–412). For sophisticated and well-informed parties, it would be hard to think of a clearer invitation to electivity than that.

The joke around Wall Street goes that the best way to tell whether a complicated financial instrument that offers no current cash flow to investors is debt or equity is simply to ask what sort of investors it is being marketed to. If they are tax exempt, it probably is debt, with corporate interest deductions and investor inclusions that (given their nontaxable status) they do not mind. If they are taxable, it probably is equity. All this may require, however, working carefully with a law firm that identifies all the bells and whistles that it deems necessary for the issuance of a favorable opinion letter (often useful in encouraging prospective investors).

Making things more complicated still is that the issuer may care about the instrument's financial accounting treatment as well as its tax treatment. Companies often favor tax-accounting "hybrids" that are debt for tax but not accounting purposes, thereby generating interest deductions against taxable income but not against the earnings reported to investors.

The IRS has recently begun trying to use corporate managers' concern about favorable accounting treatment as a friction limiting effective tax electivity, stating that in classifying instruments as debt or equity, it will consider their classification for nontax purposes, such as in financial accounting statements.[7] How much weight a court would give this new approach remains unclear. However, the issue indicates a possibility that, at least for publicly traded companies whose managers must cater to outside investor sentiment, the drive toward ever-greater effective electivity may at least be slowed down.

The Significance of Moving toward Effective Electivity

How should we think about the consequences of permitting the corporate tax rules to evolve toward ever-greater effective electivity? A good starting point is to imagine what would happen if choices such as those between corporate and noncorporate tax status, or debt and equity classifications of a financial instrument, were made explicitly elective at zero cost—in effect, by extending the approach of the check-the-box rules and assuming away any transaction costs that taxpayers may incur in the effort to maximize their benefits from such elections.[8]

For the above two choices, the chief consequences would be twofold. First, investors would be able to choose between paying tax at their own marginal rates and at the corporate rate. Second, they would be able to elect whether they were subject to the double tax (which would apply, at least on paper, if they elected to pay tax initially at the corporate rate).

At first glance, this may not sound so bad. Why not let investors use their own rates, which reflect their personal circumstances (e.g., how much other income they have), in lieu of the corporate rate? Likewise, allowing cost-free avoidance of the double tax sounds akin to permitting self-help corporate integration, thus achieving without any need for legislative action a state of affairs that most tax-policy experts would endorse.

Neither of these conclusions necessarily follows, however. With regard to the investor rate, the big problem is tax-exempts, including not just explicitly exempt U.S. institutions such as pension funds and universities, but foreign taxpayers that can avoid paying U.S. tax on inbound investment here. As Edward Kleinbard (2007c, 166) notes, "today's capital markets are supremely efficient at matching taxable issuers and nontaxable investors . . . to maximize their collective after-tax returns" at the expense of the public fisc. The ostensibly tax exempt are effectively taxable today at the corporate rate insofar as they cannot avoid investing through corporate equity, and this is not necessarily a bad state of affairs. Indeed, proponents of corporate integration often support preserving this indirect tax (Graetz and Warren 1998, 11). As for the risk of shareholder-level imposition of the second piece of the double tax, this, as noted in chapter 1, may have desirable features after all if corporate-level tax avoidance is a sufficiently serious problem.

Rules restricting effective electivity thereby function as frictions limiting taxpayers' ability to achieve socially undesirable results. To be sure, they do so at a cost. In particular, the rules tend to preserve the core inefficiencies of the corporate tax that were described in chapter 2. Additionally, they have an ambiguous but potentially bad effect on taxpayers' inclination to waste resources (from a social standpoint) by engaging in complicated tax-planning transactions. The frictions may require such transactions to be costlier than otherwise (e.g., more complicated to arrange), although for this reason they potentially reduce the number of such transactions that taxpayers engage in.

Such trade-offs are familiar fare in the existing income tax, in particular given taxpayers' ability to exploit the fundamental rule that gain and loss generally are not taken into account for tax purposes until they are realized, such as through a sale or exchange. The realization rule is no less a pillar of sand than the various special features of the corporate tax, and it periodically has had to be reinforced through rules restoring frictions that capital market innovations had undermined.[9] Even so, realization underlies corporations' ability, in some instances, to create economically fake losses for tax purposes through tax shelter transactions that amount to little more than energetic paper shuffling.

The key IRS legal tool for combating corporate tax shelters is the general requirement that loss-generating and other suspect transactions, if they are to be heeded for tax purposes, must meet minimum standards of nontax economic substance and business purpose. Such rules, in turn, "make effective electivity costlier, by requiring companies that seek a tax loss . . . to bear real economic consequences that they otherwise would prefer to avoid" (Shaviro 2007b).

Indeed, while the economic substance approach often is rationalized doctrinally, such as on the grounds that statutory language requires it or Congress intended it, I have argued elsewhere that it is really

> just a tool for accomplishing aims that have little to do with how one might define it as a matter of internal logic. Leaving aside the institutional reasons why (for courts in particular) economic substance is a particularly useful tool for deterring undesirable transactions, one might as well condition favorable tax consequences on whether the taxpayer's chief financial officer can execute 20 back somersaults in the IRS National Office on midnight on April Fool's Day, if such a requirement happens to achieve a better ratio of successful deterrence to inducing wasteful effort in meeting requirements that are pointless in themselves. (Shaviro 2000a, 223)

Reinforcing the pillars of sand in the structure of the corporate tax presents similar considerations, apart from the point that allowing investors to opt out of the corporate equity universe seems less clearly bad than allowing the deduction of fictitious losses. In any event, so long as the corporate tax retains anything like its present form, we can expect continued trench warfare over the key operative definitions, which is good news for corporate tax practitioners, albeit not necessarily for anyone else.

PART II
Economic Theory Meets the Corporate Tax

In the well-worn tale of the three blind men and the elephant, the protagonists are asked to describe the creature's shape. The first blind man feels a flank and says the elephant is built like a wall. The second feels a leg and says it is more like a tree. The third feels the tail and says it is more like a rope.

Economists often resemble the three blind men when studying the corporate tax. Given the diversity of features that affect its operation and those features' complex character, economists inevitably must work from greatly simplified models. That in itself is not problematic. Economists regularly use greatly simplified models to generate powerful insights about real-world institutions. The problem, rather, relates to the difficulty of choosing appropriate simplifying assumptions.

Simplification works best when the system being analyzed has a discernible core. For example, in evaluating income taxation, economists ask what the tax does to work, saving, and risk taking (among other key decisional margins). For each, both the concept and the direction of incentive effects are reasonably clear. An income tax discourages work and saving by taxing their fruits, and reduces the taxpayer's risk level (holding investment choice constant) by taxing gains and partly refunding losses. Thus, there is little ambiguity about the sorts of core assumptions that may work well in generating insights about income taxation.

The unique systemic features of the corporate tax are hard to describe so crisply, however. Not only are the directions of particular biases (as discussed in chapter 2) variable and ambiguous, but it is not always clear what a given bias actually is about. For example, given the pillars of sand problem and underlying conceptual incoherence, what does it really mean for an entity to be a corporation, or for an instrument to be debt rather than equity, in the view of the tax system? If the difference between debt and equity lacks clear meaning, one cannot easily be sure what favoring one over the other really amounts to in practice. So it is hard to evaluate what the corporate tax really does, and thus how economists should model it.

This poses a real dilemma for economists who must identify suitable operating assumptions about the pillars in order to model the corporate tax. Additionally, if none of the operating assumptions is generally appropriate, then we cannot adequately choose between the models. Even if one model works better than another in a given environment of corporate tax planning and practice, within a few years everything may change.

In short, economists have failed the lawyers who want their help in understanding the corporate tax because the lawyers first failed the economists by handing them an ill-posed problem. Fail to specify adequately what you are doing, and you are bound to be dissatisfied with substantive analyses of your handiwork.

Despite these caveats, the leading economic models for understanding the corporate tax are important as well as interesting. They suggest admittedly conditional answers to questions about how the corporate tax affects efficiency and wealth distribution. In addition, they have strong implications for the importance (or lack thereof) of reforms such as corporate integration, and for how any such reforms should be structured. The next three chapters will review several leading theories in the economic analysis of the corporate tax, grouping them in pairs that reach conflicting conclusions by reasoning with equally sound logic from alternative starting points.

4

"Old Harberger" versus "New Harberger" and the Incidence of the Corporate Tax

W hat is the incidence of the corporate tax? Which groups in our society would be richer or poorer, all else being equal, if it did not exist? This can be a question about different groups, such as workers, consumers, and savers, all of which we belong to in varying degrees. Or it can be a question about progressivity, denoting corporate taxation's effect on wealth distribution between richer and poorer individuals.

Understanding Incidence

Before reviewing literature on the incidence of the corporate tax as such, let's begin with a brief overview of the concept of economic incidence. Three main principles must be kept in mind in order to understand it. The first is the difference between nominal and economic incidence. The second is the importance of elasticity, or the changeability of people's tax-affecting behavior, in determining the incidence of a given tax. The third is the distinction between short-term or transition incidence and long-term or steady-state incidence.

Nominal Incidence versus Economic Incidence

When a given transaction generates a tax liability, the tax law typically specifies who among the parties must actually remit the payment to the government. We may tend to think that the tax is truly on that party, the literal taxpayer. In economic theory, however, assignment of the formal tax liability generally has no effect whatsoever on who ends up bearing its economic incidence.

A simple example may help to illustrate both this point and the related one that formal or nominal incidence is not (even if relevant) a well-defined concept. Consider a retail sales tax, such as those levied by numerous state and local governments across the United States. Suppose the tax rate is 10 percent, so that a convenience store's $1.00 sale of a pack of chewing gum generates 10 cents of tax liability. In a typical transaction, you would pay the convenience store $1.10, rather than the stated price of just $1.00, albeit with the tax component separately listed. The convenience store would then remit 10 cents to the local government—and would be required to do so whether or not it expressly made you add the sales tax to the posted price.

Seemingly, then, the convenience store is the nominal taxpayer. It is the party that actually pays the government, and may be the only party legally obligated to do so. Nonetheless, many people would view the customer as the nominal taxpayer. This reflects the convenience store's practice of stating pretax prices to customers and purporting to collect the sales tax as a separate item. The store, therefore, looks as if it is merely a collection agent, passing on to the government taxes that were due and collected from the customers.

We would have exactly the same set of cash flows, however, if retail stores posted after-tax prices and did not specifically inform customers of the tax component going to the government. This is how value-added taxes in countries around the world often operate. Can nominal incidence really be meaningful if it distinguishes between identical cash flows based on whether the store posted the pretax or the after-tax price?

Now let's consider a transaction form that actually changes the exact cash flow details and that causes nominal incidence to unmistakably lie with the customer. Suppose the cash economy had been completely supplanted by the use of personal debit cards that tax authorities could monitor electronically. Then it might be administratively feasible to collect sales tax without any stage where retail stores hold the cash. Thus, to buy a pack of gum, suppose you had to furnish your debit card to the store clerk, who would use it to transfer a dollar from your bank account to the store's, leading automatically to a further 10-cent transfer from your bank account to the local government.

With this technology in place, the store would never hold or remit the sales tax proceeds. It would have ceased to be in any literal sense a tax-payer. Yet the overall cash flow, once the transaction was complete, would still be exactly the same. Just as before, you would be out $1.10, the store would be up $1.00, and the government would be up 10 cents. The intermediate details, whether or not described as changing nominal incidence, have no effect on any of this.

The analysis of true or economic incidence leaves all such details aside in order to focus instead on the more interesting and meaningful question of who actually bears the burden of a tax, in the sense of being worse off by reason of its imposition. To explain this idea in the context of the chewing gum transaction, consider three alternative scenarios (each admittedly oversimplified and unrealistic), each offering distinctive answers to the counterfactual question of how this transaction would have changed in the absence of a retail sales tax.

Scenario 1: You would still pay $1.10 for the pack of chewing gum, but the convenience store would get to keep it all. If this is what would happen absent the tax, then in the actual situation where there is a tax, it is borne by the owner of the convenience store.

Scenario 2: You would only pay $1.00. If this is true, then you bear the tax, which is genuinely taking money out of your pocket.

Scenario 3: The price would have been $1.05, all of which the owner would have gotten to keep. Now we would say that the incidence of the tax is split between the two of you, 50-50.

Each of these scenarios ignores changes in behavior in response to the tax, such as reduced chewing gum consumption because of the price hike, or competition from new entries in the convenience store business if it becomes more profitable. Such behavioral changes, in addition to affecting prices and therefore where the tax incidence shakes out, generate excess burden or efficiency loss. The incidence of the excess burden, like that of the direct burden, could in theory be determined based on who it leaves worse off. This, however, would require knowing how foregoing the chewing gum transaction and doing something else instead would affect the parties' welfare.

Elasticity and Who Ends up Bearing a Tax

There is a story about two naturalists in Africa who are being chased by a hungry lion. "Do you really think you can outrun him?" one of them asks the other. "I don't have to," the other replies. "I only have to out-run you."

Strange as it may seem, the naturalists almost could have been talking about tax incidence. The fundamental economic precept about who among the parties to a taxable transaction will end up bearing the greatest portion of the tax is that it depends on their relative tax elasticity. Whoever runs away the fastest—or rather, whichever group most reduces its supply or demand in response to the tax burden that is being threatened—will bear it the least, while whoever is slowest (or rather, least changeable) will bear it the most. Unlike with fleeing hungry lions, however, incidence is not an all-or-nothing proposition and may end up being shared.

To illustrate with taxes rather than lions, suppose Las Vegas imposes a 20 percent tax on hotel room rentals. The natural candidates to bear this tax, at least in the first instance, are visitors who stay in Las Vegas hotels, the hotel owners, and the hotel employees. If visitors' demand for Las Vegas vacations is sufficiently fixed that higher prices will not chase them away, hotel owners can simply pass the tax on to them by adding it to the room charges. If their demand is highly elastic, however, which means that at a higher price they would come in significantly smaller numbers, then the owners cannot so easily raise prices without increasing vacancy rates at the expense of revenues.

Can the hotel owners instead take the tax out of employees' wages? This depends on supply elasticity in the labor market. The more a wage cut would reduce the hotel owners' capacity to get the staffing they want, the less feasible this is.

Will hotel owners end up taking most of the financial hit themselves? Here the elasticity question is how substantially they will exit the industry, presumably converting their properties to alternative uses, as profitability declines. The more readily they can exit, the greater the capacity of those that remain to fill enough rooms even at higher prices and to hire enough employees even at lower wages.

Short-Term versus Long-Term Incidence

Responses to newly announced tax changes often unfold slowly over time. It is not always easy to change what one is doing right away. Over time, however, a given category of behavioral response to a tax may prove far more elastic than it was initially, causing tax incidence to change gradually.

For example, suppose the United States suddenly and unexpectedly repealed the substantial income tax preferences currently enjoyed by homeowners. Overnight, real estate values presumably would decline, to the detriment of current homeowners. After all, most homes cannot easily be converted to alternative uses, and buyers would not pay as much without the expectation of tax benefits. Over time, however, as fewer (or smaller and plainer) homes were built in the new tax environment, to a degree the prices of existing homes might recover. Declining home construction would reduce the marketplace competition that existing homes faced.

While all homeowners might lose in the long term, the tax burden would fall entirely on people who owned homes at the moment when the tax law change was announced (or more precisely, when it came to be anticipated). Suppose I am considering buying a home when the tax preferences are suddenly repealed. Perhaps the value of the home that I might buy declines from $300,000 to $270,000, reflecting the loss of tax preferences worth exactly $30,000. If I am credit constrained, I might actually be glad to see the price drop. If not, I may be indifferent, since either way I get exactly the value I am paying for. If the tax preferences are worth $30,000, then presumably paying for them up front and then enjoying them over time is a break-even transaction economically. As we will see, a similar analysis applies to the corporate tax and the incidence effects of various proposals to change it.

The "Old Harberger" View of the Incidence of the Corporate Tax

With this background, we can now turn to the first enduring contribution to the economic literature devoted specifically to corporate taxation. This is Arnold Harberger's landmark study, "The Incidence of the Corporation Income Tax" (henceforth "Harberger 1962").

Harberger 1962 owes its continuing reputation not only to the author's having gotten to the subject first, but to its combining two distinct virtues. The first is its rigorous theorizing within the contours of a well-defined formal economic model. The second is its making imaginative use of real-world information, even where admittedly skimpy, in the effort to answer the most important distributional question about the corporate tax: whether its incidence is progressive. Given the corporate tax's arbitrary features, which seem likely to result in needless inefficiency, many of the people who support it, if free of the illusion that legal entities can actually bear a tax, do so on the view that it is an indirect way of increasing how the overall tax burden falls on rich people, such as those with extensive shareholdings. So the question that Harberger 1962 examines is vital to evaluating whether the existing corporate tax structure is intellectually defensible, presumably on the grounds that more straightforwardly increasing progressivity would be politically difficult.

According to Harberger 1962, the corporate tax is principally borne by holders of all capital (not limited to corporate shareholders), suggesting that it is indeed progressive. However, the reasons for its being progressive are not just nonobvious but seemingly entirely fortuitous, resting on particular observed features of the real-world division between corporate and noncorporate sectors that the paper makes no effort to explain theoretically. Given this fortuitousness, one could argue that Harberger 1962's actual main implication, if one otherwise accepts its analysis, is to show that the corporate tax could very easily fail to be progressive, notwithstanding widespread assumptions to the contrary.

Key Features of the Harberger Model

One thing almost completely lacking from Harberger 1962 is an actual description of the corporate tax. He simply states that for purposes of his model, incorporated businesses pay the tax, while all other businesses do not. The business sector therefore is treated as divided between taxed and untaxed firms. Given that the income of proprietorships and partnerships historically has always been fully taxable at the individual level, this evidently is a reference to the capacity of the double tax to penalize use of the corporate form.

Why would any business incorporate, given the assumed tax disadvantage? Harberger 1962 does not say, but one might posit that features such as limited liability are necessary in some industries. The model treats the economy as mysteriously divided between corporate and noncorporate industries, reflecting that, under its view, the selective imposition of the tax would prevent corporations from competing directly with their untaxed brethren. Imposing a corporate tax therefore is simply a means of imposing higher taxes on some industries than others.

Anticipating the objection that this model is counterfactual—there have always been plenty of industries with both corporate and noncorporate participants—Harberger argues that, as an empirical matter in his mid-1950s data set, it was largely and indeed sufficiently true. Specifically, in this data, there was strong evidence that the real estate and agricultural sectors were largely noncorporate, while most other major industries were primarily corporate (216–217). The corporate tax in the paper's model therefore was effectively a special levy on most types of industrial activity other than real estate and agriculture.

Against this background, there initially are four dramatis personae that might end up bearing the corporate tax: corporate shareholders, all holders of capital, workers, and consumers. However, Harberger swiftly dismisses corporate shareholders, although the nominal taxpayers if one credits them with the corporate-level tax as well as their own, as potential victims. He notes that capital markets tend to equalize the after-tax returns from alternative investments (215–216). Thus, suppose that all businesses earned 10 percent before tax, but that corporate businesses were uniquely subject to a 20 percent levy, reducing their after-tax yield to 8 percent. Investors would respond by exiting the corporate sector, increasing the return available to investments that remained there, and entering the noncorporate sector, driving down returns there until they precisely equaled those available after tax in the corporate sector. At equilibrium, all investors would earn the same after-tax rate of return.

This leaves three dramatis personae that might potentially bear the corporate tax. Harberger next summarily dismisses consumers as possible victims. He notes that, while consumer prices in the corporate sector should exceed those in the noncorporate sector by the per-unit amount of the corporate tax (all else being equal), consumers' ability to shift their consumption between the two types of product prevents them from losing anything overall, leaving aside the deadweight efficiency cost of the tax-induced shift. Consumers with a stronger taste for higher-priced corporate products lose, and those with a stronger taste for lower-priced noncorporate products win, but consumers as a whole break even by consuming less of some products and more of others (217–219).

Suppliers of capital and of labor therefore emerge as the two finalists in the tax-incidence struggle. Here is where the model in Harberger 1962 really goes to work. It treats all industrial activity as the fruit of jointly applying capital and labor, as distinct productive inputs to the creation of value. Both are assumed to display zero tax elasticity, so far as their overall levels are concerned. Taken literally, this would suggest that one could tax either of them at a 100 percent rate, applied across the board to all industries, without affecting the quantity supplied of either. Harberger recognizes that this assumption could be challenged, especially for capital. Wouldn't people save and invest less if the return to saving were highly taxed? He argues, however, that economic data support viewing savings levels as lacking any clearly demonstrated positive level of tax responsiveness over time (216).[1]

Under the assumption that saving has zero tax elasticity, the progressivity of a uniform tax on capital would be clear-cut, albeit established by the choice of assumption rather than by empirical analysis. If the rich disproportionately save, a tax on capital cannot help but be progressive absent any aggregate behavioral response from them in the form of reduced saving. In effect, savers end up bearing the entire burden of the tax because they are unable or unwilling to run away.

Harberger avoided so unsatisfying an approach to the question of corporate tax incidence, not only by treating capital investment in the noncorporate real estate and agricultural sectors as tax exempt, but also by relying on the fine details of the interaction between labor and capital in different industries as twin productive inputs. The incidence of the corporate tax would depend on how its imposition affected after-tax returns to each input, given their relative capacity to shift between the corporate and noncorporate sectors.

In short, the incidence of the corporate tax in Harberger 1962 depends on a subtler and more complicated version of the Las Vegas hotel example. Two key features of real estate and agriculture end up driving the analysis. The first is that they have below-average elasticity of substitution between the use of labor and of capital as productive inputs (234). The second is that they are less labor intensive than the corporate sector, using a much smaller proportion of the workforce relative to their share of capital and national income (231).

In effect, in the corporate sector, it's relatively easy to add a few more workers in lieu of a machine, while in real estate and agriculture, it's relatively hard to replace what few workers there are with extra machines. Thus, when the corporate tax drives capital out of the corporate sector and into real estate and agriculture, labor wins overall. The corporate sector now wants labor more, to a greater extent than the real estate and agriculture sectors (despite getting extra capital) now want it less. With wages therefore potentially facing upward rather than downward pressure, Harberger concludes that capital might even end up bearing more than 100 percent of the full corporate tax burden.

This conclusion, while suggesting that the corporate tax is progressive in its incidence, does not mean that Harberger 1962 suggests viewing it favorably, other than perhaps if a uniform tax on capital is ruled out for political reasons. To the contrary, by biasing investment choice between the sectors, the corporate tax creates "gratuitous deadweight loss" (Auerbach 2005, 9)—all the more gallingly if taxing all saving at a higher but uniform rate would have no efficiency costs whatsoever under the assumption that the saving level is fixed. One also might wonder about the resiliency over time of its incidence finding, given Harberger 1962's reliance on fortuitous and theoretically unexplained observations about the labor supply characteristics of different industrial sectors that happen to vary, for unknown reasons, in their compatibility with avoiding the corporate form.

Evaluating the Harberger Model

Technically impressive, creative, and resourceful though the Harberger model is, some of its continuing renown reflects a variant of the "man bites dog" phenomenon, which holds that you need to find something surprising in order for people to remember you. In Harberger 1962, what is surprising is not the conclusion that the direct incidence of the corporate tax, like the nominal incidence, falls on capital, but rather the circuitous route for getting there, relying as it does on the peculiar relationship between productive inputs in different sectors of the economy.

The problems with accepting the model today start with its not explaining why a firm would incorporate, and indeed whether corporate status is invariably tax penalized.[2] If one drops the unexplained division of the economy into corporate and noncorporate industries, the analysis in Harberger 1962 ceases to apply, and one is right back where one started, needing to ask all over again just what the corporate tax is and what it does.

More recent entries in the field have tried to do exactly that. For example, Jane Gravelle and Laurence Kotlikoff (1989, 753–755) note that there is plenty of joint production by corporate and noncorporate firms in the same industries. Accordingly, they posit that corporate status, which they continue to view as tax penalized, is necessary for "enterprises that both are very large and have a large number of owners" (756). In effect, then, what the corporate tax does is penalize production by large firms relative to that by small firms. They add as a refinement the idea that successful small firms use talented entrepreneurs, who "are more efficient than corporate managers, but since their managerial input is fixed, their output is subject to diminishing returns" as production levels rise (777).

Absent tax distortions, the balance between production by small and large firms in this model would depend purely on the trade-off between the former's superiority at small-scale production and the latter's access to economies of scale. But the corporate tax throws things off by penalizing size. Among other consequences, this greatly increases the deadweight loss of the tax, because highly substitutable production *within* industries is being affected, not just that *between* industries (Gravelle and Kotlikoff 1993, 514). Capital still loses from the corporate tax in the model, but so do workers and corporate managers. Indeed, the only winners distributionally are entrepreneurs, who benefit from the handicap that the corporate tax places on their rivals (Gravelle and Kotlikoff 1989, 766).

The possible alternative models are effectively infinite, each with its own incidence and efficiency implications for the corporate tax. A key insight from Harberger 1962 that remains valid (and always will) is that once one understands the reasons for the division of the economy between corporate and noncorporate production, idiosyncratic features of the divide can have important effects on how everything shakes out. Suppose, however, that there really is no strongly etched difference between corporate and noncorporate enterprise, notwithstanding the possible tax stakes. Then the point of main interest may simply be that double taxation penalizes some investment, presumably spread to savers generally as Harberger argues. The most important incidence question, then—for all its crude obviousness, compared to the analysis in the Harberger model—may simply be how tax elastic saving and investment are.

If saving and investment decline in response to their being taxed, this would tend to shift the economic incidence of the tax away from savers and toward workers through two mechanisms. First, with capital now being scarcer, the law of supply and demand would permit savers to demand an increased pretax return. Second, with investment slowed by the loss of available capital, advances in labor productivity would be less, tending to reduce the wages that workers could demand. So the corporate tax might fail to be progressive, through a mechanism that Harberger 1962, by positing completely inelastic saving, had ruled out.

As it happens, Harberger himself decided by the early 1990s, on similar grounds, that his pioneering analysis no longer applies. Whether or not the world is now "flat," as Thomas Friedman's recent bestselling book tells us, Harberger, in common with many other economists, concluded that globalization had dramatically changed the incidence of the corporate tax.

The "New Harberger" View of the Incidence of the Corporate Tax

Harberger 1962 assumes a closed economy, or one in which labor and capital cannot enter or leave the taxing jurisdiction in response to stimuli such as the corporate tax. Since that era, however, worldwide capital mobility has become ever more extensive and important. The change suggests that, even if saving levels do not alter meaningfully in response to the taxation of capital, the amount invested in a given taxing jurisdiction, such as a country, may respond significantly. At the limit, with perfect international capital mobility, no country with a small (relative to the world) open economy can unilaterally impose any tax burden on capital whatsoever, whether through a uniform levy or the corporate tax.

The Small, Open Economy Scenario

A simple chart may help to depict this scenario. In figure 4.1, capital is assumed to flow freely around the world in pursuit of the prevailing rate of return, which is 6.5 percent. Thus, in a small open economy such as Country X, all investments that earn at least 6.5 percent, but only those investments, are made. Also, since the reach of Country X's tax system is

Figure 4.1. Taxing Inbound Capital in a Small Open Economy

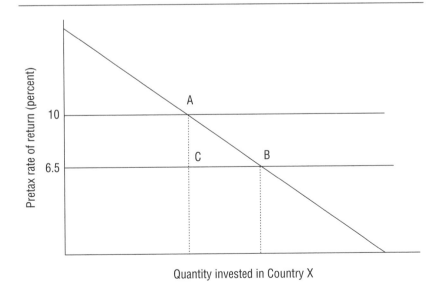

Quantity invested in Country X

small relative to the size of worldwide capital markets, nothing that X does can affect the prevailing rate of return. Local resource owners, who control either their labor or the use of land and natural resources, are assumed to be unable or unwilling to move out of the country in response to after-tax price changes, reflecting the power of local ties such as family, neighborhood, and language. However, the locals capture any return to a given investment opportunity that exceeds the required 6.5 percent rate, since if one investor were to demand more there would always be another who was willing to accept the prevailing worldwide rate.

Absent any tax on capital, the amount invested is that shown at B. The entire triangle above the 6 percent line to the left of B represents profits accruing to local resource owners after paying the 6.5 percent rate to those furnishing the capital. Suppose, however, that Country X imposes a 35 percent tax (via the corporate tax) on the furnishers of the capital. As a result, a 10 percent pretax return is now necessary in order for such furnishers to get the 6.5 percent after-tax rate that they can readily procure by investing elsewhere.

The consequence of the 35 percent corporate tax is that investment declines from the amount shown at B to that at A. The incidence of the tax falls entirely on the local resource owners, who now earn only the amount shown by the triangle over the 10 percent line to the left of A. They lose the profits represented by the rectangle between the 6.5 percent and 10 percent lines, because of the higher interest rate that they now need to pay, while the profits represented by the triangle ABC simply go unrealized (representing the deadweight loss of the tax).

The furnishers of the capital, although they are actually sending tax payment checks to the treasury of Country X for 35 percent of their pretax profits, bear none of the incidence of the tax. After all, they still earn the same 6.5 percent after-tax return that would have accrued to them if the corporate tax did not exist. The assumed perfect supply elasticity of capital, which can freely go wherever a 6.5 percent return is available and avoid all circumstances where it is unavailable, is what permits complete shifting of the incidence of the tax to local resource owners, who are assumed to be sitting on a fixed set of differentially profitable investment opportunities.

Application to the U.S. Corporate Tax

Many economists believe that the above scenario substantially or even completely holds today with respect to the U.S. corporate tax. Thus, most recent studies find that "immobile factors (labor and/or land) bear most, if not all, of the long-run incidence of the corporate tax in the open economy due to capital flows across borders" (Gravelle and Smetters 2001, 2). A recent survey of economists at leading universities found an average estimate that capital now bears only 40 percent of the tax (Fuchs, Krueger, and Poterba 1997). Harberger (1995) has himself argued emphatically that an open economy scenario, rather than the analysis he offered in 1962, now applies. Thus, he no longer accepts the "old Harberger" view that holders of capital bear the burden of the corporate tax.

The conclusion following from the small open economy scenario—that local resource owners, including workers, bear the burden of the corporate tax—is theoretically irrefutable if alternative investments around the world are sufficiently interchangeable to lead to equalization of expected after-tax returns, and if nothing else happens to the labor-capital mix (in the fashion of Harberger 1962) to create a surprising detour in how tax incidence plays out.

Jane Gravelle and Kent Smetters (2001, 2006) suggest two considerations limiting the requisite capital mobility for the open economy model fully to apply. The first is that "capital does not flow freely across borders . . . [reflecting] legal, accounting, language, and cultural differences between countries. In particular, investors want to invest in companies that they understand within a legal framework that they understand" (2006, 15). Further, while cross-border investment by domestic and foreign companies could create full capital mobility despite investors' home-country bias in the choice of corporate vehicle, the empirical literature suggests that its tax elasticity is limited as well (21).

Second, if there really are distinct corporate sectors (such as manufacturing) and noncorporate sectors (such as agriculture), as posited by Harberger 1962, then limited substitutability between the products in different sectors, as well as variations in the products' cross-border substitutability, may similarly limit the elasticity of capital flows. In the Gravelle-Smetters model, capital ends up bearing the long-run incidence of the U.S. corporate tax, even though the tax applies only to specified industrial sectors at home amid a worldwide open economy.

Other models, by contrast, tend to get the more intuitive result that the burden mostly shifts to labor, the less mobile productive input.[3] In addition, a set of recent studies using international data to explore the relationship between corporate tax rates and wage levels suggest that labor may indeed bear significantly more of the incidence of the corporate tax than does capital.⁴ Thus, while the debate about the incidence of the corporate tax is ongoing and unlikely to be resolved definitively any time soon, it does appear to be trending strongly toward the view that labor rather than capital bears the largest share of the burden.

What Difference Does It Make whether the Long-Run Incidence of the U.S. Corporate Tax Is Progressive?

Once one has looked at enough economic models created to shed light on the incidence of the corporate tax and has come to realize just how inscrutable the incidence issue remains, it is natural to ask, "So what? Do we really need to resolve all these abstruse questions about whether, say, labor or capital is the input that can more freely shift between agriculture and manufacturing, in order to determine what we think about the corporate tax and what, if anything, we ought to do about it?"

It is natural to be frustrated by the ineluctable complexity of the real world we live in, layered on top of the maddeningly ill-posed problem that economists face when they try to model the corporate tax. Yet there is a simple reason why we really should want to understand the long-term incidence of the corporate tax. The current rules are not inevitable, and proposals to modify them significantly are actually on the table. We face not only short-term political decisions, such as what to do about the scheduled 2011 expiration of the 15 percent tax rate for dividends, but broader strategic questions concerning the direction in which the tax system ought to be heading.

Again, it is hard to think of a good rationale for the current structure of the corporate tax unless, perhaps, it increases progressivity and other, more direct routes to the same goal are politically blocked. Further, even if we can achieve the same level of progressivity with or without the current structure, we may want to know just what (if anything) we would need to do elsewhere in order to make corporate tax reform distribution-neutral—arguably, a prerequisite to persuading groups with different distributional preferences to unite in supporting it.

Meanwhile, life goes on without our knowing the answer to the corporate tax incidence question. Indeed, political groups on both the left and the right often seem untroubled by the question as they gird up for battle over the expiring tax cuts. Or they may focus on issues of long-term incidence for narrowly tactical reasons. For example, "political 'conservatives' inside the Washington Beltway sometimes prefer assigning the full incidence to capital, thereby allowing them to claim that the tax code is already sufficiently progressive" (Gravelle and Smetters 2006, 1).

If one wonders how the question of true long-term incidence could seemingly have so little political traction, an important part of the answer is that politics is mainly about the short run. And here there really is no ambiguity about the distributional consequences of change. Just as homeowners clearly would lose (absent deliberate transition relief) if their tax breaks were suddenly and unexpectedly repealed, so corporate shareholders would clearly win from the overnight adoption of full-fledged corporate integration. The day before adoption of a surprise change, they would have held stock that could not generate dividend payments to them without a shareholder-level tax, and that was priced on the basis of this assumption. The day after, they suddenly would be able to get tax-free dividends—potentially making the stock more valuable, even if no dividends were currently being paid. This is the sort of distributional change that everyone can understand, with no economic models needed.[5]

This prospect of transition gain sounds nice if one is a corporate shareholder but otherwise is hard to rationalize as a matter of distribution policy. Whether one wants the overall tax system to be more progressive or less, why hand to a given group what is arguably a windfall gain, just because its members happen to hold a given set of assets at the moment when people first realize that the law is going to change? And if the transition effect is the clearest—and perhaps even the largest—distributional consequence of adopting corporate integration, then perhaps the question of whether we ever should have adopted the current corporate tax is no longer all that policy relevant. To a degree, it is water under the bridge. One might argue that, instead, the main question for policymakers ought to be whether the ongoing efficiency consequences of the corporate tax are great enough to support reform if one is agnostic about the long-term distributional effects and averse to handing anyone a transition windfall.

As it happens, this efficiency question is right at the heart of the next big issue that I examine in the economic literature concerning corporate taxation. This is the battle between the "old view" and the "new view" of the consequences of taxing corporate distributions to shareholders.

5

The Old View
versus the New View
of Dividend Taxation

If one thing seems obvious about U.S. corporate taxation, it is that by including a dividend tax, it discourages dividends. This may be good for corporate managers, who "have a preference for retaining earnings beyond the optimal level from the shareholders' perspective" (Chetty and Saez 2007, 2), but it does not sound good for anyone else and is an important part of the efficiency case against the current system.

Beliefs that are obviously true tend not to get distinctively named. There is no special term, for example, to describe people who believe that the sun generally rises in the morning. So we learn something surprising from the fact that today, in the corporate tax literature, there is actually a name for the view that the dividend tax discourages dividends. It is called the "old view" or (more kindly) the "traditional view."

What Is the New View, and Why Does It Matter?

The "new view"—discovered independently by three leading economists about 30 years ago (see King 1977; Auerbach 1979; Bradford 1981)—rigorously and irrefutably proves that, under specified circumstances, the dividend tax actually does not discourage companies with accumulated earnings from paying out dividends, and indeed from doing so sooner rather than later if that is what they otherwise prefer.

One can question how applicable the new view is to a given state of the world, but one cannot question how true it is under the preconditions that it identifies any more than one can question the "view" that, in an equilateral triangle, each internal angle is 60 degrees. The new view, like the theorem about equilateral triangles, states a logically necessary consequence of its assumptions. It is a tautology, not a falsifiable theory like the belief that cutting taxes this year will boost economic growth. Further, it is a tautology with at least some real-world descriptive relevance, although just how much is disputed and may vary over time. Except under rare circumstances, such as those prevailing on the day before a preannounced permanent repeal of the dividend tax, the new view strongly suggests that, as a practical matter, "the tax treatment of dividends is less generally unfavorable than the traditional view would have it" (Andrews 2007, 1). So the new view is worth examining closely as a precursor to considering corporate tax reform.

How can a dividend tax help but discourage dividends? The answer has to do with inevitability. If you are rational and farsighted, you will only try to avoid things that are, in fact, avoidable. If something is going to happen eventually no matter what, and if postponing it offers no mitigation of the impact, then you might as well just accept it and spend your time worrying about other things. At the heart of the new view, accordingly, is the point that if a given tax is unavoidable and deferring it does not reduce its impact, it is irrelevant so far as one's incentives are concerned.

To develop this point, the new view describes the consequences of a hypothetical tax instrument in the form of a uniform corporate distributions tax. This is a flat-rate tax that applies to all corporate distributions to shareholders. The single assumed rate applies no matter when a given distribution is made—there is assumed to be no legal change over time. And it applies no matter how the distribution is made—there is assumed to be no distinction between the taxation of dividends and share repurchases.

In truth, we do not really have such a tax. The actual corporate distributions tax has had frequent rate changes over time and treats share repurchases differently than dividends. In addition, given the tax-free basis step-up at death, share repurchases can be used to avoid shareholder-level taxation altogether. The new view therefore describes the consequences of a counterfactual state of affairs. However, even assumptions that are not completely true may be illuminating insofar as they are partly true (or can be made so).

The assumption of a uniform distributions tax includes the notion that all retained corporate earnings will be distributed eventually, leading to shareholder-level tax liability at some point. To be sure, there is no due date when earnings have to be distributed and the corporate enterprise brought to an end. In theory, however, the reason people save and accumulate wealth (including valuable shares of stock) is to consume it eventually, even if the end date—say, for all of the Rockefeller family's wealth finally to be fully consumed—seems likely to lie many generations in the future. And if we like, rather than assuming that all corporate earnings will eventually be distributed, we can assume instead that, from the shareholders' standpoint, nondistribution to avoid the tax makes no difference—for example, because they would have to pay a corporate distributions tax in order to get their hands on all of their money. This might be the case, if, in the presence of a 30 percent distributions tax, a shareholder with a claim on $100 of earnings that were in corporate solution was no better off than an individual with $70 in her own bank account, given the tax cost of extracting the corporate funds.

The distributions tax can, of course, be deferred by keeping undistributed earnings in corporate solution. And if one idea is fundamental to income-tax planning, it is that deferral of taxes generally benefits taxpayers. Suppose you will pay the government $100 of tax at some point in time. Deferring the tax for a year, if the after-tax interest rate is six percent, lowers the present value of the tax liability to $94.30, which is the amount one would have to set aside today in an interest-bearing account, in order to have the full $100 in a year. Alternatively, one can think of the one-year deferral as equivalent to the combination of (1) paying the full tax today and (2) getting to borrow $100 interest-free from the government for a year.

Since deferral is generally so valuable to taxpayers, why doesn't deferring the tax on corporate distributions reduce its bite? If it did, the new view would be mistaken, as current (or at least accelerated) distributions would indeed be disfavored by the tax system. The key difference between deferral in the corporate-distributions setting and elsewhere in the income tax is that a sooner distribution, by getting the money out of corporate solution, prevents subsequent earnings from facing the corporate-level tax.

To illustrate, consider two taxpayers that are deciding whether to incur tax liability now or in a year. The first holds an appreciated asset—say, a painting—that has a basis of zero and a value of $100. The second taxpayer holds corporate stock with a basis of zero and a value of $100, all from undistributed corporate earnings, and is deciding whether all of the earnings should be distributed now or in a year. Further, assume a tax rate of 50 percent, both for corporations and shareholders, on dividends and capital gains, and an annual pretax rate of return of 10 percent that applies to all assets. As we will see, in these circumstances, a year of tax deferral benefits the first taxpayer, who is deciding when to sell the painting, but not the second one, who is deciding when to receive the dividend.

(a) Timing of Asset Sale
  (i) Sell now—Selling the painting now for $100 would leave $50 after tax. Invested at the 10 percent rate of return, this amount would grow in a year to $55 before tax, or $52.50 after tax.
  (ii) Sell in a year—In a year, the painting will be worth $110 (given the 10 percent rate of return), leaving $55 after tax once it is sold. A year of tax deferral therefore ends up increasing the holder's after-tax wealth, even though all of the income has now been taxed.
(b) Timing of Dividend Distribution
  (i) Distribute now—Distributing all corporate earnings now would leave the taxpayer with $50 after tax. This amount would grow in a year to $55 before tax, or $52.50 after tax.
  (ii) Distribute in a year—By holding the $100 of undistributed earnings for a year, the corporation gets to earn another $10 before tax, or $5 after tax, leaving it with $105. Distributing this full amount to the shareholder leaves only $52.50 after payment of the dividend tax. A year of tax deferral with respect to the distributions tax therefore ends up having no effect on the holder's after-tax wealth, which is $52.50 either way.

The reason deferral fails to help the second taxpayer, unlike the first one, is that there is a benefit as well as a cost to distributing the corporate earnings sooner. The benefit is that it gets them out of facing double taxation. Pay out the $100 of undistributed earnings today and, while you will pay the tax on that amount sooner, at least all subsequent returns will be subject to tax only once, rather than twice.

To put it another way, the benefit of deferral is precisely offset by the detriment of ultimately having more corporate earnings to distribute. Both are creatures of the same interest rate. If deferring this year's dividend tax reduces its present value by five percent (the after-tax interest rate), but the amount to be distributed simultaneously grows by five percent, then the shareholder has accomplished precisely nothing by waiting.

Hence, the new view of dividend taxation shows that a uniform distributions tax has no effect on the timing of dividend distributions. However, the limits of what it shows, even under its assumptions, should be kept firmly in mind. Even with a uniform distributions tax, the new view does not prove (or even suggest) that the timing of corporate distributions is a matter of general indifference. For example, if the corporation's pre-tax rate of return differs from that available to shareholders, there is good reason to keep the money wherever it will earn more. Likewise, a uniform distributions tax does not assure tax neutrality as to the timing of corporate distributions. If the corporate and individual tax rates differ, shareholders have an incentive to keep the money where the tax rate is lower. In either case, however, the distributions tax, while responsible (given the corporate-level tax) for double taxation, is not creating a lock-in of corporate earnings, contrary to what seems to have been the universal old-view assumption.

What if the New View's Assumptions Were True?

In evaluating why the new view matters, we can start by asking what would follow if it were true. That is, suppose share repurchases really were given the same tax treatment as dividends, that the tax rate for both was permanently set in stone at a single fixed rate, and that the tax-free basis step-up at death, at least for shares of corporate stock, had been eliminated. A uniform distributions tax would then truly be in place. How would this change or clarify our thinking about corporate taxation?

In this scenario, two of the four main distortions caused by the corporate tax (discussed in chapter 2) would be eliminated. As demonstrated by the new view, there would no longer be any tax bias between distributing and retaining corporate earnings.[1] Also, as an assumed precondition for the analysis, the distinction between dividend payments and share repurchases (or proportional versus disproportional repurchases) would be eliminated.

To be sure, the other two big distortions would remain: the choices between corporate and noncorporate entities, and between debt and equity financing. These, however, are choices about how to make new investments. Should a new business be incorporated or not? How should a corporation finance a new plant? For valuable corporate equity that is already out there, however, the new view suggests that the distortions caused by the corporate tax are water under the bridge. The structure of the corporate tax does not affect (under the new view) decisions about whether to distribute or retain the value of such equity.

Considering just how much corporate net equity is out there, such tax-indifference about the timing of distributions implies a huge reduction in the amount of distortion that seems likely to result from the corporate tax. According to a prominent measure, the Dow Jones Wilshire 5000 Corporate Index, the total market capitalization of all publicly traded U.S. corporations recently stood at approximately $15 trillion. Under the old view, all of this net equity is being tax induced to stay in corporate solution even if it could be used more profitably elsewhere. Under the new view, this is not a problem. Corporate assets may be getting misused from a social standpoint because of other problems, such as tax preferences or shaky corporate governance, but not because of the structure of the corporate tax. So the importance of major corporate tax reform, such as the adoption of corporate integration, may suddenly seem a lot smaller.

A further implication of the new view concerns the likely relationship between corporate share prices and the value of underlying corporate net assets. A well-known measure, Tobin's q (for quotient), describes the ratio between the market value of a company's stock and the replacement value of its assets (see Tobin 1969). Thus, if Microsoft's market capitalization (the value of all its shares) were $330 billion and its asset replacement value were $300 billion, its Tobin's q would be 1.1. If its market capitalization fell to $270 billion without any asset change, its Tobin's q would be 0.9. The lower the Tobin's q, the worse the shareholders are doing given the underlying assets.

The new view's implications for Tobin's q, and thus for shareholders' economic well-being, are best described by assuming that, but for the tax on corporate distributions, the ratio would always be exactly 1.0—that is, corporations would always be worth exactly the replacement value of their assets. Suppose this were the case, and that the uniform tax rate on corporate distributions was 35 percent. In this scenario, $100 of net equity in corporate solution would always be worth exactly $65 to shareholders, since this would be all they could extract after paying the dividend tax. This, in turn, implies that the stock of a corporation with $100 in the bank, all from corporate earnings, and no other assets or liabilities would sell for exactly $65. Tobin's q would therefore be 0.65.[2]

In this scenario, whatever the long-term incidence of the corporate tax given the behavioral response issues explored in the Harberger model and elsewhere, one thing is clear: a surprise overnight repeal of the corporate tax, completely unanticipated by financial markets, would hand a huge windfall gain to shareholders. Tobin's q would suddenly jump from 0.65 to 1.0. An incorporated $100 bank account, previously worth only $65 due to the distributions tax that everyone assumed to be permanent, is worth $100 if we suddenly take that tax away.

Under the new view, therefore, eliminating the distributions tax not only would be pointless from an efficiency standpoint so far as old equity is concerned, but would have huge distributional effects that appear to be anomalous. Why would we want to hand existing corporate shareholders a huge windfall gain?[3] Only for new equity, entering the corporate tax regime after announcement of any policy change, would the case for corporate integration have any positive weight at all.

One last implication of the new view concerns corporate governance. However bad governance may be, as suggested by the myriad scandals of the Enron era, at least the corporate tax system isn't making things worse via lock-in. Such a conclusion would, however, make one wonder about the historical evidence that corporate managers pushed for the dividend tax (Bank 2003, 514–515), and have slyly continued to welcome it (Arlen and Weiss 1995), as an excuse for retaining earnings beyond the optimal level from the shareholders' standpoint. Does the new view, though admittedly based on a hypothetical system rather than the actual distributions tax we have, either undermine this view of the historical record or suggest that important players misunderstand the actual incentives in place? And would this, in turn, have further implications for how we ought to think about corporate taxation and underlying economic behavior?

Why Does the New View Matter in the Absence of a Uniform Distributions Tax?

Clearly, the new view would matter a lot if it really did rest on an accurate description of our corporate tax institutions. But is it merely a fanciful detour from assessing those institutions, given the lack of a uniform distributions tax? The answer is no—that is, the new view really does matter—for three reasons: (1) its model of the distributions tax is partly true rather than wholly false, (2) it dramatically reorients our thinking about dividend taxation, and (3) we can make it either more or less true through changes in current law and in people's expectations. Let's explore each of these reasons in more detail.

Partly True

Skeptics of economic models often are too prone to say, "Your assumptions are not 100 percent true, so we can act as if they were 100 percent false." An example would be to say that because market competition typically is imperfect, all economic reasoning about markets' capacity to satisfy consumer demand can be thrown in the trash. With respect to the new view, while we do not actually have a uniform distributions tax, we do have a widely applicable one. For companies with generally positive earnings and generally rising stock prices, distributions to shareholders will tend to be taxable no matter when made and no matter how made (leaving aside the special case of share repurchases right after the tax-free basis step-up at death). Thus, just as posited by the new view, shareholders really should be comparing the distributions tax they would pay today with the one they would pay in the future, keeping in mind that deferral is not valuable as such if the earnings subject to the double tax grow at the regular interest rate.

Further, in making this comparison, the lack of a uniform distributions tax does not necessarily mean that there is some degree of lock-in after all. That would require that the future distributions tax not merely be different than the current one, but lower in present value-adjusted terms. Without the tax-free basis step-up at death (and its common exploitation through share repurchases), there would be little reason for generally expecting the tax hit generally to decline over time. In principle, tax rates can rise as well as fall. In times when rates seem likely to rise, the corporate tax system may actually encourage sooner rather than later distributions. While such a scenario would diverge from the neutrality claim of the new view, it would directly contradict the lock-in claim of the old view.

Changing Our Thinking

The new view teaches us that incentive effects on corporate distributions depend not on whether the distributions are taxable, but on the relationship between current and expected future taxes. Consider the argument for adopting corporate integration via dividend exemption, as a means of eliminating tax biases regarding the timing of distributions. Dividend exemption would indeed have this effect (leaving aside for now the question of how share repurchases would be taxed), if people expected it to remain in place permanently. But so would any other permanent adoption of a uniform rate. The timing neutrality would result from the rate's being constant over time, not from its being zero. Without the expectation of permanence, dividend exemption might even reduce timing neutrality by inducing a rush to take maximum advantage of the unusually low rate (in historical terms) before it went away.

More generally, the new view helps us to understand the importance of expected policy stability over time to corporate distribution incentives. Gyrating distribution taxes would make the new view's neutrality result especially false, but for reasons that it explains. Suppose, for example, that the tax rate on dividends is expected to vary randomly over time, with little rhyme or reason and only limited advance predictability. This scenario might create lock-in after all, but for a new-view-compatible reason. If rates are bouncing around, then distributing corporate earnings today involves sacrifice of the option to wait for a lower rate at some unknown time in the future.

Affecting How True It Is

The accuracy, at any time, of the new view's assumption of a uniform distributions tax is an empirical question. Rather than being a fixed feature of the world, it is something that policymakers can actually affect. One way of making the new view either truer or less true is to address the relative treatment of dividends and share repurchases, including through the indirect effects of the basis step-up at death. Its truth or falsity at any given moment may also be affected by political economy factors that lead to greater or lesser expectations of policy stability.

Empirical Tests of Ostensible New-View Models

Despite the reasons for considering the new view relevant to tax policy thinking even if it does not currently rest on an accurate description of the U.S. corporate tax system, economists have naturally wanted to test it empirically. This requires expanding the basic tautology into a full-blown model of corporate behavior that generates actual predictions, which then can be checked for descriptive accuracy.

Testing the new-view model is potentially valuable: it can help increase our knowledge about the world. The problem, however, is that a simple if-then statement—if there is a uniform distributions tax, then here is what follows—does not immediately generate testable real-world predictions. Perhaps for this reason, economists who want to perform empirical tests of the new view have loaded it with all sorts of almost fungal incrustations, some known to be false and others merely irrelevant to the core tautology that gives it such analytical power.

Among the characteristics that the new view typically acquires in these models and empirical tests are the following:

(a) The new view is treated as assuming or even predicting that there are no share repurchases, and that only dividends are used to distribute profits to shareholders (U.S. Treasury Department 1992, 267; Gordon and Dietz 2007, 8). Such an assumption admittedly is required for the new view to hold entirely, given the distinct tax rules for the two types of distributions, but calling something that is clearly false a prediction of the new view verges on the absurd (Andrews 2007, 6).

(b) The new view also is treated as assuming that paying current or steady dividends offers no nontax benefits, such as reassuring capital markets that the company is doing well (U.S. Treasury Department 1992, 267). This assumption may make it easier to test a crisply defined new-view model, since nontax benefits, which presumably vary over time, might complicate distribution patterns and the behavior over time of the Tobin's q share-price discount. Why, however, should our understanding of how future expected corporate distribution taxes affect current distribution policy be entangled with assumptions that can fairly be described as childishly naïve?

(c) The new view also ostensibly assumes, in some of the models, that corporate managers faithfully serve shareholders rather than trying to promote their own objectives (U.S. Treasury Department 1992, 523). The same objection applies here.

(d) Once we assume that dividend payout patterns are irrelevant to firm value, and hence also irrelevant to noble and selfless managers, it becomes natural to assume that they will simply be a residual, each year equaling the excess of the company's profits over the amount that it wanted to invest. Given that profits tend to be volatile, both absolutely and relative to investment patterns, this appears to generate the empirically false prediction that companies' dividend payouts will be volatile rather than relatively stable (Gordon and Dietz 2007, 8).

(e) New-view models typically assume that firms use retained earnings to finance new investments, rather than using new equity issues as assumed in old-view models (Chetty and Saez, 1). This assumption helps add to the apparent importance of the issue the new view emphasizes, since the alternative to investing retained earnings is distributing them, and the degree of tax neutrality regarding when to distribute would therefore be a key consideration. By contrast, the new view and old view cohere in recognizing that the appeal to investors of new equity issues would be reduced by the prospect of paying a double tax. Again, however, it is hard to see why the question of how close we are to having a uniform distributions tax should be entangled with that of where companies happen to be getting their investment dollars from.

Further complicating the empirical tests, they often involve defining the old view as well as the new view, so that two sets of rival predictions can be compared. What exactly is the old view, however? If not simply a failure to recognize the new view's core insight about uniform distributions taxes, it presumably amounts to the claim that if the alternative to paying taxable dividends this year is *never* to pay a distributions tax, then there is lock-in that rises with the applicable tax rate. This claim is every bit as logically impeccable as that of the new view concerning uniform distribution taxes (albeit less surprising and counterintuitive). Once again, however, the urge to construct complete, easily tested models has encouraged adding features that muddy analysis of the true difference between the two views.

The old view assumption about expected future distribution taxes makes the current payment of dividends impossible to explain—since, from a tax-planning standpoint, it is madness—unless associated with nontax benefits that might involve either maximizing share value or managerial self-dealing. So the clearly correct points that firms' dividend policies might affect either share value or managerial pursuit of self-interest get folded into old-view models, even though logically consistent with either theory.

This setup gives the old view a natural leg up in the empirical contest, since being associated with realistic assumptions about extraneous matters can only help. Perhaps we should not be surprised, then, that according to some observers, the weight of empirical evidence does indeed favor the old view (U.S. Treasury Department 1992, 269). Others, however, find the new view performing better, at least in particular settings (Auerbach and Hassett 2005).

Even without any extraneous bias in the modeling setups, no one should imagine that empirical work can, as some observers hope, resolve in any stable or permanent sense the controversy as to which assumption about future dividend taxes is more applicable (U.S. Treasury Department 1992, 268). The relative truth of the competing hypotheses depends on the prevailing state of practice and belief concerning corporate distributions at any given point in time. That which is truer today may be less true tomorrow, whether because of a change in practices or in market expectations about future dividend-tax rates.

Does It Matter Why Companies Pay Dividends?

Since the old view and the new view are theories about dividend taxation, one might think it matters greatly why publicly traded companies actually pay dividends. In fact, it doesn't matter to the truth of the new view as such, since the tautology it states about the incentive effects of a uniform distributions tax would be true in any event. However, theories concerning why companies pay dividends are crucial to assessing the actual efficiency consequences of departures from tax neutrality with respect to the form and timing of corporate distributions.

If corporate managers fully served shareholders' interests, rather than having self-serving aims that they could advance without being fully observed, distribution decisions would depend, in the absence of tax bias, purely on where the funds could be used most profitably. Companies would retain funds on which they could earn a higher rate of return than that directly available to the shareholders, while distributing funds that the shareholders were better situated to use. In this zero-agency-cost scenario, lock-in resulting from the corporate tax system's failure to levy a uniform distributions tax would make it rational, in some cases, for companies to retain funds that the shareholders otherwise could have put to better use. Likewise, tax-preferring share repurchases might cause firms to favor them over dividends even when transactionally more costly and otherwise equivalent at best.

Adding real-world corporate governance problems to the model requires revisiting the efficiency analysis. Their most obvious and straightforward implication would be that they increase the efficiency cost of failing to levy a uniform distributions tax. Empire-building managers who are keen to retain excessive funds may all too readily seize on lock-in as an excuse for avoiding taxable distributions even where the shareholders would benefit from them after tax. Likewise, as noted in chapter 2, the more favorable treatment of share repurchases gives managers an excuse for using them to profit at the public investors' expense from inside information about share value (Fried 2005, 1328).

Might something be missing from this analysis, however? If share repurchases both are tax favored and benefit managers, then it becomes even more of a mystery that they have not historically been used more, relative to dividend payments. Perhaps there is a behavioral explanation, such as that shareholders dislike having to decide whether they want to tender shares or not, anticipating that (due to loss aversion) they would subsequently regret having guessed wrong about where the stock price was headed more than they would enjoy having guessed right (Shefrin and Statman 1984). However, numerous economists have concluded that the efficiency analysis of how lock-in affects dividend decisions in light of agency costs is more complicated than it initially seems.

In particular, a variety of "signaling" theories treat dividend payments as credibly communicating that the firm that pays them is of high quality, thus exerting upward pressure on the stock price. The essence of a credible signal of high quality is that it scares off "big talkers." Anyone can claim to be high quality, since talk is cheap. But if you have to back up the claim by doing something that would be costlier to you if you are actually of low quality, then the liars will tend to be filtered out and the signal of high quality may actually work (Spence 1974). A signal succeeds insofar as it creates a separating equilibrium in which only the high-quality truth-tellers benefit on balance from using it, rather than a pooling equilibrium in which everyone (or no one) benefits.

Why would paying dividends credibly signal high quality? One explanation is that since investors react adversely to reducing regular dividend levels, establishing a high payment rate credibly signals that one expects sufficient future earnings to maintain dividend payments (Joos and Plesko 2004, 2). A second is that by reducing cash on hand, dividends show managers' willingness to resort to the discipline of capital markets if they need to raise more funds (Easterbrook 1984). Perhaps the most provocative dividend signaling theory, however, holds that the very wastefulness of paying dividends, from a tax standpoint, is what makes them a credible signal of firm quality. This is the "money-burning" theory of dividends, originally suggested by Douglas Bernheim (1991).

A few analogies may help make this theory intuitively more comprehensible. Some have argued that the United States defeated the Soviet Union in the decades-long Cold War by boosting military spending to levels that the Soviets felt they had to match, and that, while wasteful for both economies, were affordable only by the United States. Or suppose that rich people engage in wasteful, conspicuous consumption in order to signal their status, knowing that others cannot afford to imitate them. These are both classic money-burning theories.

For a variant showing that money burning (or its equivalent) can work even if none of the players understands it, consider the evolutionary puzzle of the male peacock's tail, which imposes a handicap by reducing maneuverability while increasing conspicuousness to predators (Ridley 1993, 148). Why would male peacocks evolve with such tails, or female peahens evolve to prefer them? The prevailing explanation is that only high-quality males can survive, at sufficient rates, having handicapping themselves with large and showy tails. Once females "learn" this, the tail bearers make up for their reduced survival rates by having more offspring.

Lest one think this requires too much cleverness on the part of the peahens, there is actually no requirement in the theory that they understand why they prefer the showier males. So long as those males truly are genetically higher quality than their rivals despite their handicap, natural selection will favor the females that blindly and automatically choose them. Returning to dividends and money burning, this is an important point in favor of the theory's potential plausibility, since surveys of investors that prefer high-dividend firms would be unlikely to produce the explanation that they were impressed by the wastefulness of bad tax planning.

As applied to dividends, the money-burning theory holds that only high-quality firms can offer investors sufficient financial returns over time despite wasting so much money by triggering extensive double taxation. Investors, being (one hopes) more cognitively advanced than peahens, are credited with learning over time that high-dividend firms often tend to be good ones. Or, at the least, experience does not dissuade them from such a view, even if they initially adopted it for naïve reasons or out of impatience for immediate cash in hand.

Money-burning theory radically transforms the apparent efficiency consequences of lock-in. If paying immediate dividends is not tax discouraged after all due to a uniform distributions tax, the theory collapses. One can't have an effective differentiating signal if adopting it imposes no costs. This means, however, that under new-view conditions, firms lose a mechanism for increasing the efficiency of capital markets by conveying accurate and credible information to investors through an activity that, while wasteful from their standpoint, is socially just a transfer because it raises revenue for the government. In short, under the money-burning theory of dividends, the lock-in that results from imposing an avoidable dividend tax is "potentially Pareto-improving" (Bernheim and Redding 2001, 466)—it can make everyone in the society better off. The only limit is that just as the peacock's tail has an optimum size, above which the survival costs exceed the mating-selection benefits, so a rising degree of lock-in from the dividend tax would at some point become excessive.

Since the other dividend-signaling theories rely on imposing costs other than from increased tax liability, they could survive making current dividend payments tax neutral rather than tax discouraged. Even under those theories, however, lock-in from dividend taxation can increase the efficacy of dividend signaling with respect to stock prices (Bernheim and Wantz 1995, 533). Thus, the other theories may join money burning in support of the surprising conclusion that lock-in may actually be good, and that at a minimum it is not as bad as it seems. However, the empirical persuasiveness of the dividend-signaling theories remains contested (see, e.g., Skinner 2003), even after several decades of study.

Implications of the Old View–New View Debate for Corporate Taxation and Its Possible Reform

If wishing were enough to make it so, we would probably live in a new-view, not an old-view, world. Unless dividend-signaling theories have sufficient weight to the contrary, lock-in, which a uniform distributions tax would avoid, increases the efficiency costs of the corporate tax. The new view shows that the distortions from double taxation can be limited to new equity, rather than extending as well to old equity with its current market capitalization of about $15 trillion.

The most straightforward case for making the new view truer relies on the usual efficiency argument for tax neutrality. However, managers' preference for retaining excess earnings might suggest that, if anything, we should want to encourage, rather than discourage, current corporate distributions of earnings. Thus, the current rules creating lock-in might be even worse than the usual case for tax neutrality suggests, by leaning in precisely the wrong direction. On the other hand, dividend-signaling theories, and in particular the money-burning theory of dividends, suggest that the existing corporate tax, by creating some lock-in, may verge on getting it right, albeit apparently by accident.

If one accepts the new-view case for making the form and timing of dividend payments tax neutral, then elimination of the double tax through corporate integration not only loses some of its importance, but may affirmatively become a bad idea. Lock-in under current law may increase if people anticipate future legislation under which the dividend tax would completely disappear. Reform efforts might then optimally place more emphasis on making dividend-tax rates stable over time than on making them zero. Such efforts might also focus on reducing the disparity between the tax treatment of dividends and share repurchases, such as by eliminating the tax-free basis step-up at death.

6

Debt and Equity
Trade-Off Theory versus
the Miller Equilibrium

Capital finance theory considers how firms optimally would, and actually do, finance their investments. The financial instruments that firms use can vary infinitely in their terms—relating, for example, to their upside variability, downside risk, priority over other claims, enforcement procedures, and effects on voting control. However, given the historical prevalence of the classic debt and equity forms, along with the continuing prevalence of legal rules (in tax and elsewhere) shoehorning as many financial instruments as possible into these two categories, much of capital finance theory is devoted to the question of how firms should and do choose between debt and equity financing. Each instrument typically is assumed for this purpose to have all of the classic characteristics of its type. Thus, debt gives a fixed return, gets paid first, creates enforceable claims that extend to bankruptcy, and provides no voting rights; equity is opposite on each point (see, e.g., Harris and Raviv 1991, 350).

As we will see, it is extremely important to both capital finance theory and the corporate tax that the real world of financial instruments is much more variable and complicated than this, and becoming increasingly so over time. However, since classic debt and equity remain important primary components of capital markets, we can accept for now the traditional bimodal view of the world in which these two instruments, rather than the underlying attributes that they bundle in particular ways, are treated as the fundamental subatomic particles of finance.

Capital Structure and the Modigliani-Miller Theorem

Capital finance theory began as the domain of people who often had practice backgrounds, rather than being mainly theoretical economists, and who brought maxims from experience to bear on the question of how firms should and do choose between debt and equity financing. Early theorists' holy grail was the optimal capital structure, or the mix between debt and equity that, for a given firm, was precisely calibrated to maximize share value. This analysis relied on the view that firms should minimize the cost of capital, which followed a U-shaped curve, first declining and then rising as leverage, or the percentage of debt financing, increased (Melnyk 1970, 332). This assumption of a U-shaped curve relied on the notion that investors start out preferring debt to equity because it gets paid first, but at some point begin to get nervous about the prospect of default on debt as leverage rises above a safe level.

Theoretical economists subsequently attacked this view with a pithy analogy from a less health-conscious era than ours:

> Under perfect markets, a dairy farmer cannot in general earn more for the milk he produces by skimming some of the butter fat and selling it separately, even though butter fat per unit weight sells for more than whole milk. The advantage from skimming the milk rather than selling whole milk would be purely illusory; for what would be gained from selling the high-priced butter fat would be lost in selling the low-priced residue of thinned milk. (Modigliani and Miller 1958, 279)

In other words, if debt is like cream because it brings the right to be paid first, then it "thins" the equity from the first dollar onward, requiring additional factors in the model if the idea of an optimal capital structure, based on a U-shaped cost of capital as leverage rises, is to be accepted.

Modern capital finance theory began with a famous article by Franco Modigliani and Merton Miller (1958) directly rejecting the traditional idea of an optimal capital structure, or in any event requiring any such idea to be differently and more precisely justified. Modigliani and Miller showed that in an efficient market, and ignoring taxes, bankruptcy costs, and asymmetric information (such as corporate managers' inside knowledge about their firms' prospects), the value of a firm is unaffected by how it is financed.

Their sophisticated mathematical proof relied, in a move that proved highly influential in financial economics, on the arbitrage opportunities that would arise if firm value diverged from the dictates of their capital-structure irrelevance principle. Thus, in the butter and milk example, if slightly thinned milk were being sold for the same price as whole milk, sophisticated arbitrageurs could in theory take "long" positions in whole milk (agreeing to buy it) and "short" positions in slightly thinned milk (agreeing to sell it), leaving them with no net cash outlay but a bit of free cream once they had removed the permissible amount from the milk they bought. This would amount to giving them free money if they then sold the extracted cream, attracting more and more exploitation of this opportunity until the relative mispricing of thinned milk was eliminated.

Another intuitive way to explain the Modigliani-Miller theorem is to ask, "What is the value of a firm?" Surely it is the expected value of the net cash flows that it can produce, using its available capital and other resources, and adjusting value as needed for the presence and significance of any risk. A firm's capital structure merely determines how its net cash flows (and the risks pertaining to them) are to be divided up between the parties that supplied its capital. Thus, it merely allocates value, rather than directly affecting it. Similarly, consider a large pizza, which we presumably can agree will be the same size whether the man at the counter slices it into 8 wedge-shaped pieces or 12 mostly rectangular ones.

The importance of the Modigliani-Miller theorem is easily misunderstood. It does *not* show (or purport to) that the choice between debt and equity never matters, in the sense of affecting firm value. Rather, it shows where we need to look in order for the debt-equity choice to matter. In particular, it directs attention to the issues it expressly rules out—taxes, bankruptcy costs, and asymmetric information—as potential sources of capital-structure relevance. Modigliani and Miller thereby spawned an extensive subsequent literature on how and why firm value might end up being affected after all by the relative proportions of debt and equity used.

From Modigliani-Miller to Trade-Off Theories

If one thing seemed clear from the start, once Modigliani and Miller had transformed capital finance theory, it was that the debt-equity choice is anything but a matter of indifference from a tax standpoint. Given the double taxation of equity-financed corporate investment, compared to the single level of tax on debt-financed investment, one would think that 100 percent debt financing is optimal under the model. This implication was unsettling, given its being so clearly counterfactual. To explain practice's departure from the seeming dictates of theory, Modigliani and Miller

(1963, 442) suggested a general "need for preserving flexibility . . . [through] the maintenance by the corporation of a substantial reserve of untapped borrowing power." Analysts found this unsatisfying and began searching for stronger countervailing considerations to explain the use of equity despite its apparent tax disadvantages. Under the theory, these presumably would have to relate either to bankruptcy costs or to asymmetric information.

Bankruptcy costs emerged first, in what probably remains the best-known theory explaining the use of equity despite its tax disadvantages. Under what is often called trade-off theory, the downside of using debt is that the bankruptcy proceedings it can trigger, if the company defaults on obligations to debt holders, waste valuable resources (Kraus and Litzenberger 1973). By contrast, when equity holders fall short of getting the returns they expected, while this is regrettable for them, at least the waste associated with bankruptcy proceedings is avoided. Thus, a company should be expected to keep on issuing debt, erecting a "tax shield" via the interest deductions against corporate-level income tax liability, but incurring ever-rising bankruptcy risk, until the trade-off turns negative—that is, until the marginal increase in expected bankruptcy costs from issuing another dollar of debt outweighs the marginal tax savings.

Under this view, the efficiency cost of tax favoring debt over equity is clear. The Modigliani-Miller capital-structure irrelevance principle, if not modified by the factors that their analysis left out, might suggest that it really doesn't matter. Tax favoring debt over equity is no costlier socially than favoring instruments printed on blue paper over those printed on gray paper if the debt-equity choice is trivial. But trade-off theory suggests that the tax bias matters because it induces companies to take on socially excessive bankruptcy costs in the pursuit of tax advantages.

A second prominent theory to explain the use of equity identified a trade-off in the realm of agency costs given asymmetric information. Michael Jensen and William Meckling (1976) were among the first to note that debt and equity may each have an advantage over the other in addressing a particular incentive problem that can lead to bad business choices. Managers and shareholders have a conflict of interest in that the former "do not capture the entire gain from their profit enhancement activities, but they do bear the entire cost of these activities" (Harris and Raviv 1991, 300). Meanwhile, managers get all of the benefit and only a portion of the cost from such activities as diverting company resources to their own pockets and engaging in empire building for its own sake.[1]

The use of debt can address this conflict of interest by avoiding further dilution of the managers' claim on residual profits.

A second conflict of interest lies between shareholders and creditors. The former can benefit from choosing risky, "heads we win, tails you lose" investment projects that have a big upside, from which they would capture all the extra profits, but that on the downside would lead to bankruptcy. Equity issuance can avoid this problem because the people supplying the new cash are purchasing the same financial position as those already in control (301).

The choice of which conflict of interest to mitigate causes companies seeking new capital to face a trade-off. Mitigating either one worsens the other. Agency cost trade-off theory, as I will call this, therefore does not share the implication of bankruptcy trade-off theory that equity is generally better than debt, tax considerations aside. It suggests, rather, that there is a role for each. If debt and equity each convey declining marginal benefit, with respect to the agency costs that they address, as their use increases, then, for any given company, there is an optimal balance where the debt-equity mix is just right, and expected value therefore highest. A company seeking new capital would have an incentive to seek this optimum, since the amount investors would be willing to pay presumably would depend on how much they expected their ultimate return to be reduced by waste attributable to bad incentives.

Despite this difference between the two trade-off theories, they are alike in suggesting that a tax bias in favor of debt will lead to inefficiency. Under agency trade-off theory, the problem is that overuse of debt will lead to a failure to balance properly between the two competing margins. While managers will be cheating shareholders less than if the balance were just right, the social gain from this will be exceeded by the social loss from inducing shareholders to cheat creditors more.

A third well-known capital finance theory, pecking order theory, has the empirically awkward implication of suggesting that (taxes aside) debt is generally better than equity, making the use of equity even harder to understand given the apparent tax bias. This theory holds that companies may have difficulty financing even genuinely meritorious projects, because outsiders may with good reason fear that the insiders seeking their cash have reason to exaggerate likely profitability (Myers and Majluf 1984). This creates a "pecking order" of preferred financing sources, as capital becomes costlier the more people must be compensated for this fear. Internal funds are best because (ignoring manager-shareholder conflicts) the people supplying them have, by definition, the best available information. Low-risk debt comes next, because it relies on investment quality only in the special case of default. Equity is worst because it fully relies on company performance—seemingly suggesting, counterfactually, that no one but insiders would ever use it.[2] Consequently, the theory "requires an exogenous debt constraint" in order to work (Harris and Raviv 1991, 306). One would have to know more about the functioning of this debt constraint in order to evaluate the efficiency cost of tax encouraging the use of debt, but, in any event, pecking order theory has done poorly in empirical tests (see, e.g., Frank and Goyal 2003).

Then there are signaling theories that treat debt issuance as credibly communicating that the issuers are of high quality, thus permitting them to charge more for the financial instruments that they issue. Debt may signal high quality in two ways. First, it suggests that the corporate insiders are not worried about bankruptcy, which might be quite bad for them—for example, if managers would lose their jobs and reputations. Second, it suggests that insiders don't want to share the variable upside with outsiders, preferring just to offer the market rate of interest (Harris and Raviv 1991, 311). In either case, the signal's being costlier to low-quality than high-quality firms creates the possibility of a separating equilibrium, or at the least of some significant positive correlation between issuance and true quality.

The signaling theories, while easier than pecking order theory to reconcile with a world in which equity is common despite its apparent tax disadvantages, resemble it in making the efficiency costs of the tax bias hard to gauge. Presumably, everyone will use more debt if it is tax favored. The question of interest, however, is how effectively the signal works to separate the wheat from the chaff with the tax system's thumb on the scales, as opposed to without it. This is hard to tell in the abstract. While tax favoring debt over equity may seem likely to make the signal generally weaker, it arguably increases the relative appeal of debt to high-quality firms, which are more likely to expect future earnings against which they can anticipate deducting their interest expenses.

Throughout the discussion so far, the common assumption has been that the tax system disfavors equity, and that a good explanation of how companies set their capital structures must sufficiently explain why it is so frequently used. In bankruptcy trade-off theory, which is perhaps the most prominent theory, the assumption of tax bias is not merely an important background fact but actually part of the model. It would therefore make a huge difference if this assumption were discredited.

While this large literature was still developing, Merton Miller re-entered the fray to suggest exactly that. Debt is not tax favored after all, he argued, and indeed the capital structure irrelevance principle can be extended to include taxes in the model. As we will see, the importance of his argument to contemporary thinking about corporate tax reform exceeds its degree of acceptance in the capital finance literature.

The Miller Equilibrium

Miller launched his provocative counterstrike in favor of capital structure irrelevance at a 1977 presidential address to the American Finance Association. He focused on bankruptcy trade-off theory—at that time the best-developed, and still today probably the best-known, attempt to go beyond Modigliani-Miller's restrictive assumptions. Miller seems to have viewed trade-off theory not as advancing the ball by adding realistic features to his coauthored model, but instead as a retrograde revival of what he thought was the discredited traditional analysis of optimal firm leverage (Miller 1977, 262).

Beyond thus seeming to find trade-off theory unwelcome, Miller believed that it fell short empirically in two critical respects. First, debt-equity ratios did not appear to change historically with marginal tax rates as they should have if the theory were true. In recent decades, "[corporate] tax rates had quintupled—from 10 and 11 percent in the 1920s to 52 percent in the 1950s" (264). If the tax rate is five times as high, then each dollar of interest deductions saves five times as much in taxes as previously. If companies were leveraging to shield their earnings from the corporate tax until the point where the marginal benefit of the last dollar of tax savings precisely equaled the marginal cost of increased bankruptcy risk, then one might have expected to see much more leverage in the 1950s than the 1920s, but the record did not seem to show this (or to respond as predicted in other periods).

Second, the expected bankruptcy costs that firms ostensibly were trading off against tax savings seemed too small to explain prevailing debt-equity ratios. Thus, a study had found that bankruptcy's direct cost averaged about one percent of the filing firms' asset value as of seven years before the time when they filed (263). Even keeping in mind indirect bankruptcy costs, but also that most firms never enter bankruptcy, this seemed far too low a cost to explain firms not levering up more when (depending on the marginal rate) they could save 30 to 50 cents of taxes per dollar of added interest expense.

Given the seemingly radically unequal weight of the two components that trade-off theorists claimed were being balanced against each other, Miller suggested, it "looks suspiciously like the recipe for the fabled horse-and-rabbit stew—one horse and one rabbit" (264). He concluded from the anomalies that "the tax advantages of debt financing must be substantially less than the conventional wisdom suggests" (266). To explain why this might be so, he offered illustrative reasoning based on three simplifying assumptions: (1) bonds are riskless, offering a fixed return with no chance of default, (2) shareholders pay no tax at the individual level, and (3) investors face progressive marginal rates that range from below the corporate rate to above it (268). Thus, suppose that investors' rates are either 0 percent or 40 percent, while the corporate rate is 30 percent.

Under these circumstances, the only significant difference between debt and equity is that debt-financed income is taxed at the investor's rate, while equity-financed income is taxed at the corporate rate. Without risk in the picture, the debt can pay interest equaling exactly 100 percent of the earnings that it is invested to generate. Thus, debt-financed earnings are zeroed out for tax purposes at the corporate level through use of the interest deduction, but reappear at the investor level as fully taxable interest income. Meanwhile, equity-financed earnings are fully taxed at the corporate level but never reappear as taxable income at the investor level.

The tax-planning implications are clear: investors facing a 0 percent marginal rate will invest in corporations through debt, thus preserving the use of their low rate despite investing through a taxable entity. For taxpayers subject to a 40 percent rate, things are better still. They don't just get to preserve their otherwise applicable tax position, but to better it by substituting the corporation's lower marginal rate for their own.

Without risk in the model (or voting rights for stock), debt and equity are the same. If corporate earnings are certain, debt as well as equity can be designed to pay them out exactly. Within its assumptions, therefore, Miller's view is as unanswerably correct as the new view within its very different (and indeed, inconsistent) assumptions. So if we want to ask why the Miller view wouldn't be true, the only possibility is that its core assumptions fail to describe with sufficient accuracy the actual corporate tax. In other words, risk must matter, as it can potentially give meaning to the debt-equity choice, or perhaps it is voting rights that matter, or else the difficulty of avoiding the second level of tax. Or perhaps factors excluded from the model add important complications—in particular, either bankruptcy costs (although he argues these are low) or agency cost trade-offs, which he acknowledges but does not emphasize (262).

Reflecting his professional interests, Miller emphasized the corporate-finance rather than the tax-policy implications of his model. In particular, he noted that for the corporate sector as a whole, it implied an equilibrium debt ratio based on the relative investment dollars from investors with tax rates above, not below, the corporate rate. (Hence, it is often called the "Miller equilibrium.") However, no individual firm would have an optimum debt ratio. Low-leverage firms would target investors in high tax brackets, while high-leverage firms would target tax-exempts, but one clientele is as good as any other, so firm value wouldn't be affected by firms' debt versus equity choices (269).

Within the corporate finance literature, Miller's theory has not fared especially well. As a descriptive matter, it cannot easily be reconciled with the facts that tax-exempt pension funds often have large stockholdings, or that investors commonly have mixed portfolios of debt and equity. In addition, no evidence has been adduced that overall debt-equity ratios fluctuate, as Miller's model would predict, with the relative size of investor clienteles paying tax at more than the corporate rate, as opposed to less. In particular, widespread equity holding is hard to explain when the top corporate rate equals or exceeds that generally applying to individuals, as is the case today. As a model for thinking about tax policy, however, the Miller view is considerably more promising, as we will see next.

The Miller Equilibrium and Tax Policy

From a tax-policy standpoint, the Miller view suggests an important shift in our thinking about corporate taxation. Rather than viewing the U.S. system as something that burdens investors, relative to simply taxing all corporate income at once, we should think of it—insofar as the application of a double tax can be avoided—as something that benefits them. By reason of the debt-equity distinction, what the corporate tax does is offer an election to be taxed either at one's own rate or at the corporate rate, whichever is lower.[3]

As a general rule, taxpayer elections are a bad idea for the tax system. If taxpayers respond to them by expending resources in order to determine which choice will enable them to pay the least amount of tax, then we may get the unholy combination of less revenues plus more waste.[4] Normally, we think of added inefficiency as an unavoidable byproduct of getting *more* revenue, not less.

In addition, if the otherwise applicable rate structure was picked for good reasons, then allowing taxpayers to opt out of it, through the use of corporate equity investment, may be anomalous. Thus, suppose Congress made 40 percent the top marginal rate for individuals but set the corporate rate at only 30 percent, perhaps to keep it competitive with the corporate rate in other countries. The use of equity investment without threat of a second level of tax would enable taxpayers in the top bracket to avoid paying tax at the expected 40 percent rate, which presumably would be a bad thing if one favored the nominal rate structure. (And if one did not favor it, then putting in a 30 percent top rate directly presumably would be preferable, so as not to implicate entity choices or debt versus equity choices.)

Since the taxpayer election is not explicit, but instead depends on financial instrument choice, it potentially has a cost. How costly it is depends on the interaction between (1) how the tax system identifies debt and equity, and (2) what sort of economic characteristics the taxpayer, along with counterparties such as the corporation and other investors, want the financial instrument to have. As we saw in chapter 3, the tax rules may afford considerable electivity to taxpayers, especially if they are willing to steer a course somewhere in the middle. And the easier it is to marry the economics one prefers with the tax label one prefers, the more effectively elective and therefore Miller-like the state of affairs should be. Where taxpayers can get the label they want, be it debt or equity, but at the cost of changing their preferred economics at least a little, the cost of this departure from their preferences is akin to a fee for making the preferred election. However, unlike an actual cash fee, the change in preferred economics involves deadweight loss, rather than a transfer to the government.

Thus, the relevance of the Miller view depends not only on taxpayers' ability to avoid (or at least minimize) the second level of tax, but also on their ability to achieve their nontax objectives independently of whether a given financial instrument is classified by the tax system as debt or as equity. Just as with the new view of dividend taxation, the Miller view's degree of truth and relevance is not a timeless historical constant, but can vary over time. And the truer the Miller view is, the greater the importance of changing corporate taxation to treat debt the same as equity, as opposed to emphasizing other elements (such as the double tax) in the corporate integration program. One also can directly affect how true the Miller view is by strengthening or weakening either the shareholder-level tax or the tax rules for distinguishing debt from equity. In contrast to the case with the new view, however, making the Miller view completely true seems likely to be a bad idea from a tax-policy standpoint, given the problems with unlimited taxpayer electivity.

A further tax-policy implication of the Miller view concerns its interaction with Harberger-style analysis of the incidence of the corporate tax. It is plausible that the analysis in chapter 4 would not change if the corporate tax were effectively negative (or a subsidy) as compared to the taxation of other business activity. Thus, the Miller view might imply that holders of capital capture the benefits of debt-stock electivity under "old Harberger," while workers capture most of the benefit under "new Harberger." This would certainly be an ironic result for the U.S. corporate tax if it purported to burden capital, and thus aid labor, through the double corporate tax, but instead got both the burden versus benefit question and the incidence question backwards, causing it to have the desired distributional result after all.

PART III
The International Dimension

The term "international taxation" arguably is a misnomer. Only nations and their subdivisions levy taxes, not the international community as such. Nonetheless, the term has a well-understood meaning in practice. The international tax rules of a given country, such as the United States, concern how it taxes outbound investment by its residents and inbound investment by other countries' residents. For outbound investment, the questions are what foreign income should currently or ultimately be taxable at home, and what account to take of other countries' taxes on this income. For inbound investment, the question is to what extent domestic taxes should be imposed on foreigners.

Twenty years ago, international taxation was a niche specialty, both in corporate tax practice and in policymaking circles. Today, this has changed: international taxation has gone mainstream. Inbound and outbound capital flows are so pervasive that corporate financing transactions, for example, routinely involve one or the other. Likewise, in the policy world, the taxation of cross-border capital flows has become too large a piece of the corporate-tax picture to ignore. While the taxation of outbound investment by U.S. multinationals is at center stage, even seemingly domestic questions, such as what the U.S. corporate tax rate should be, depend in large part on the international picture. This part of the book therefore discusses, first in chapter 7, the basic U.S. international tax rules along with their rationales and main effects, and then in chapter 8, the chief tax-policy dilemmas presented by the design of these rules.

7

U.S. International Tax Rules
The Basics

M ost people, if attending a sit-down wedding and asked by the server if they want the meat or the fish, would think it bad manners to answer "both." Many countries, however, are not so bashful when designing international tax-policy rules. Faced with two plausible grounds for asserting tax jurisdiction—the residence of the taxpayer and the source of the income—frequently they do indeed answer "both." Problems caused by the overlap, plus the dilemma of which to favor insofar as a country mainly emphasizes one, form the grist for a surprisingly rich set of policy issues and dilemmas in international taxation. The U.S. rules offer a case in point.

The Multiple Components of U.S. International Taxation

Being firmly (at least formally) in the "both meat and fish" camp, the United States purports to tax all worldwide income of U.S. residents, along with the U.S.-source income of foreign residents. For individuals, U.S. residents are defined based on legal status as a citizen or permanent resident, or alternatively, time spent in the United States. Obviously, no such test could work for corporations, so they count as U.S. residents if they were incorporated here, which generally means in a U.S. state (most commonly,

Delaware). This exclusive focus on the place of incorporation makes the United States somewhat of an outlier, as other countries typically rely, whether additionally or instead, on corporations' place of management or principal business location (Ault and Arnold 2004, 349–350).

Taxation of U.S. Companies

While U.S. corporations theoretically are taxable on their worldwide income in the year it is earned, in practice they get a tax benefit known as deferral for the foreign-source income of their foreign subsidiaries. To explain, when a U.S. corporation decides to operate in a foreign country, it has two options. One is simply to open an office there, commonly referred to as a "foreign branch," although it is not formally distinct from the domestic company. The second option is actually to incorporate a new company in the foreign country, presumably as a wholly owned subsidiary of the U.S. parent. The use of subsidiaries, rather than branches, is prevalent among large U.S. (and other) multinationals, reflecting the legal advantages that use of a subsidiary can have—for example, limited liability at the parent level if the local firm goes bankrupt.[1]

The origin of deferral for the foreign-source income of foreign ubsidiaries, but not branches, was purely formal or legalistic. Foreign branches are not in any way legally distinct from their domestic parents. Thus, income earned by a U.S. company through a Paris branch is no less includable than that earned through a New York or Miami branch. By contrast, since the subsidiary is a separate legal person, technically its income is not that of the parent company, even if the parent owns 100 percent of the stock and the practical differences from branch status are trivial. If the subsidiary has positive earnings, in theory that merely indicates that perhaps the parent's stock in it is likely to have appreciated in value. And asset appreciation generally has no tax consequences for taxpayers until the economic gain is recognized through a transaction such as a stock sale or the receipt of a dividend.

In 1962, the Kennedy administration, recognizing that foreign subsidiaries ("controlled foreign corporations," or CFCs) can be a lot like branches, proposed to end deferral and make their income currently includable by U.S. corporate parents. U.S. multinationals protested vigorously, arguing that their ability to compete with foreign companies that did not have to pay U.S. tax would be adversely affected. The dispute led to a compromise, the retention and precise contours of which remain controversial to this day, under which deferral generally was retained, but subject to a significant exception. U.S. companies were made currently taxable on a new term of art, their CFCs' "subpart F income" (named for the new rules' placement in the Internal Revenue Code).[2]

The rules of subpart F are complicated. In general, however, the income that it makes taxable falls into either of two categories. The first is passive income, such as interest and dividends earned on portfolio assets, as distinct from the proceeds of an active business that the U.S. company controls. The second is a disparate set of items with the common theme of appearing to reflect suspected tax avoidance activity abroad. An example is the rule treating "foreign base company sales income" as subpart F income.[3]

While the exact technical details of the foreign base company sales rules lie far beyond the scope of this book, a brief description is in order since the underlying concept is so pervasive and controversial in U.S. international tax-policy debates. Suppose that a U.S. manufacturer ("Clever-Co") wants to sell U.S.-produced consumer items (say, widgets) in Europe, but subject to as little European tax as possible. It therefore sets up a subsidiary in a low-tax European country, such as Luxembourg, which buys the widgets from Clever-Co for one price, then resells them at a substantial markup to fellow subsidiaries in high-tax European countries such as Germany and France. Further, suppose the Luxembourg subsidiary ("Lux-Co") exists more on paper than as an actual enterprise with employees and business functions, and thus does very little to earn the markup that it pockets under the corporate group's official bookkeeping.

As an aside, intercompany prices such as those charged by Clever-Co to Lux-Co and by Lux-Co to the other European affiliates are commonly called "transfer prices." They may superficially look just like any other prices that buyers pay to sellers in transactions. But since transfer prices (by definition) involve buyers and sellers that are commonly owned, they tend to be a matter of complete economic indifference to the supposed counterparties, tax consequences aside. To be sure, reported transfer prices may be challenged by U.S. or foreign government tax authorities, on the grounds that they differ from the "true" transfer price that would have been agreed to at arm's length. Transfer-price manipulation can lead to improper shifting of income between related parties, presumably to locate income in low-tax rather than high-tax countries.

The Lux-Co scheme, if successful, is European tax planning at its finest. Clever-Co gets to shift non-U.S. taxable income from Germany and

France to Luxembourg, where the tax rate is much lower. Germany and France might conceivably defeat the scheme by challenging the transfer prices reported on the inter-European sales for German and French tax purposes, but this may be unlikely in practice. Even the U.S. tax authorities often have a tough time challenging reported intercompany transfer prices, and other countries' tax authorities generally have not tried as hard.

Under the foreign-base company sales rule, however, simply by reason of the transaction's structure and without any inquiry into the European transfer prices, the profits that Lux-Co reaps from on-selling U.S. property to affiliates in other countries are treated as currently taxable to its U.S. parent, Clever-Co, precisely as if Lux-Co had immediately sent the money back home as a dividend. The likely upshot, if Clever-Co is well advised, is that it will not even attempt the transaction to begin with (or else will find a way to escape the reach of the foreign-base company sales rule), since immediate U.S. taxation would eliminate the net tax benefit. Accordingly, barring successful avoidance of subpart F, the result may be that Clever-Co simply pays more tax in Europe than it would have if the rule did not exist, and still retains the full benefit of deferral for U.S.-tax purposes. We will return later in this chapter to the question of why the United States might have chosen to impose such a rule, given the plausibility of the scenario in which only the European tax authorities end up directly benefiting from its imposition.

Taxation of Foreigners on U.S.-Source Income

In addition to taxing U.S. companies on their worldwide income subject to deferral, the United States taxes foreign companies (as well as individuals) on their U.S.-source income. In general, for business activity in the U.S., foreign companies are taxed on their U.S. activity in much the same way that U.S. companies would be taxed on such activities, albeit with a few significant differences in defining various cross-border elements. For passive income earned here, such as interest and dividends paid by U.S. companies, foreigners generally face a 30 percent gross withholding tax that is collected from the U.S. payer. This withholding tax, which falls on gross income unreduced by any deductions, is imposed in lieu of the U.S. income tax, on the view that collecting the latter from foreigners would be difficult. However, numerous countries have tax treaties with the United States providing that both countries will exempt the others' residents from their own withholding taxes. Tax planning that relies on exploiting and effectively expanding treaty exemptions, as well as on various other manipulations, has created a widespread sense in the tax bar, according to Edward Kleinbard, Chief of Staff of the U.S. Congress's Joint Committee on Taxation, that "only fools pay withholding taxes on dividends today" (Young 2007, 1111).

In general, the U.S. rules taxing foreigners on their U.S.-source income face a fundamental challenge: the difficulty of defining income's source. Just as "residence" is hard to make meaningful with respect to legal entities such as corporations, so "source" is an idea that verges on having "no there there" (as Gertrude Stein famously said of Oakland, California). Suppose I perform services entirely in the United States and entirely for U.S. customers. Then it is easy to conclude that the service income must be U.S. source. As soon as the facts get more complicated, however, not only may the "truth" about source be hard to discern, but it is not clear what source even means. We saw in chapter 1 that "income" has been defined economically as the taxpayer's consumption plus her change in net worth (Simons 1938, 50). There is no similarly orienting economic definition for the source of income.

Passive income is hard to place anywhere, in a meaningful economic sense, given the lack of any underlying activity that can clearly be associated with it. Thus, suppose I earn interest income, ostensibly in the Cayman Islands, via a bank that is registered there and maintains a Caymans post office box. In theory, one might think that the funds I have credited to this bank are actually being used somewhere by a borrower (since banks make money from the spread between their lending and borrowing rates). Money is fungible, however, and thus we cannot really say where my funds are being used unless we focus on arbitrary and manipulable details of cash flow.

Lacking a better approach, the U.S. tax rules generally base the source of passive income on the residence of the payer. Thus, interest and dividends paid by U.S. companies, but generally not by foreign companies even if those companies are owned in whole or part by U.S. individuals or entities, are treated as U.S.-source income.[4] However arbitrary this may be, one might think U.S.-source income would at least be hard to avoid in cases where one actually wants to hold debt or stock in a particular U.S. company. As we will see in chapter 9, however, financial innovation makes it ever easier to have the economic equivalent of an investment stake in a U.S. company without being caught by the U.S. rules.

One also might think that business income would be easier to source than passive income, at least if it arises from the activities of people that are in actual physical locations. While this may be true to a degree, it is not nearly true enough to avoid big opportunities for tax planning, along with high compliance and administrative costs. The basic problem goes back to transfer pricing and the arm's length standard on which IRS scrutiny of reported transfer prices attempts to rely. Suppose a French firm acquires a U.S. firm, creating increased joint profits due to the synergies that arise from their sharing management, financing, access to valuable intangibles such as their trade names, and so forth. To be concrete, suppose the two companies previously earned $10 million a year each, but now earn a total of $25 million a year. The extra $5 million could be called their "synergy income" from the merger. But what is the source of this synergy income— the United States or France?

The officially reported location of the income will depend on transfer pricing as between the French and U.S. companies, along with how they allocate expenses that create shared benefits, such as financing and head-quarters costs. But where does it really arise, given that it reflects the synergistic combination of the two? This is not an answerable question.

Even if officials in the two companies bargained with each other at arm's length regarding how to split the extra $5 million, there is no way to know how these negotiations would have come out. Further, such bargaining would be inconsistent with what modern economic theory understands as the core reason for the existence of large firms, including multinationals. As first set forth by Ronald Coase (1937) in his famous article, "The Nature of the Firm," economic production arises within firms, rather than through arm's length relationships between contracting parties, when it is more efficient to organize production in a hierarchical rather than a price environment. Further, in real-world cases, even the bargaining range may be unclear, rather than being limited to a specified amount of synergy income. For example, where a French firm establishes a new U.S. subsidiary, as distinct from merging with a preexisting company as in the above example, there may be no way to tell how much would have been earned had the U.S. firm instead been a stand-alone entity.

The swiftly rising importance to modern economic production of intangible assets, such as patents or proprietary production techniques, has made the difficulty in sourcing income ever greater. The question of where intangible value, such as that from developing know-how or a patent, arises is harder to answer than the question of where, say, factory assembly takes place. So the shift from hard assets to intangibles as the source of value creation makes the tax system's job of sourcing income even harder.

Foreign Tax-Credit Rules

The existence of both residence and source taxation, not only in the United States but in many countries around the world, creates the potential for crippling overtaxation of cross-border enterprises relative to those in just one country. Thus, suppose the United States has a 35 percent corporate income tax, while Australia has a 25 percent corporate income tax, applying in each case both to the worldwide income of resident companies and to foreigners' income from inbound investment. In addition, suppose that the only adjustment either country makes for taxes paid to the other country is to make them deductible when paid by a domestic firm on outbound investment, on the view that the taxes reduced the firm's profits. Finally, suppose that both the U.S. firm ("U.S.-Co") and the Australian firm ("Australia-Co") earn $100 pretax in each jurisdiction.

Before tax, the companies' income would be as follows:

	Source	
Company	United States	Australia
U.S.-Co	$100	$100
Australia-Co	$100	$100

After tax, however, they would retain the following:

	Source	
Company	United States	Australia
U.S.-Co	$65	$48.75
Australia-Co	$48.75	$75

Clearly, under these circumstances, cross-border investment would be severely penalized, most likely to the economic detriment of both the United States and Australia. Thus, for a U.S. firm, the gap between the 35 percent rate it would face at home and the effective combined 51.25 percent rate it would face in Australia would steeply tilt the odds in favor of its investing at home, even when it had the opportunity to earn a lot more before tax in Australia. Likewise, a given investment in either country that a firm from the other country could make far more profitably than a home firm would nonetheless end up being made by the home firm unless the difference in pretax profitability was big enough to overcome the huge tax penalty for cross-border investment. Further, the penalty results not from what either country is doing standing alone—each is taxing every taxpayer it identifies at a uniform rate, without any discrimination between such taxpayers—but from the interaction between the two countries' overlapping source- and residence-based tax bases.

Countries have developed two main solutions to the overlap problem. The first is to exempt the foreign-source income of one's residents, thereby moving toward a purely source-based system that will not overlap with other countries' taxation of one's residents unless two countries claim the same income as domestic source. The United States arguably gestures in this direction by providing deferral, although the exemption ends when a U.S. firm repatriates its income (or has subpart F income). The second response is to provide foreign tax credits for the taxes that residents pay to foreign countries on the income from their outbound investments. This the United States does more generally.

Tax credits are dollar-for-dollar reductions in tax liability by reason of creditable expenses incurred. Thus, with a full foreign tax credit, if you pay $30 of tax abroad, you reduce your domestic liability by that full $30. In effect, the taxpayer gets all of its money back from paying the foreign taxes. Of course, this only happens once the foreign-source income is actually taxable in the United States—one cannot claim current foreign tax credits with respect to earnings that remain untaxed here by reason of deferral.

If the United States and Australia both provided unlimited foreign tax credits, the final after-tax tally for U.S.-Co and Australia-Co would look as follows:

	Source	
Company	United States	Australia
U.S.-Co	$65	$65
Australia-Co	$75	$75

The United States, observing that U.S.-Co had earned $100 and paid $25 of tax in Australia, would calculate a $35 tax bill for that income based on the U.S. rate, reduce the amount due by the $25 foreign tax credit, and collect $10. Meanwhile, Australia would determine that Australia-Co should have paid $25 on its U.S.-source income. Given the $35 foreign tax credit, what Australia would do, if it offered unlimited foreign tax credits, is actually pay $10 to Australia-Co, fully making up for the higher U.S. rate out of its own pocket.

In practice, no country is that generous in determining the allowable use of foreign tax credits. Rather, credit-granting countries, including the United States, generally limit permissible foreign tax credits to the amount of domestic tax that would otherwise have been due on the foreign-source income. In the above example, what Australia would actually do (and what the United States would do in the same circumstances) is allow only $25 of foreign tax credits, fully offsetting the $25 Australian tax that would have otherwise have been due, but not going a penny further. The excess (i.e., unused) foreign tax credit of $10 would be kept on the books and potentially used in another year to offset domestic tax liability with respect to foreign-source income.

Hence, the actual final picture—disregarding potential use by Australia-Co of the excess credit—would be that U.S.-Co and Australia-Co end up after tax as follows:

	Source	
Company	United States	Australia
U.S.-Co	$65	$65
Australia-Co	$65	$75

One last point to keep in mind is that multinational companies devote a great deal of effort—imperfectly obstructed by various foreign tax-credit rules—to "cross crediting," or finding ways to use excess credits from one set of outbound investments against the domestic tax liability (net of credits) that otherwise would remain with respect to other such investments. Thus, suppose Australia-Co also invested in a relatively low-tax country, such as Singapore, earning $100 and paying $15 of local tax. If this investment stood alone, Australia-Co would pay $10 of Australian tax after netting the Singapore tax credits against its domestic liability. But by pairing this investment with that from the United States, Australia-Co complies with the foreign tax-credit limit by having, overall, $50 of foreign tax credits with respect to $200 of foreign-source income.

Why Tax Worldwide Income on a Residence Basis?

Since so many of the problems in international taxation reflect imposing tax on both residence and source income and then trying to coordinate the two, it is worth asking what rationales underlie each piece of the system. Starting with worldwide residence-based taxation, the case for it is compelling, and indeed verges on being overwhelming, if we ignore entity-level taxes, such as the corporate tax, and imagine a world where all income taxes were imposed directly on individuals. Under these circumstances, both distributional policy and concern about efficiency would strongly indicate that residents should be taxed on their entire worldwide incomes.

Distributionally, the tax system relies on income as a comprehensive measure of material well-being in order to decide how the burden of paying for government should be distributed. Marginal rates that vary with overall income are an important part of this story. Progressivity typically results from applying graduated marginal rates, or those that rise with income. If individuals' foreign-source income is not included, this central goal of tax policy cannot be accomplished properly. Thus, recall the earlier example involving the United States and Australia, but with the U.S. income tax (1) assumed to fall directly on U.S. individuals who own stock in U.S.-Co, rather than being imposed at the entity level, and (2) standing at 35 percent only for high-income individuals. Under these circumstances, failing to tax U.S. individuals' foreign-source income might prevent effective imposition of the intended U.S. marginal rate structure.

From an efficiency standpoint, taxes generally cause the least harm when imposed on relatively immutable characteristics, so that people cannot substitute deadweight loss for revenue raising by changing their behavior to avoid tax. For individuals, even in an era of globalization, residence decisions remain relatively tax insensitive, at least in a large country like the United States. People's ties of culture, language, family, community, and career remain too strong for tax-induced expatriation to be common. By contrast, investments can easily be moved around, but with a worldwide residence-based tax, that makes no difference. Residence-based taxation that ignores source therefore has an important efficiency advantage if the tax is being imposed directly on individuals.

With an entity-based, corporate-level tax, the case for worldwide residence-based taxation weakens significantly. Even with home-country bias in investment portfolios—that is, people tend to invest disproportionately in securities from their own countries—the distributional story loses considerable force. Assuming we know the incidence of the corporate tax, we may want to apply rates that reflect domestic distributional considerations to home companies' (and thus home investors') worldwide income. However, the corporate rate will not necessarily match the individual rates that we are trying indirectly to apply, unless all shareholders are in the same marginal rate bracket (in which case applying that rate to corporations gets things exactly right).

From an efficiency standpoint, the case for worldwide residence-based taxation likewise is weaker for a corporate-level tax than for one directly on individuals. Corporate residence is not necessarily a fixed characteristic. If the tax system's definition relies on where, in substance, a company is actually managed, it potentially may piggyback on the reluctance of managers to move. However, discerning where centralized management truly occurs can be difficult. In many countries purporting to apply such a test, it has devolved into a more formalistic inquiry into such readily manipulable considerations as where the annual board meeting takes place (Ault and Arnold 2004, 350). Needless to say, even for managers who do not want to move, it is no great hardship to schedule annual board meetings in the Cayman Islands, which have numerous luxury hotels and average daily temperatures of about 80 degrees Fahrenheit throughout the Northern Hemisphere's winter.

The U.S. tax law's reliance on place of incorporation to determine corporate residence may make corporate residence even more tax responsive. Several years ago, there was a big U.S. political controversy about corporate inversion transactions, in which a U.S. multinational parent would make itself the subsidiary of, say, a newly created Caymans company, and also would cease to own directly the group's foreign subsidiaries. Adverse publicity forced a few companies to cancel their inversion plans, and others were prospectively deterred by anti-inversion legislation. For a new company that plans properly upfront, however, avoiding U.S.-resident status is not especially difficult. To be sure, it means doing without domestic corporate law, such as that of Delaware or one's home state. This might add to the costs of getting legal advice, or it might disconcert investors who are more comfortable with U.S. corporate law regimes. Perhaps it would affect one's ability to lobby Congress effectively, if legislators and their aides distinguished between domestic and foreign companies. Yet increasingly, as worldwide capital markets continue integrating, incorporating abroad grows easier and less potentially costly.

Taking U.S. incorporation as given, imposing the corporate tax on worldwide income potentially has an efficiency advantage in that it can eliminate U.S. companies' incentive to invest abroad instead of at home, or to treat income from cross-border operations as foreign source, in quest of lower tax rates. However, as the efficiency issues here are considerably more complicated, I defer discussing them until chapter 8.

Why Allow Deferral of Foreign Subsidiaries' Foreign-Source Income?

Deferral is hard to defend directly. While potentially discouraging U.S. companies from repatriating earnings where this would permit more profitable use of the funds, in practice the tax is highly avoidable. Companies have developed various tax-planning techniques over the years that give them substantial practical access to the underlying funds, albeit at a positive transaction cost, without requiring a dividend payment to the U.S. parent, or any other form of taxable realization (Altshuler and Grubert 2001, 26). According to one recent estimate, the repatriation tax raises only about $5 billion of revenue annually, an extremely low yield given the estimated $100 billion repatriation tax base (Grubert and Mutti 2001, 21). On balance, observers generally agree that its efficiency costs are "extremely high relative to the revenue raised" (Blumenthal and Slemrod 1996, 48)—almost the definition of a bad tax from an efficiency standpoint.

The problem with eliminating treatment of repatriation as a taxable event relates to the question of what would replace it. The most obvious possibilities are (1) full worldwide taxation of U.S. companies without regard to repatriation, and (2) eliminating the U.S. tax on U.S. companies' foreign-source income. Politically, however, as well as intellectually among tax-policy experts, neither of these polar opposite choices has dominated the other. Deferral has accordingly persisted as a compromise or ceasefire in place, even though a good argument could be made that either of the polar alternatives would be better than where we are now.

Why Tax Subpart F Income?

Taking deferral as given, the rationale for taxing subpart F income depends on which of the two main categories one is considering. That passive income does not have an economically meaningfully location suggests that it likely will not be taxed anywhere, absent action by the residence jurisdiction. After all, while a small island nation that arguably is in the tax-haven business, such as the Caymans, could only host a few factories that generate active business income, there is no natural limit on the number of Caymans mail drops that could purport to generate locally sourced interest or dividend income. For this reason, even countries that generally exempt foreign-source income from bearing any domestic tax often limit the exemption to active business income and tax residents' passive or portfolio income on a worldwide basis (Ault and Arnold 2004, 378).

Subpart F's application to items, such as foreign-base company sales income, that involve suspected tax avoidance activity abroad is considerably more controversial. After all, why not encourage U.S. companies with mainly U.S. shareholders to minimize the taxes they pay to foreign governments? Indeed, as we will see in chapter 8, the issue of whether subpart F should thus be applied goes right to the heart of the core dilemmas in setting international tax-policy rules. However, if one is worried about investment fleeing the United States as resident companies seek lower-taxed opportunities abroad, then subpart F rules of this kind may play an important role. The rule might thus be rationalized as responding to concerns about tax flight.

Again, only so much real business activity can fit into tax havens such as the Caymans or Luxembourg. But if one can locate such activity in larger, more highly-taxed countries such as France and Germany and still end up for tax purposes with income in the havens, the incentive to shift investment outside the United States is stronger, all else being equal. The application of subpart F potentially addresses this.

Why Tax on a Source Basis?

The rationales for source-based taxation, no less than for residence-based taxation, are powerful:

- Suppose inbound investors benefit from goods and services supplied by the government, such as maintaining roads, controlling crime, and educating workers. Indeed, suppose inbound investment actually increases the host government's cost of providing these services. Then there is a strong case for requiring investors to pay for the benefits they receive or the costs they impose (although domestic-source income is not necessarily a good measure of the appropriate service charge).
- Taxation is a means not just of raising revenue, but of exerting regulatory control over domestic economic activity. Not taxing inbound investment by foreigners might be anomalous from this perspective.
- From the standpoint of auditing and enforcement, the government that operates where business activity is actually occurring may be

better situated than the faraway residence jurisdiction to measure and collect a given income tax.

- Without source-based taxation, foreigners may be able to invest locally at lower tax rates than those residents would face, even taking into account any worldwide residence-based taxation by their own home jurisdictions. One would hate to be the politician who was running for office on a platform that called for taxing only residents (including voters) and exempting foreigners. But even if one is concerned neither about the crass politics nor about equity issues, there are potential economic distortions if different potential investors would face different tax rates upon making the same investment. (Again, more on this in chapter 8.)

The arguments for source-based taxation of inbound investment by foreigners necessarily imply, with respect to residents, that the case for taxing outbound investment, as in a full worldwide system, is weaker than that for taxing residents' home investments. Thus, there would be an intellectual conflict between the cases for residence- and source-based taxation even if they did not overlap in practice. That they do overlap makes things even worse. This brings us to the rationale for the foreign tax-credit rules, which do not automatically follow as the optimal reconciliation device even if one agrees that something ought to be done to mitigate double taxation.

Why Provide (Limited) Foreign Tax Credits?

To explain the rationale for the foreign tax-credit rules, one must address both why credits are offered to begin with and why they are limited to the U.S. tax liability on the U.S. measure of foreign-source income. The arguments for these two aspects of the rules resemble the arguments for residence-based and source-based taxation in being difficult to reconcile with each other.

Providing foreign tax credits. Offering a dollar-for-dollar refund (in effect) of U.S. companies' overseas tax liabilities appears, at first glance, to be a startlingly generous policy. Where foreign tax credits do not run into the credit limit (and ignoring the effects of deferral), they can make U.S. companies completely indifferent to reducing the taxes they pay to foreign governments. Likewise, the credits can make foreign governments completely indifferent to the risk that higher taxes will discourage U.S. companies from investing in their jurisdictions. Instead, Uncle Sam—or perhaps one should say Uncle Sugar—pays the full freight, at the expense of U.S. taxpayers generally.

This degree of generosity has two main rationales. The first is that the United States is cooperating with other countries, offering what might otherwise be overgenerous double-taxation relief because they are reciprocating by doing the same thing (whether via foreign tax credits or exemption). Everyone wins if all countries recede comparably from the full revenue claims they would otherwise make and if profitable cross-border activity therefore avoids being seriously tax deterred.

The second rationale is very different in spirit. It holds that foreign tax credits should be thought of as an aggressive trade subsidy for U.S. companies, permitting them to compete abroad by relieving double taxation. Under this rationale, unlike the first one, offering foreign tax credits might make sense even if other countries imposed unlimited double taxation on their resident companies.

Limiting foreign tax credits. If foreign tax credits are so good, why limit them? The usual answer, rooted in the worldwide-cooperation rationale for offering them in the first place, is that our generosity can only go so far. Unlimited credits might permit foreign governments, by raising their taxes on U.S. multinationals (though this would be hard to do selectively in a credit-generating income tax), to drain the U.S. Treasury and prevent us from collecting revenues even on the domestic tax base. Likewise, under the competitive rather than cooperative rationale for foreign tax credits, the argument would be that aid to our multinationals should only go so far, eliminating their extra burden from double taxation but not actually subsidizing them relative to the baseline of paying full source-based U.S. taxes only.

One problem with this argument is that it fails to rationalize the exact manner in which such exploitation is limited. Suppose a U.S. multinational earns $1 million at home and $1 million of currently includable foreign-source income, generating (at a 35 percent U.S. rate) $700,000 of pre-foreign tax credit U.S. liability. In this scenario, up to $350,000 of foreign tax credits will be currently allowable. How much difference is there, really, between (1) the dollar of revenue that the United States loses when foreign tax credits permissibly increase from $349,999 to $350,000, and (2) the dollar that the United States would lose if credits were permitted to increase from $350,000 to $350,001? Isn't a dollar just a dollar either way?

To put the point more broadly, our limiting foreign tax credits suggests that there is a trade-off between competing considerations—that is, between the cooperative or competitive benefits of offering credits on the one hand, and the revenue loss or adverse incentive effects on U.S. companies and foreign governments on the other hand. If we are trying to optimize U.S. tax policy in how it balances these competing considerations, why would the optimal system feature a sudden shift, at what is arguably an arbitrarily selected point, from 100 percent reimbursement of foreign taxes to 0 percent reimbursement? Mightn't some other, perhaps more gradual and intermediate, percentage reimbursement scheme do better than our actual one in balancing the competing considerations? Perhaps the only good argument for the exact structure of the foreign tax-credit limit is that it appeals intuitively, however irrationally, to the widespread "sentiment that reducing a set of taxes . . . to zero is less objectionable than allowing them to be negative" (Shaviro 2007c, 169).

The unholy combination of deferral plus the foreign tax-credit limit does much to make the U.S. tax rules for outbound investment by our multinationals so administratively costly, relative to the revenue raised. Recall that credits only become available once the associated income is repatriated, and that cross crediting is a fundamental tax-planning tool for avoiding the limit. Taxpayers therefore time their repatriations to match the high tax to the low tax so that the two are in perfect balance. One can "liken the process to a master distiller blending a perfect tax liqueur, in which the blended product bears tax at precisely 35 percent, so that no residual U.S. tax is due and no excess credits are generated" (Kleinbard 2007a).

8

International Tax Policy Dilemmas

If you were lost somewhere and could not ask for directions, two resources you might welcome are a compass and a map. The compass would help you to go in the right direction, while the map would permit you to see in detail how to get from one site to another.

Domestic corporate tax policy, as set forth in chapters 1 through 6, could be described as requiring one to navigate without a map. Given the murkiness of its landmark concepts, such as corporate versus noncorporate entity or debt versus equity, one cannot easily discern what it actually does or how changing its rules would play out on the ground. But at least from an efficiency standpoint, its compass for tax policy navigation is fairly clear. Taxing everything neutrally, at least against the baseline of a uniform income or consumption tax, seems likely to be the way one would want to proceed. By definition, such neutrality would eliminate wasteful tax bias as to the various choices that the structure of the corporate tax potentially makes meaningful.[1]

The Lack of a Clear Framework

When one shifts from the domestic corporate tax to international tax policy, the task of navigating grows significantly harder. Now not only the map is missing, but also the compass. In the international realm, it ceases to be clear what tax neutrality means, and thus in what direction one should generally be trying to steer tax policy.

The main problems in applying a neutrality ideal to international tax policy are twofold. First, as soon as countries have different tax rates, one cannot create neutrality at all of the principal margins. Recall the example from chapter 7 where the United States has a 35 percent rate while Australia has a 25 percent rate. Under these circumstances, cross-border investment simply cannot be taxed neutrally as compared to *both* of the one-country alternatives. Thus, with respect to an investment by U.S.-Co in Australia, one cannot both (1) set the tax rate at 35 percent so U.S.-Co will face the same tax rate whether it invests in the United States or in Australia; and (2) set the tax rate at 25 percent so U.S.-Co will face the same tax rate on that investment as would Australia-Co. Rather, one has to choose between these two alternatives, or perhaps try to balance them and accept only partial achievement of each.

Second, international tax policy involves a multiple-sovereigns problem. In domestic tax policy, one can set a national-level tax rule that will apply to everyone. Internationally, however, a country can only set its own tax policies. While it can bargain with and otherwise try to influence governments in other countries, in the end the merits of its policy choices may depend on the actions of decisionmakers outside its control. The role of multiple sovereigns creates a situation where strategic interactions between governments, whether cooperative or competitive, are important. Such interactions are hard to model and predict, and may play out inconsistently over extended time frames, yet they may be critical to the question of what any one country should do.

With multiple sovereigns that might either compete or cooperate, one faces the question—absent in purely domestic tax policy—of whether to think about efficiency, and consequent economic welfare from minimizing distortions, in global terms or in purely national terms. In other words, to use the terms of art from the literature, should international tax policy aim to maximize worldwide welfare or merely national welfare?

From a philosophical standpoint, surely worldwide welfare has considerable appeal. People from everywhere in the world should matter equally from an ethical standpoint, and nationalism is special pleading akin to nepotism. However, the selfless beneficence of a disinterested philosopher is hard to sell politically or sustain internationally. It invites exploitation by others less scrupulous. Arguably, therefore, at least within the limits of civilized behavior, countries should be expected and perhaps even internally encouraged to act purely from the standpoint of national, rather than worldwide, welfare.

This, however, merely frames, without resolving, the choice between normative standards. Whenever a given approach to international tax policy would increase worldwide welfare, it creates at least a theoretical possibility of a Pareto improvement, or a transaction that would leave everyone better off and no one worse off. Thus, suppose a given U.S. policy—say, mitigating double taxation by offering foreign tax credits—would cost the United States $5 billion but make the rest of the world $50 billion better off. In theory, a deal in which other countries compensated the United States for adopting the policy, through payments of more than $5 billion but less than $50 billion, could leave everyone better off.

To be sure, cash transfers like this may be politically unrealistic. Suppose, however, that other countries' compensation instead took the form of their being likewise public-spirited in their tax policies, such as by similarly mitigating double taxation at a positive cost to themselves, but conditioned on reciprocity. We then might have a situation where each country, considered in isolation, appeared to be acting with surprising altruism, but in fact was doing what was best for itself. Addressing worldwide welfare would simply be a handy way of advancing national welfare, with the two being reconciled by countries' positive-sum, cooperative, strategic interactions.

Only, now the next question might be, "Is it sometimes advantageous to cheat, from the standpoint of designing one's own tax rules to promote worldwide welfare?" Countries' international tax rules are hard even for domestic experts, much less foreign governments, to understand. So the optimal level of cheating, from a national-welfare standpoint that embraces beneficence purely due to others' reciprocity, seems unlikely to be zero. Thus, the point is not that national and worldwide welfare perfectly cohere in the design of tax rules for cross-border investment, but rather that their complicated relationship includes a possibility of substantial overlap. Thus, both must be considered, even if the national perspective ultimately governs, in the international tax policy realm.

*   *   *   *   *

We have, therefore, two core uncertainties in international tax policy: how to define neutrality, and—even if it could be defined—how to navigate between worldwide and national welfare considerations in implementing it. In practice, both uncertainties would have to be resolved before one could derive clear conclusions about international tax policy. Resolving just one would leave all of the main policy choices that dominate the current debate still wide open.

International Tax Policy and Worldwide Welfare

Suppose initially that the only question of interest was how best to maximize worldwide economic welfare through international tax policy, on the view that countries' cooperative behavior should aim at the highest possible target. In keeping with the usual efficiency idea that taxes should not alter parties' incentives, one would then have to choose between the two big margins—in the earlier example, equalizing U.S.-Co's domestic and outbound tax rates, or equalizing U.S.-Co's and Australia-Co's tax rates on investing in Australia. These two possible neutralities generate no fewer than three alternative worldwide efficiency norms that can be used in orienting international tax policy.

Capital Export Neutrality

The norm of capital export neutrality (CEN) holds that taxpayers should face the same tax rate no matter where they invest (Richman 1963). In consequence, they will choose the investment offering the highest pretax return, since this investment will also have the highest after-tax return if everything is taxed at the same rate (and at less than a 100 percent rate). Thus, taxpayers will not substitute less profitable for more profitable investment opportunities by reason of location-based tax-rate differences.

In the earlier U.S.-Australia example, CEN requires a 35 percent rate on U.S.-Co even if it invests in Australia, and a 25 percent tax rate on Australia-Co even if it invests in the United States. One way to achieve CEN is through purely residence-based taxation. Even with duplicative residence- and source-based taxation, however, CEN can still be achieved if residents' worldwide income is taxable immediately at home (without deferral) and residents get unlimited foreign tax credits. Existing international tax rules fail to achieve CEN due to the absence of these two features from the law.

The only difference between the two alternative ways of achieving CEN lies in who gets the revenue. Thus, if U.S.-Co earns $100 in Australia, the U.S. would get the entire $35 under residence-based taxation, but under a foreign tax credit approach would only get $10, with Australia getting the other $25. Likewise, when Australia-Co earns $100 in the United States, under residence-based taxation the United States would collect nothing and Australia would get $25, while under an unlimited foreign tax-credit system the United States would collect $35 and Australia would actually pay out $10. The two methods are equivalent, from a CEN standpoint, because taxpayers are presumed to care only about how much money they get to keep—not about who gets the taxes they pay.

What makes CEN a worldwide-welfare approach, rather than one directly serving national welfare, is its indifference to who gets the tax revenue. When the United States offers foreign tax credits, it acts as if paying taxes to Australia were just as good, from a U.S. national-welfare standpoint, as paying taxes to the U.S. government. In fact, however, it is not just as good from Americans' standpoint, because they get to use the money only if it is paid to their own government.

Despite CEN's supporting unlimited foreign tax credits, its main implications, when invoked in actual tax-policy debates, are pro-government. It supports ending deferral, or at least expanding subpart F, so that U.S. companies will derive less tax savings from investing in low-tax countries abroad. It also supports aggressively challenging taxpayers' use of transfer pricing to shift taxable income into low-tax jurisdictions. Further, when taxpayers attempt cross crediting so they can avoid being caught by foreign tax credit limits, it arguably supports trying to stop them. While the opportunity to cross credit lessens the undue bias (from a CEN standpoint) against investing in high-tax jurisdictions, it also provides an undue incentive, once one has the potentially disallowed credits, to invest in low-tax jurisdictions even if the income earned in them is currently taxable in the United States.

Capital Import Neutrality

The norm of capital import neutrality (CIN) holds that an investment should face the same tax rate no matter who makes it (Horst 1980, 794). As traditionally posited, however, it focuses not on the firm that makes a given investment, but on the nationality of the saver that provides the capital that gets invested. Thus, one should think of it as either (1) ignoring entity-level taxation and assuming that individuals are taxed directly on their investments, even through corporations, or (2) relying on home-country bias in investment portfolios, which would suggest that American firms raise money mainly from American savers.

CIN would result from imposing purely source-based taxes, which (in terms of the earlier example) would cause an investment in Australia to face a 25 percent rate, and one in the United States to face a 35 percent rate, no matter who made it. Again, however, the point of interest from the standpoint of CIN is not who gets the revenue, but which country's tax system sets the applicable overall rate.[2]

The rationale for CIN is that it prevents tax rate differences from inducing the wrong person to save. To illustrate, suppose a given investment in Australia would earn 10 percent before tax. Under a CEN-based system, an American would earn 6.5 percent after tax from making this investment, while an Australian would earn 7.5 percent.

In conventional economic theory, people decide whether to save based on the trade-off between present and future consumption. Saving today means that you do not get to consume until later, which is a bad thing if you are impatient. Even assuming impatience,[3] however, you will agree to save now, and thus defer your consumption, if the payoff is high enough. Thus, consider that, at a 7.5 percent after-tax rate of return, your money will double about every seven years. Tightening your belt now in order to live better in the future might well be worth it even if you would otherwise prefer to consume now.

Suppose that a given American would save so long as she could earn at least 6.6 percent after tax, while an Australian would save so long as he could earn at least 7.4 percent. Evidently, the American attaches less personal disutility to saving, since she is willing to do it even in exchange for a smaller reward. If, however, returns to her saving would be taxed at 35 percent, while those of the Australian would be taxed at only 25 percent, then only the latter will agree to fund an investment that pays 10 percent before tax. By failing to provide CIN, therefore, we get the "wrong" saver— the one that minds saving more, as measured by the parties' reservation prices. Only by taxing all prospective savers at the same rate can we avoid this scenario.

In U.S. tax-policy debates, CIN generally is invoked to support a pro-taxpayer rather than a pro-government stance, on the view that U.S. companies should not face U.S. taxes on their outbound investments on top of the local, source-based taxes that all of their competitors are paying. For example, it arguably suggests that deferral does not go far enough, and that foreign-source, active business income should generally be exempt from U.S. tax. This reflects not just that resident corporations in low-tax countries pay no other country's residence-based tax, but that other big countries typically do not apply subpart F–type rules very broadly even if they purport to tax their residents' worldwide income. Even permitting aggressive transfer pricing can be supported on CIN grounds if other countries are not stopping their resident corporations from doing it.

Capital Ownership Neutrality

A recent entry to the field, capital ownership neutrality (CON), focuses on the firm level, rather than the investor level, and holds that ownership decisions should not be distorted by tax considerations (Desai and Hines 2003, 494). Thus, if U.S.-Co would be the most productive and therefore most profitable owner of a particular investment in Australia on a pretax basis, CON requires that tax considerations not lead to a different ownership pattern, such as the investment's being owned by Australia-Co.

CON, like CIN, is satisfied by purely source-based taxation. Thus, if all investments in the United States are taxed at 35 percent, while all those in Australia are taxed at 25 percent, then there is no tax advantage to having Australia-Co, rather than U.S.-Co, make a given investment in Australia. CON's leading proponents, economists Mihir Desai and James Hines, state that CON does not require source-based taxation or its equivalent, and indeed is satisfied whenever "income is taxed at rates that, if they differ among investors, do so in fixed proportions. Thus, CON would be satisfied if investors from certain European countries face home and foreign tax rates that are uniformly 1.2 times the tax rates faced by all other investors" (494–95).

Among the implications is that purely residence-based tax systems, in addition to satisfying CEN, would also satisfy CON. Thus, assume again that the U.S. rate is 35 percent and the Australian rate is 25 percent. Suppose the pretax rate of return on all investments (without regard to ownership) is 10 percent, meaning that, with worldwide residence-based taxation, U.S.-Co would always earn 6.5 percent after tax, while Australia-Co would always earn 7.5 percent. Under these circumstances, both U.S.-Co and Australia-Co would pay exactly $100 for an investment that earned $10 before tax, whether located in the United States or in Australia. So tax considerations would not distort ownership patterns even though U.S.-Co faced a higher tax rate than Australia-Co on all investments, including those made in Australia.[4]

Worldwide residence-based taxation ceases to satisfy CON, however, if we change the hypothetical a bit. Suppose we assume a residence-based tax purely on legal entities, such as corporations, and effectively (perhaps due to tax planning) no tax at the investor level. This, as readers may recall from chapter 6, is exactly the assumption that proponents of the Miller equilibrium make as to equity-financed corporate investment. A given investor is pondering whether to finance an investment in Australia through U.S.-Co or Australia-Co, in either case by purchasing newly issued stock from the company.[5] Suppose that U.S.-Co would earn a 10 percent annual return before tax from the investment, whereas Australia-Co would earn only 9 percent. With residence-based rather than source-based corporate-level taxation, the investor will nonetheless choose Australia-Co, since its after-tax return is higher (6.75 percent instead of 6.5 percent), thus violating CON.

Likewise, suppose U.S.-Co is considering two different ways of locating a portion of its production activity in Australia, in either case through the use of preexisting Australia-Co's employees and factory. The first method would be to acquire Australia-Co, by exchanging shares of U.S.-Co stock for the Australia-Co stock currently held by that firm's owners. The second would be to establish an arm's length contractual relationship with Australia-Co. Perhaps the difference, taxes aside, boils down to whether it is more efficient to organize production in a hierarchical or in an arm's-length, price-driven environment (as suggested by Coase's theory of the firm). If the United States and Australia both levy worldwide residence-based taxes without deferral, then tax considerations will put a thumb on the scales in favor of an arm's length contractual relationship so that the Australian company's income will be taxed at only 25 percent. Once again, this may lead to a violation of CON, unless avoided by levying a source-based rather than a residence-based corporate tax.

In tax-policy debate, CON, like CIN, generally is invoked to support the pro-taxpayer view that U.S. multinationals' outbound investment generally should not be taxable here. Again, this reflects that other big countries typically do less than we do to tax their multinationals' outbound investment, causing U.S. firms' ownership of foreign businesses to be increasingly tax discouraged if the United States expands the reach of its worldwide tax or challenges aggressive tax planning that other countries permit.

Resolving the Choice between Worldwide Standards

Since CON was not introduced to the literature until 2003, for decades the academic tax policy debate about how best to promote worldwide welfare through international tax policy lay purely between CEN and CIN. A strong (if not quite universal) consensus held that the argument for CEN was stronger than that for CIN.[6] Reasons included the following: (1) investment choice, which CEN addresses, is generally more tax sensitive than savings choices, which CIN targets; (2) countries can unilaterally achieve CEN by granting unlimited foreign tax credits, but with existing tax instruments they cannot unilaterally achieve CIN; and (3) an income tax automatically discourages saving in any event, but need not discriminate between investment choices.

Academic viewpoints therefore strongly supported expanding U.S. taxation of U.S. multinationals on their outbound investments, such as by repealing deferral. Congress's reluctance to do this encouraged the view that it was merely responding to the interest-group power wielded by U.S. multinationals. Even proponents of shifting to a "territorial" system, in which U.S. companies would no longer be taxed on their active business income earned abroad, often relied on the political unfeasibility of expanding deferral, along with the low revenue yield (relative to the tax-planning costs) that resulted from taxing repatriations (Grubert and Mutti 2001).

CON's introduction has changed the intellectual balance of forces. As we will see, however, the argument for emphasizing it instead of CEN rests on claims about the two standards' relative compatibility with pursuing U.S. national self-interest, not on their relative importance on the worldwide stage. Proponents of CON have not as yet made substantial progress in quantifying its importance either in absolute or relative terms, although they note that the modern theory of the firm (derived from Coase's work) suggests that ownership arrangements are extremely important.

Making the analysis more difficult is that the relevant "ownership," like residence and source, is not an economically well-defined concept. U.S. tax consequences depend on whether U.S. tax law defines a given set of economic arrangements as involving a relationship with a branch, a foreign subsidiary, or an independent third party. True economic relationships between parties may not neatly divide into the within-firm and arm's-length contractual baskets, and even where they do, may be hard for the tax system to observe accurately. So it is unclear here, as with residence and source, to what extent and how the formal rules matter.

The Unilateral National Perspective

Even with greater consensus about worldwide welfare, the implications for U.S. international tax policy would depend on its relationship to national welfare. Worldwide gain may require cooperation for any one nation to benefit from pursuing it. Unilaterally pursuing national welfare not only is an alternative to cooperating, but sheds light on the costs of cooperating and the likelihood of its paying off.

Unfortunately for those who would like life to be simple, the question of how the United States would best promote its national economic welfare if acting unilaterally is as bitterly contested in the literature as the worldwide welfare question. Two main empirical issues underlie this divide: (1) the effect of outbound investment by U.S. multinationals on the level of domestic investment, and (2) the question of how U.S. firms' "competitiveness" is affected by U.S. tax policies and affects U.S. economic welfare.

Does Outbound Investment Reduce Domestic Investment?

National Neutrality

Under the traditional view of international tax policy that identified CEN and CIN as the main worldwide welfare considerations, the implications of acting unilaterally were considered clear. Not only should resident companies' worldwide income be taxed without deferral, but foreign taxes should not be creditable against domestic liability. Instead, they should merely be deductible in computing domestic tax liability. The resulting worldwide double taxation, and consequent discouragement of cross-border enterprise, simply is not worth addressing absent reciprocal forbearance (such as the allowance of foreign tax credits) by other countries.

To illustrate this standard, known as national neutrality, consider again the case of U.S.-Co, which is deciding whether to invest in Australia or in the United States, in either case earning $100. Suppose initially, however, that there is no Australian tax. Why does national self-interest counsel taxing this foreign-source income instead of exempting it? The answer is that we want companies to invest on a pretax basis, because taxes paid to the U.S. authorities, which to the companies are a cost like any other (such as wages or rent) are from the U.S. national standpoint merely a transfer of resources from one pocket to another.[7] Exempting overseas investment from the otherwise applicable tax would cause companies to prefer such investments to domestic ones, even when less profitable before U.S. tax, because companies naturally view taxes paid as a cost rather than a transfer.

When we add Australian taxes to the mix, however, the analysis differs from that of U.S. taxes because Australians, rather than Americans, are the ones who get the money. Australian taxes therefore really are a social as well as a private cost from the U.S. national standpoint, no less than paying wages to Australian workers. Thus, if U.S.-Co would earn $100 before tax and $75 after paying source-based Australian taxes, taxing it in the United States on the basis of its having earned $75 preserves the incentive to seek the highest pretax profit, as correctly defined from a purely nationalistic standpoint.

Exponents of the view that national neutrality offers the proper definition of unilateral U.S. self-interest in setting international tax policy usually do not propose that the United States follow its counsel by making foreign taxes merely deductible rather than creditable. Instead, it is more of a reductio ad absurdum, intended to show that cooperation must indeed be robust, given how widely credits (or exemption) are followed around the world. The implication is that, even though offering foreign tax credits might seem naively overgenerous, in fact the United States is not being exploited, but rather is participating in an extraordinary international success story. Reuven Avi-Yonah (1996, 1301–3) calls the prevailing international tax regime in some respects "a miracle. . . . Taxes are the last topic on which one would expect sovereign nations to reach a consensus. . . . Nevertheless, and contrary to a priori expectations, a coherent international tax regime exists that enjoys nearly universal support."

One problem with this point of view is its arguable disconnect from actual national politics. The United States adopted foreign tax credits unilaterally, and apparently without serious thought about worldwide efficiency, national neutrality, or reciprocity (Graetz and O'Hear 1997, 1043–44). Contemporary U.S. tax politics suggests little inclination to repeal foreign tax credits, much less any sentiment that we are being self-sacrificing in deference to other nations in a spirit of international cooperation. To the contrary, calls for a more unilateral and self-interested policy usually take the pro-taxpayer side and focus on issues of competitiveness (discussed below). Other countries likewise do not appear to regard full double taxation as tempting, or to be dissuaded from it solely by fear of retaliation.

One could try to explain this, however, on the grounds that domestic firms' political clout (and perhaps the intuitive unseemliness of double taxation) restrain countries from doing what they "should" do from a purely self-interested perspective. It would hardly be big news, after all, to observe countries pervasively declining to implement what economists regard as good policy. For example, there is widespread academic support for scaling back tax preferences (thus permitting tax-rate reduction without overall revenue loss) and for corporate integration, but countries generally do not listen—responding, apparently, to internal political dynamics that outweigh academic arguments about national welfare.

Exemption (or National Ownership Neutrality)

The logic behind national neutrality, while irrefutable within its own terms, rests on a crucial though unstated assumption. It treats the taxpayer's decision regarding where to locate a given investment as having no expected effect on any other locational decisions regarding investments, by this taxpayer or any other. Thus, the United States loses tax revenue if U.S.-Co places a given investment in Australia rather than in the United States because the income is earned there instead of here. This would not be the result if either (1) U.S.-Co's foreign and domestic investments were complements rather than substitutes—that is, if making the one increased the likelihood of making the other, rather than crowding it out, or (2) U.S.-Co's investing abroad meant that someone else would take the empty U.S. slot instead.

Suppose that, on average, a U.S. firm's decision to make a given investment overseas has *no* effect on the amount invested in the United States, and thus on U.S.-source taxable income and U.S. tax revenues. National neutrality would entirely cease to hold. Instead, as Desai and Hines (2003, 496) note, "with unchanging domestic tax revenue, home-country welfare increases in the after-tax profitability of domestic companies." They therefore propose, as an efficiency benchmark for unilateral, nationally minded international tax policy in lieu of national neutrality, a policy of exempting residents' outbound investment from domestic tax on the view that, in effect, it generates free money and thus should not be discouraged. Desai and Hines call exemption of outbound investment "national ownership neutrality" (NON), but to minimize jargon I will simply call it "exemption."

How can domestic investment be unaffected by a U.S. company's investing abroad resources that could instead have been invested at home? There are two main scenarios, each of which may occur some of the time. First, U.S. companies, rather than having an effective budget limit on the amount they can invest that is dictated by their own finite resources, may instead operate by going to international credit markets and raising funds whenever they have a sufficiently good idea. Accordingly, rather than having to choose between investments, they get to "pitch" as many as they like and make all those that have sufficiently demonstrable merit. While they have to pay market interest to whomever provides the funds, they capture the excess over the market rate (in economic parlance, a rent) that reflects their special skills, assets, or intellectual creativity. In this scenario, domestic investment may even be a complement rather than a substitute for foreign investment—if, for example, skills developed or ideas validated abroad can then be brought home using further funds from international capital markets.

Second, when a U.S. firm does not invest at home, that may leave an opening for foreign firms that would not otherwise exist. Suppose, for example, that a given commercial block has a fixed number of storefronts, all of which are bound to be leased by someone. If a U.S. firm goes elsewhere and worldwide demand for space on the block is high enough, someone else will come in instead. And if the fixed-storefronts metaphor seems inadequate to describe the real world of multinational capital flows, one might think instead in terms of niches for profitable investment. For example, the fewer the restaurants in a given area, the greater the likely market demand by customers (all else being equal) to eat in a new restaurant that comes in. Or, if a region has a given-sized workforce, the fewer the factories already there, the greater the appeal to a prospective employer of locating there. Under this scenario, worldwide investment is like a giant game of musical chairs, and that a given country's firms locate in one place, rather than another, simply does not matter so far as the number and location of seats filled is concerned.[8]

Hines (2007, 19) notes a "flurry of recent evidence suggesting that outbound foreign direct investment may not reduce the size of the domestic capital stock, but instead possibly increase it." In particular, a set of firm-level or industry-level studies analyzing data from Australia, Canada, Germany, and the United States have failed to find any association between outbound investment and reduced domestic investment. While no one claims that these studies are as yet conclusive, at a minimum they lend significant empirical support to the assumptions underlying support for exempting outbound investment, in lieu of national neutrality, as the preferred unilateral policy from a national-welfare standpoint.

Evaluating the Choice between National Neutrality and Exemption

Even without the above empirical evidence, the logic of viewing outbound investment as not entirely a substitute for domestic investment would be compelling. In particular, a view of investment in a particular location as involving niches, such that each new entrant marginally discourages other prospective entrants, has intuitive appeal. Even if outbound investment proves, through further research, to have *some* negative correlation with the level of domestic investment, national neutrality appears likely to be quite wide of the mark in effectively assuming one-for-one substitution of foreign for domestic investment.

While this seriously undermines national neutrality's appeal as a unilateral benchmark, the case for exemption does not necessarily follow, even if we assume zero aggregate substitution between domestic and outbound investment. Being an efficiency benchmark is not the same as being an affirmative policy guide. After all, a lump-sum tax, such as a uniform head tax, may stand as an efficiency benchmark relative to income or consumption taxation, but no one seriously proposes adopting it. In the case of exemption, the issue is not balancing distributional goals against efficiency (as in the case of the head tax), but rather minimizing total inefficiency given that a higher domestic tax rate, to pay for the revenue loss from adopting exemption rather than a worldwide system, would be worse in other respects.

The conundrum remains even if we assume that outbound investment offers Americans free money from the excess of its expected earnings over either (1) the market interest rate one pays for the extra funds, or (2) the rate of return one would have earned (in lieu of a foreigner's earning it) by occupying one of the fixed niches for domestic investment.

As noted in chapter 1, the taxation of economic rents generally is assumed to be efficient, because free money remains free money after tax, even if reduced in amount. In addition, even if taxing outbound investment has some discouraging effect, because the profits are not pure rents, one must keep in mind that *any* tax on productive activity, by distorting incentives, is likely to reduce national welfare in some respects. It remains unclear, therefore, how outbound investment would best be taxed from a unilateral national standpoint, although clearly the old consensus about national neutrality can no longer be sustained.

Domestic Firms' Competitiveness

Even more than revenue, the hot-button issue in debates about U.S. national welfare considerations in taxing outbound investment goes to the question of "competitiveness." U.S. firms complain that they are unfairly disadvantaged, relative to their foreign competitors, if they face tax burdens from the U.S. system exceeding the domestic burdens that the competitors face. They further claim that this is not merely unfortunate for them, but adverse to U.S. national welfare. In particular, reducing their profits may make U.S. individuals poorer, given the home-country bias in people's investment portfolios (Hines 2007, 35). The competitiveness argument can be made in a couple of different ways.

Competitiveness, Version 1.0

American firms argue that they cannot compete effectively in foreign markets if, because of U.S. taxes imposed on top of local source-based taxes, they pay tax at a higher rate than their foreign rivals. Thus, suppose again that U.S.-Co faces a 35 percent tax rate, as compared with Australia-Co's 25 percent, as they contemplate competing in a given foreign jurisdiction. Can U.S.-Co compete effectively, given its higher tax rate?

The view that U.S.-Co faces a serious competitive disadvantage in these circumstances is intuitively appealing. By analogy, suppose it had to pay higher wages for the same workers, or higher electricity costs for the same electricity usage. Then Australia-Co, all else being equal, might be able to charge lower prices and drive U.S.-Co from the market if the two were otherwise equivalent. But paying a higher tax rate on net income is different, and does not necessarily operate in this way to create competitive disadvantage.

In particular, the difference in tax rate does not give Australia-Co an opportunity to underprice U.S.-Co. Whether a business's tax rate is 25 percent or 35 percent, its goal in setting consumer prices is to pick whatever price will maximize its pretax profit. After all, the higher the pretax profit, the higher the after-tax profit will be at any tax rate below 100 percent.

Thus, suppose that U.S.-Co and Australia-Co both initially face the same 35 percent rate, and that Australia-Co charged consumer prices that resulted in its earning $100 million a year. Presumably, Australia-Co has determined that either raising or lowering its price would reduce profits, even though the former would increase its profit margin per sale while the latter would increase its sales. Lower its tax rate to 25 percent, and there is no obvious reason why this calculation would change.[9]

Now consider U.S.-Co's perspective. To be sure, its owners are less well off paying tax at 35 percent rather than 25 percent. It means they make less money. Anyone that had a choice between paying the two tax rates would choose the lower one. But U.S.-Co and its owners still can pay their bills and remain in business, generating a pretax profit and matching the after-tax return that they would have earned doing anything else that is subject to the same tax rate.[10]

If we add real-world complications, the view that U.S.-Co faces no competitive disadvantage may be challenged. Suppose, for example, that firms with good investment opportunities need to rely on internally generated financing because of the difficulty of persuading third-party lenders that one's prospects are actually good. Australia-Co will be able to generate after-tax profits at a higher rate than U.S.-Co, all else being equal, and thus will have a tax-generated advantage in funding its growth. However, the importance of this factor is unclear for large multinationals that in practice rely heavily on global credit markets for new funds.

Accordingly, the traditional competitiveness argument concerning a higher tax rate's implications for U.S. multinationals does not necessarily succeed. One certainly appreciates that the shareholders and managers would rather pay the lower rate that they see being paid by their rivals, rather than the higher one that may be imposed on them. But if they can nonetheless compete effectively, there is no obvious U.S. national welfare implication, since the U.S. government gets the extra tax revenue that the firms' U.S. owners (or other affected U.S. individuals, if the incidence shifts) are losing.

Competitiveness, Version 2.0

A newer version of the competitiveness argument changes the focus from the firm level to the investor level. Suppose U.S.-Co and Australia-Co are competing for new equity capital that they would use to fund a new investment anywhere outside the United States. Clearly, all else being equal, investors would rather put their money in a company that is taxed at 25 percent than at 35 percent. Thus, Australia-Co has a competitive advantage over U.S.-Co in raising equity capital.

The analysis does not apply to debt, so long as interest deductions are allowed at the corporate level when the income is taxed, since in that case the investor's tax rate is the relevant one, and presumably is the same no matter through whom one invests. While it makes sense as to equity, there remains a missing link in connecting it to U.S. national welfare.

The argument for such a link requires that U.S.-Co's preexisting owners, who are assumed to be mainly Americans due to home-country bias, lose out on the opportunity to capture rents because Australia-Co gets the extra financing instead. However, if U.S.-Co and Australia-Co are competing to make investments that would offer extra-normal returns, one might think these rents would be competed away, and thus would not be available to the prior shareholders in any event.

After all, either company should be willing to accept anything exceeding the normal return that is available elsewhere, and thus should not be outbid by the other so long as a penny of potential rents remains. This presumably includes any competition for scarce new equity capital, which can be offered at an increasingly favorable issue price until the last penny of rents for existing equity is gone. So it is unclear whether the new competitiveness argument, though plausible at the firm level, strongly implicates unilateral national welfare. At most, it adds to the old competitiveness argument by showing that U.S. companies are disadvantaged as to two of the main three vehicles for raising funds—retained earnings and new equity financing. This would only leave new debt financing as a vehicle for raising capital on even terms with lower-taxed foreign firms. As noted in chapter 6, debt financing presents the greatest incentive problems as between shareholders and the prospective sources of new capital, since shareholders get the entire upside but creditors share the downside.

So the competitiveness issue appears to boil down in large part to the following question: Are U.S. companies, with predominantly U.S. shareholders, liquidity constrained with respect to exploiting overseas rents in a manner that would ease discernibly if they did not face higher tax rates than their foreign competitors? That is, would increased company-wide retained earnings and access to equity markets make a noticeable difference in their ability to exploit rents, to the benefit of U.S. resident individuals that were shareholders? Much research on this question still needs to be done, and until it is resolved, the merits of competitiveness arguments will remain unclear.

A Unilateralist Bottom Line?

The rise of powerful objections to national neutrality as a unilateral national welfare standard, and the strengthening of competitiveness arguments on behalf of U.S. firms, leaves the unilateralist perspective in some disarray. Exemption gains force as a plausible approach, relative to the scenario where even granting foreign tax credits (and thus limiting domestic tax to the spread between domestic and foreign rates) seemed overgenerous unless it stimulated reciprocal forbearance by other countries. But the idea that the United States could benefit from unilaterally moving closer to the pole of worldwide residence-based taxation cannot be dismissed, given the possibilities that (1) outbound investment is not fully replaced by new inbound investment, (2) taxing outbound investment would not greatly affect the rents ultimately enjoyed by U.S. individuals, and (3) where rents are not involved, U.S. national welfare is not greatly affected if foreign firms rather than U.S. firms make particular foreign investments.

Suppose, for example, that U.S. Congress decided to change current law on a revenue-neutral basis by either (1) raising the corporate rate but eliminating all taxation of U.S. companies' foreign-source, active business income, or (2) lowering the corporate rate but repealing deferral. Even assuming no effects on other countries' tax policies, no existing economic model convincingly establishes that one of these two approaches would be better than the other.

The Ongoing Dilemma of U.S. International Tax Policy

Current U.S. international tax policy has two very clear ways it could go: toward full worldwide taxation (subject only to foreign tax credits) via the repeal of deferral, or toward a territorial system in which U.S. companies' foreign-source, active business income is entirely exempt from U.S. tax. Instead, as Keith Engel (2001, 1525) puts it, we are "stuck in the middle with subpart F" plus the rules taxing repatriations.

Given the inefficiency of the deferral regime, many would agree that either pole would be preferable to the midpoint where we have found ourselves stuck for so many decades. Yet the stalemate seems powerfully rooted in U.S. politics (1562). This reflects more than just the theoretical uncertainties, which may have only limited political influence. It reflects as well the eternal battle between (1) multinationals' political power, backed by intuitively appealing competitiveness arguments that draw on the notion that "our guys" deserve a "fair chance," and (2) the intuitive case for "neutral" treatment of U.S. taxpayers, reinforced by emotionally salient concerns about "runaway plants" that lead to lost U.S. jobs, if the United States permits resident companies to reduce their worldwide tax burdens by visibly relocating investment abroad.

Even if the twin poles are politically unavailable, however, debate about whether the United States should move marginally in one direction or the other is ongoing. Battles about the scope of subpart F and deferral, about taxpayers' ability to take advantage of foreign tax credits, and about defining U.S.-source versus foreign-source income continually roil the tax-policy realm through both proposed legislation and debate concerning how the U.S. Treasury should use its regulatory and rulemaking discretion. These battles make one wish for an effective compass showing which way we should ideally head. But again, the compass is missing.

Two considerations arguably counsel against steering too definitely toward the worldwide taxation pole rather than the exemption pole. The first is that even if tax penalizing U.S. firms compared to their foreign competitors is relatively innocuous from a U.S. national-welfare standpoint, it also fails to do any good, even from a worldwide-welfare perspective rooted exclusively in CEN, if companies around the world respond sufficiently by simply swapping around their ownership positions. Second, U.S. corporate residence rests on too slender a reed to bear much weight as foreign incorporation becomes ever more acceptable even among U.S. investors. The case for moving toward a pure worldwide system would be stronger if U.S. corporate residence were made harder to avoid for companies that are managed by U.S. individuals that are reluctant to move.

Insofar as worldwide capital mobility increases the competitive pressures faced by the U.S. income-tax system, one could argue that lowering the corporate rate (including for inbound investment by foreign companies) is more clearly indicated as a policy response than exemption.

Reducing the domestic corporate rate would unambiguously tend to draw more business activity here, and to discourage the use of transfer pricing to shift reported profits out of, rather than into, the United States. It also might not reduce progressivity if (as discussed in chapter 4) the incidence of the tax increasingly falls on workers rather than savers.

Many of the United States' leading trading partners have significantly reduced their corporate rates in recent years, reflecting such factors as the competitive pressure exerted on western European countries by low rates in eastern Europe (U.S. Treasury Department 2007, 6–8). The United States, while less immediately subject to such competitive pressures, clearly faces them in the long run. However, this is but one dimension of the broader question of how U.S. corporate-tax rules should respond to 21st-century economic and political conditions—a question that part four of this book will take up more broadly.

PART IV
Where Is the Corporate Tax Headed?

The U.S. corporate tax has been quite stable for a long time. For example, the top marginal rate has been 35 percent for the last 15 years, and was 34 percent for several years before that. During this same period, there has been only one significant structural change, albeit a very important one—the 2003 enactment of the (potentially expiring) rate cut for dividends.

Given the recent track record of stability, it might be natural—at least, leaving aside the dividend tax issue—to think that things are likely to stay roughly unchanged. Expecting more of the same is classic inductive reasoning, and often leads us in the right direction. But not always. Bertrand Russell (1959, 63) noted:

> Domestic animals expect food when they see the person who usually feeds them. We know that all these rather crude expectations of uniformity are liable to be misleading. The man who has fed the chicken every day throughout its life at last wrings its neck instead, showing that more refined views as to the uniformity of nature would have been useful to the chicken.

Analogously, if not quite so direly, important things may actually change soon in U.S. corporate taxation, despite the long period of legal stability. In particular, as chapter 9 will show, a number of important trends suggest that the future need not, and perhaps even cannot, play out simply as an extension of the past. Chapter 10 then considers corporate integration, the most dramatic structural change to the corporate tax to have received substantial attention in recent years. Finally, chapter 11 discusses other possible new directions for the U.S. corporate tax.

9

The Emerging Brave New World

Three emerging trends suggest that the future of the corporate tax may look very different from its past. In brief, the trends are ongoing financial innovation, rising worldwide capital mobility, and changing U.S. political dynamics that may yield worrisome legal instability in the year-to-year content of the corporate tax.

Each of these trends is ongoing, and we may not be headed to dramatic breaking points on any of them. Yet, while in a sense there is nothing new under the sun, differences merely in degree can eventually turn into differences in kind. Something that starts out as simply more of the same can gradually become transformative.

Ongoing Financial Innovation

"Pillars of sand" problems in the structure of the U.S. corporate tax have been with us from the start. As early as 1911, and again in 1925, the U.S. Supreme Court had to address the applicability of the tax to companies that were not formally incorporated but that seemed suspiciously similar to publicly traded corporations (Bittker and Eustice 2006, 2–3). Income tax litigation about the distinction between debt and equity was familiar by the 1930s.[1]

As late as the 1970s, arguably little had changed. In the 1980s, however, aggressive financial innovation emerged, as "capital markets developed high-yield debt, zero coupon debt, hybrid debt, floating rate debt, money-market preferred [stock] and liquid yield option notes" (Hariton 1994, 500), significantly weakening the debt-equity divide by permitting debt to behave more like risky equity. Financial innovation really got going in the 1990s with the rise of derivatives, or financial instruments with payoffs that depend on the value of something else (such as stock or option prices, or inflation or interest rates). Derivatives helped decisively finish off the old world in which "public markets issued a limited variety of instruments," and created instead one in which "corporations can offer investors any set of rights that can be described by words, subject to any conceivable set of qualifications, and in consideration of any conceivable set of offsetting obligations" (500–501). Traditional debt and equity retain their market niches, but even these may diminish over time. Meanwhile, the LLC boom in state entity law, offering businesses a formally noncorporate structure with classic corporate features such as limited liability, was making corporate classification by the U.S. federal income tax system more complicated even before the Blackstone going-public transaction (discussed in chapter 3) placed in doubt the effectiveness of the existing publicly traded line.

This process of unraveling what had once been tolerably clear distinctions has continued to unfold in the 21st century. It has been turbocharged by securitization, or the issuance of financial instruments that are backed by particular, and often otherwise illiquid, assets. Among other effects, securitization has vastly increased the values being traded in financial markets. Thus, consider credit default swaps, designed to pool mortgage risks. Between 2000 and 2008, the market for these instruments grew from $900 billion to $45.5 trillion, thus becoming (at least nominally) twice the size of the U.S. stock market.[2] Credit default swaps are now important enough to have played a starring role in the financial meltdown of 2008.

Financial innovation, by making capital markets larger and more complete, undermines many of the frictions on which the tax system relies. For example, why hold equity if it is tax disadvantaged domestically or if it triggers a withholding tax on dividends paid to foreigners? One can replicate its economics, without the adverse tax consequences, through derivative contracts, such as those that use or mimic options in a given type of stock. In the future, perhaps, why be publicly traded as the term is defined for corporate classification purposes? Even Blackstone was concededly publicly traded, and relied on the applicable statutory definition of passive income to avoid corporate status. However, future companies may not need public tradability if mechanisms emerge to create investor liquidity without it.[3]

One key implication of having ever more complete financial markets is that the Merton Miller view, in which the corporate tax (via the debt-equity choice) offers investors an election between using the corporation's tax rate or their own, should become ever truer. Likewise, increasing the electivity of tax status as a corporation should work toward limiting the reach of the corporate tax to cases where falling under it is tax beneficial. A point to keep in mind, however, is that while all this sounds like it is good for investors, a "new Harberger" view suggests that workers capture the benefit of investors' increasingly using the corporate tax to achieve reductions in the applicable marginal tax rate.

A second set of implications of ongoing financial innovation goes to U.S. international taxation. Even without changes in worldwide capital mobility (the trend I discuss next), financial innovation may affect how international tax rules apply in practice. For example, U.S. corporate residence becomes an ever slimmer reed on which to base the application of worldwide, residence-based tax liability if companies can increasingly replicate the benefits of Delaware incorporation without actually selecting it. Further, the tax consequences assigned to cross-border capital flows, such as in taxing U.S. companies on repatriations from abroad or foreigners on the receipt of U.S.-source passive income, become more avoidable if the flows grow ever harder for the tax system to observe. Accordingly, the U.S. international tax rules would increasingly be stressed by financial innovation even if the true underlying capital flows were, in substance, completely unchanged.

Rising Worldwide Capital Mobility

As I noted some years ago, "in the international taxation literature, one cannot so much as scan an opening paragraph without substantial danger of 'learning' once again that we live in an age of globalization [and ever rising] worldwide capital mobility" (Shaviro 2002, 317). While the observation struck me as having become distressingly trite, this was only because it was (and is) so true.

Others have noted, with similarly unmistakable accuracy, that "greater capital mobility and international tax competition allow investors to escape taxation easily by shifting capital to low- or no-tax jurisdictions" (Avi-Yonah 2000, 1575). They worry that this significantly undermines the progressivity of the existing income tax. The usual policy prescription, if one favors progressivity, is international cooperation to prevent corporations from taking advantage of tax competition to demand lower tax rates for investing and/or to shift their activities into lower-taxed environments.

For three reasons, this prescription can be questioned. First, it may be extremely hard to accomplish. There are hundreds of separate national governments, each (at least among those that are reasonably well functioning) potentially with something to gain from offering lower rates than their neighbors in order to attract extra business investment and tax revenues. Even if everyone ought to cooperate, being a lone hero does not necessarily pay. In this regard, one should consider not only the possibility of losing business investment and tax revenue to other countries, but also the evidence (discussed in chapter 4) that corporate taxes may be borne by local workers if investment can readily leave in response to the tax.

Second, the progressivity of the corporate tax may be unclear even if one can use worldwide cooperation to recreate the "old Harberger" closed-economy scenario on a worldwide scale. Even leaving aside the specialized sectoral factors in application of the corporate tax that Harberger showed could lead to surprising incidence results, his assumption of a zero savings response to the tax can be challenged. The more saving declines in response to a tax on capital (an empirical question that remains contested in the economics literature), the less progressive a tax on capital income, whether corporate or otherwise, is likely to be.

Finally, as long as wealthy individuals are relatively immobile, rather than personally migrating from high-tax to low-tax countries, it is theoretically possible for a country to achieve however much progressivity it likes (absent a savings response) whether corporations shift their investments from high-tax to low-tax countries or not. Almost by definition, a worldwide residence-based income tax on individuals, if enforced effectively in practice, would prevent mere shifts in where one invests from reducing progressivity. Indeed, even with foreign tax credits, tax competition never gets off the ground if resident individuals will end up being taxed at locally determined rates no matter what they pay on a source basis abroad. The progressivity threat from tax competition with respect to corporate investment is entirely a function of measuring tax liability at the entity level while permitting postponement or even permanent avoidance of the investor-level tax. This reflects the balance of forces in domestic tax politics, rather than just following ineluctably from worldwide tax competition or even from the administrative advantages of entity-level tax collection.

If worldwide tax competition, based on an entity-level tax, is a given, then one would certainly expect the United States to face increased pressure to participate in the competitive process by cutting its corporate rate. The political forces favoring such a shift have indeed been gaining strength in recent years, reflecting not just the political power of business interests (although that may be a factor) but the substantive arguments of national self-interest that weigh in favor of joining in. For example, lowering the U.S. rate would encourage (or reduce discouragement of) both actual investment in the United States rather than in other countries, and tax reporting of geographically ambiguous income as U.S. source rather than foreign source. Real shifts in economic activity and reporting shifts in the location of taxable income can both be sources of national benefit, albeit at the expense of other countries' welfare (which generally is the motivation for engaging in tax competition).

However, even if reducing the corporate rate significantly below the top individual rate is unambiguously a good idea, it would increase the tax policy challenges posed by managing the relationships between the corporate and individual systems. For example, it would tend to make the Merton Miller view more relevant by increasing the tax-rate advantages that high-bracket individuals gain from investing through corporate equity in lieu of using either corporate debt or noncorporate entities. A significant rate spread might also increase the grounds for wanting to use the investor-level tax (whether or not it was integrated with the corporate-level tax) as a way of ensuring the application of desired tax rates to such individuals.

Possible Changes in U.S. Political Dynamics

The years of relative political stability for the U.S. corporate tax did not just happen by chance. Rather, this stability had underlying structural and intellectual causes. If the reasons for stability persist, then—even if there is a sharp, one-time regime change in the corporate tax, such as the adoption of corporate integration or a dramatic rate cut—one might well expect renewed stability within the general contours of the new regime. If the underlying political dynamics change sufficiently, however, then all bets are off concerning year-to-year stability in the future, whether we experience a dramatic regime change or not.

Political forecasting is always hazardous. British Prime Minister Harold Wilson once remarked that even a week is a long time in politics, and an assessment of long-term legal stability requires looking many years into the future. Any attempt to predict where tax politics is headed requires "stepping deep into the speculative wilderness" and hence is only for the "bold at heart" (Shaviro 2008b, 3).

It seems clear, however, that there is reasonable cause for concern that the future of U.S. corporate taxation may prove significantly less stable than the recent past. There are three main reasons for this concern: the rise of more polarized and political party-driven tax legislative politics, the growing popularity of temporary tax legislation, and the threat that rising budget deficits will create serious fiscal sustainability problems.

Starting with the first of these factors, in recent years, both the internal cohesion and the ideological differences between the Democratic and Republican parties have increased sharply in the U.S. legislative process (Fiorina 2006, 241–242). The Republicans in particular have "started to act like a traditional, ideological European political party, maintaining strict party formation in all voting . . . [and] punishing internal dissenters from the party line" (Gilman 2004, 2). While Democrats have not as yet moved nearly so far in this direction, they as well have recently shown significantly greater party cohesion in legislative voting than they did in earlier decades (Fiorina 2006, 240).

Stronger party-line voting may cause the U.S. tax legislative process to function more like that in a parliamentary system than was previously the case, especially when the president's party controls both houses of Congress. Thus, consider the difference between 2001 and 2003 on the one hand, when the Republican leadership passed White House-derived major tax legislation with almost no Democratic support, and 1986 on the other, when fundamental income-tax reform passed only with great difficulty even though the leaders of *both* parties supported it (Birnbaum and Murray 1987). While a more top-down legislative process may make significant tax changes easier to enact than they would be in a more dis-aggregated and decentralized system, it does not necessarily imply instability, or that policy will regularly lurch back and forth as party control oscillates. After all, tax politics in European countries with parliamentary systems are not necessarily unstable by U.S. standards.

What makes a more parliamentary-style U.S. tax legislative process potentially a source of instability is the particular dynamics of recent political competition between the Democratic and Republican parties. Ordinarily, in a two-party system, each party has political incentives to move toward the center as a way of competing for the median voter, whose preferences might be expected to lie between those of either party's ideologues (see Downs 1957, 117). As a result, "a two-party electoral system [can] be prone to yielding competing candidates who, as George Wallace famously complained in the 1960s, had 'not a dime's worth of difference' between them" (Shaviro 2007a, 129). Even when party differences were clear, such as during Ronald Reagan's presidency in the 1980s, this phenomenon often helped to produce centrist, bipartisan cooperation (131). Thus, the parties collaborated, during Reagan's and George H. W. Bush's presidencies, not only on the 1986 tax-reform legislation (which included a corporate rate cut from 46 to 34 percent), but on repeated deficit reduction measures that raised taxes in coordination with cutting government spending. However, such bipartisan deals stopped being made in the early 1990s, when the Republicans moved sharply to the right and began following a political strategy known popularly as "energizing the base" (131–34), or getting the most ideologically fervent voters sufficiently motivated to turn out in force.

From the standpoint of competing for the median voter, the Republicans' political lurch to the right during the presidencies of Bill Clinton and George W. Bush may seem surprising and anomalous. Yet it was both deliberate and, at least for a considerable period, politically successful, reflecting that an "energizing the base" strategy has an advantage potentially offsetting its abandonment of the political center. If relatively extreme voters are "far more sensitive to ideological distance in deciding whether to vote than those in the middle of the spectrum" (133), then abandoning the political center can "pay" for the loss of moderate votes by sharply increasing voter turnout among those whose views lie closer to the fringe.

This tactical shift has been accompanied, whether as cause or effect, by the emergence of far greater ideological differences between the parties regarding what U.S. tax policy generally, including with regard to corporations, should look like. Corporate integration, for example, is a Republican political cause largely rejected by Democrats. This gulf contributes to the current state of uncertainty concerning the 15 percent dividend rate that is scheduled to expire after 2010. Likewise, shifting from income to consumption taxation, which (as we will see in chapter 10) would have huge implications for the corporate tax, is almost purely a Republican cause. On the other hand, Democrats have on several recent occasions advocated moving U.S. international taxation closer to being a true worldwide system,[4] whereas Republicans tend to favor moving toward exemption (or at least staying put). Overall, the range of disagreement is simply much greater than it used to be.

Whether tax policy dissensus between the parties is more tactical or more ideological in its causation, it carries the clear implication that rule oscillation and instability may be greater in the future than they were in the past. If such features as the corporate rate, the dividend rate, and the capital gains rate start bouncing up and down more sharply and frequently than they have historically, or if major structural changes in the system start getting enacted and then repealed, corporate tax planning may be greatly affected. Companies may more often need to think explicitly about not just the current rules, but also the likely near-future rules.

Making things worse is the growing congressional practice of enacting temporary tax legislation that threatens or even guarantees year-to-year change. Sunsetting, or the practice of enacting tax laws that are scheduled to expire even if the proponents avowedly plan to make them permanent, was rare until the George W. Bush administration, when it became standard operating procedure, applied not just to the rate cut for dividends, but to most of the tax cuts that were enacted (Viswanathan 2007, 657). Its main purpose was to bypass budgetary constraints in the form of Senate procedural rules that would have required supermajority support for tax cuts applying more than 10 years out (667). Secondarily, sunsetting permitted proponents of controversial changes to minimize admitted long-term revenue costs through what I have elsewhere called

> a cynical game of "bait and switch." First, [Congress] would enact a tax cut with a sunset, estimated (by reason of the sunset) to cost only, say, $350 billion over ten years. Next, when proponents moved to eliminate the sunset, as they had promised in advance to do, they could accuse any critics of the new proposals of trying to "raise taxes." In short, the baseline [for measuring revenue cost] would be deceptively shifted without an honest accounting at any time. (Shaviro 2007a, 50–51)

This is not the behavior one expects in a healthy policymaking environment where political competition coexists with a shared interest in stable governance. Rather, it reflects the degree to which partisan and ideological divisions can promote shortsighted and irresponsible behavior that inevitably makes business planning much more difficult and uncertain.

Temporary tax legislation also can promote instability when it is meant all along to expire. A prominent recent example was the ostensibly one-time dividends-received tax holiday, for repatriations of foreign-source income from controlled foreign corporations, that Congress passed in 2004. U.S. multinationals took advantage of this tax holiday, which (for one year only) reduced the applicable tax rate on repatriations to 5.25 percent, to send home "more than $300 billion of their $804 billion of accumulated nontaxable earnings at the end of 2004 in their overseas operations" (Weiner 2007a, 853). This resulted in immediate incremental tax revenues of $7 billion, although the long-term net-revenue cost may have been as much as $39 billion (853). While a truly one-time-only tax holiday presumably would not affect companies' subsequent repatriation decisions, the obvious lesson is that if it happens once, it can happen again, leading to increased lock-in and economic distortion if companies respond by waiting for the next special offer.

Arguably, the broader lesson of the 2004 tax holiday for foreign dividends is even more discouraging than its promotion of anticipatory lock-in for the future. Congress's willingness in 2004 to use time-inconsistent budgetary gimmicks to raise short-term revenues and gratify lobbyists (see Weiner 2007b, 855) may tell us something about the contemporary tax legislative process. Ostensibly one-time tax holidays, no less than the pervasive use of sunsets for provisions that the proponents insist should be permanent, simply were not a feature of prior U.S. political eras.

The final factor raising concern about corporate tax-law stability goes to the increasingly threatening overhang of the long-term U.S. fiscal gap. Current U.S. tax and spending policy appears to be unsustainable due to the inadequacy of projected revenues to pay for projected spending. Indeed, the shortfall was recently estimated to have a present value, in current dollars, of $98 trillion, or about 8.76 percent of the present value of all projected future U.S. gross domestic product (Auerbach, Furman, and Gale 2007, 773). The implications are sobering. Putting the U.S. budget on a sustainable long-term course would require

> a permanent reduction in noninterest spending of 34.2 percent or a permanent increase in revenues of 50.8 percent. . . . Narrower means of closing the gap would be even more draconian—an 82.1 percent increase in income taxes, for example—and eliminating all discretionary spending would not suffice. Because the fiscal gap measures the size of the required *immediate* fiscal adjustment, the required adjustment also rises if action is delayed (773).

In this sort of fiscal environment, I have argued that "nothing is really safe, and no government commitment can be taken for granted for more than a few years. With even Social Security and Medicare likely to be on the chopping block, none of the players can afford to rely on political inertia to protect what they now have" (Shaviro 2007a, 50).

While the implications go well beyond the expected future course of U.S. corporate taxation, they clearly extend to it. Surely the new view is a lot less true in this sort of unstable political and fiscal environment than in one where broad political consensus and ample net revenues entrench the prevailing status quo. The problems are obviously much larger, however. Should corporate rate cuts, if enacted, be expected to persist? Is any one regime for U.S. international taxation likely to prove stable? Will Congress, at some point, be tempted to engage in short-term revenue grabs wherever the money seems politically and administratively easy to get? How will businesses respond if U.S. fiscal problems worsen and the day of reckoning appears to be growing closer? These are questions that we cannot answer today.

Corporate Integration

Given how little sense the corporate tax's four main distortions appear to make, it is natural to ask if we could do away with them by adopting corporate integration. As we will see, however, the issues of how and even whether to adopt integration, under real-world political and administrative constraints, are more ambiguous than one might think. Clearly, a system that taxed all business income once, at rates that did not depend on such anomalous factors as organizational form or financial-instrument design, would potentially be very appealing. Things get more complicated, however, when one actually focuses on concrete integration proposals and their likely effects, in particular given the United States' long-term budgetary and political stability problems.

To What Problems Might Corporate Integration Be the Solution?

Sometimes we hear of a solution in search of a problem, which someone offers to a baffled world despite the lack of any discernible need for it. Examples include the George W. Bush administration's endless advocacy of tax cuts, interminable concert tours by the Rolling Stones when they are past age 60, and the live-action theatrical movie version of *Scooby-Doo.*

Corporate integration lies on the opposite end of the spectrum from those unneeded initiatives. In practice, at least from the standpoint of ready accessibility, integration tends to involve too many solutions in pursuit of too many problems. Even if one agrees that the existing corporate tax rules are unnecessarily complicated and inefficient, and that double taxation of equity-financed corporate income makes no sense, the question of how to rationalize the system has a wide range of possible answers, each differing in its response to the underlying distortions and pillars of sand that might reasonably motivate reform.

The most common answer to why we might favor corporate integration focuses squarely on the double tax. This answer is too narrow, however, given that, as demonstrated by debate concerning both the new view and the Miller equilibrium, the structure of the existing corporate tax may affect tax burdens and economic decisions even if the shareholder-level tax is never actually paid. A better way to think about corporate integration, therefore, is as a suite of proposals designed to ease or eliminate, in varying degree, one or more of the four main distortions (discussed in chapter 2) created by the current system. I therefore start by briefly reviewing the current intellectual state of the play concerning these distortions.

Entity choice. Classification as a C corporation mainly depends on whether one chooses either to be formally incorporated, as in the case of an enterprise that makes use of Delaware corporate law, or to access worldwide capital markets by being publicly traded. Efficiency would be enhanced if corporate integration, by conforming the overall tax treatment of corporate and noncorporate entities, permitted these choices to be made based purely on their merits from a pretax economic standpoint. Accomplishing this in full would require not only eliminating the double tax, but conforming the marginal tax rates that apply to corporate and noncorporate income.

Debt versus equity. Insofar as the choice between debt and equity matters economically—for example, because of its effect on default risk or on how incentives are aligned as between insiders and outsiders—one would like it as well to be tax neutral. And even if taxpayers can achieve the economics they want independently of the financial instrument labels they choose for tax-reporting purposes, disparity between the tax treatment of debt and equity can lead to undue electivity between paying tax at the corporate rate or at one's own rate.

Distributing versus retaining earnings. Corporate governance problems suggest that lock-in of corporate earnings, resulting from the expectation that current distributions would bear a higher tax burden than future ones, is undesirable. Further, fiscal and political instability suggest that having a deferred shareholder-level tax, the rate of which can change at any time, may be a recipe for tax-driven distribution decisions (aimed at taking advantage of low-rate years), violating the principle of tax neutrality.

Form of distribution. Tax bias between dividends and asymmetrical share repurchases may matter for corporate governance reasons—for example, if managers use the latter to benefit from inside information regarding "true" share value. While basis recovery for share repurchases creates divergence between the two in any event, the tax disparity would generally increase if (contrary to 2008 law) the dividend rate were raised above the capital gains rate.

Why Isn't Corporate Integration Easy?

Eliminating *all* of the distortions that result from the structure of the corporate tax would be easy in theory, but it is not so easy in practice. Under a comprehensive, purely individual-level tax on economic income, defined as the taxpayer's consumption plus her change in net worth (Simons 1938, 50), people holding financial instruments of any kind in business entities of any kind would pay tax annually based on the instruments' change in market value during the year. Nothing else would matter. Thus, none of the legal distinctions that underlie the four distortions in the existing corporate tax would make any difference to tax liability, except insofar as they affected pretax net worth (which the taxpayer would want to maximize in any event).

Once we have a realization-based income tax, however, things are not so simple. Indeed, there would be problems even if corporate taxable income, as determined on a realization basis, were allocated and taxed directly to shareholders without any requirement of a shareholder-level realization event. This "flow-through" approach, from the entity to its owners, is generally used in taxing partnerships under current U.S. law. Even if such an approach were used for corporations, however, some or all of the four main corporate tax distortions might nonetheless continue to exist.

For example, the debt-equity distinction would still matter if anyone classified as a debt holder was outside the income allocation regime even if the value of her instrument depended in part on corporate performance.

Corporate debt instruments frequently have special features that make them equity-like in this sense. An example is convertible debt, or that which the holder has an option (perhaps only under specified circumstances) to exchange for a determinate number of corporate shares. For that matter, even straight debt is to a degree equity-like insofar as there is a chance of default, since this makes corporate performance among the determinants of current value.

Partnership tax rules are notoriously flexible and manipulable, however, making it often quite easy to allocate gross income to partners with low marginal rates and deductions to partners with high marginal rates (Shaviro 1995, 704). Thus, applying the flow-through approach of partnership taxation to corporations might be considered inappropriate, even if it were feasible. Several leading studies have concluded, however, that applying it to publicly traded companies would involve undue complexity given both the frequency with which capital interests may change hands and the myriad forms that these interests may take (U.S. Treasury Department 1992; American Law Institute 1993).

With perfect solutions being, as a practical matter, unavailable, proponents of corporate integration have had to settle for advocating mechanisms that work only to a degree. All of the leading proposals aim for the equivalent of one level of tax on corporate income. In cases where tax is collected at both the entity and owner levels, the proposals typically coordinate or reconcile the amounts levied at each, so that, at least in general, there will not be a true double tax.

All of these proposals have in common, however, a need to address a number of key design issues wholly apart from whether the double tax is generally being eliminated. Given these issues' importance, as well as their potential impact on the four distortions, I briefly survey them before turning to the main details of the proposals themselves.

Tough Choices Associated with Corporate Integration

The decision to adopt corporate integration would place several vexing and potentially divisive policy issues at center stage as design choices were being made. One of these, the problem of how to handle the transition to an integrated system, is endemic to enacting legal change. In other cases, however, the problem is that the current design of the corporate tax happens to affect other, seemingly distinct policy choices—relating, for example, to the breadth of tax exemption for institutions such as pension funds, or to the question of how generous tax preferences should be. Corporate integration would potentially disrupt the current state of play in such areas, even though its main rationales are largely unrelated to their optimal resolution, thus complicating the question of how to structure it.

Transition

Current corporate shareholders acquired their shares when the double corporate tax was in place and presumably considered likely to remain so. As we saw in chapter 5 (concerning the new view), insofar as share prices reflect the expectation of an eventual distributions tax, the windfall gain to shareholders from sudden and unexpected repeal of this tax could be substantial. In illustration, suppose that an incorporated $100 bank account was considered certain to face a 35 percent distributions tax at some point in the future. Suddenly and unexpectedly repealing that tax would lead to more than a 50 percent increase in the share value (from $65 to $100).[1]

Especially in an era when we face grave fiscal sustainability problems, the motivation for providing such a windfall is unclear. Additionally, if repeal of the shareholder-level tax started to be anticipated prior to its actual enactment, then, during the interim period, lock-in of corporate earnings might increase. Why pay a dividend tax today if the tax might disappear tomorrow? (On the other side of the ledger, advance anticipation of corporate integration would also reduce discouragement of new corporate equity during the interim period by suggesting that the double tax might disappear.)

In theory, there are mechanisms for eliminating the windfall gain, such as by limiting the benefits of integration to postenactment new equity, or by imposing an offsetting one-time tax on old equity at the time of enactment.[2] If, however, such mechanisms prove to be untenable, whether politically or administratively, then the main implication of disliking the windfall gain is that it might reduce the appeal of adopting corporate integration to begin with.

Treatment of Tax-Exempt Shareholders

Various shareholders in taxable U.S. corporations are not themselves legally or effectively taxable. Examples include tax-exempt charitable organizations (such as universities with huge endowments), pension funds that hold tax-favored retirement savings on behalf of their investors, taxpayers with loss carryovers from other taxable years that make them effectively exempt from U.S. income taxation at the margin, and foreigners who are not subject to U.S. tax (for example, due to a tax treaty between their country of residence and the United States).

Under present law, these shareholders effectively are taxed at the entity level when they earn income through a taxable U.S. corporation. Also, while (in accordance with the Miller equilibrium) this gives them a strong motivation to invest via debt rather than stock, they do not always do this, reflecting the continuing difficulty of getting the same economics with either label. Thus, for example, Harvard University's $35 billion endowment has a substantial stock component.[3]

If corporate integration were implemented via curtailment of the entity-level tax, the tax-exempts would benefit from effective elimination of the taxes they currently (albeit indirectly) pay. This arguably is a policy change unrelated to the motivations for corporate integration, if we think of exemption as different from the positive marginal tax rates that individual investors presumably ought to pay on their shares of corporate income.[4] Thus, unless there were a politically and administratively feasible vehicle for preserving the indirect levy on tax-exempts, any aversion to expanding their degree of tax benefit from the current system would weigh in favor of taxing corporate income at the entity level rather than the owner level. This, however, would need to be weighed against any grounds for otherwise preferring the application of shareholder-level tax rates, such as to avoid biasing taxpayers' choice of entity or financial instrument.

Corporate-Level Tax Preferences

Under current law, the benefit of tax preferences enjoyed at the corporate level often is lost when tax-favored income is distributed to shareholders. Thus, suppose a corporation holds municipal bonds (issued by U.S. state and local governments), the interest on which is generally exempt from U.S. income tax. If the corporation distributes this tax-free interest income to shareholders, the shareholders are taxable upon the receipt of a dividend, exactly as if they had received any other type of corporate-level income.

Corporate integration potentially would disrupt the current state of play concerning the degree of benefit derived from tax preferences, notwithstanding that the motives for adopting it might have nothing to do with the question of how generous they ought to be. In particular, simply eliminating the shareholder-level tax might make the tax preferences enjoyed by corporations effectively larger. One way of trying to preserve the current balance is to condition the excludability of corporate distributions to shareholders (if that is the integration method adopted) on the income's having previously been taxed at the corporate level. The Bush administration's 2003 proposal to eliminate the dividend tax would have done this.

Such an approach, however, creates lock-in of tax-preferred earnings at the corporate level (unless new-view considerations apply) and also may discourage use of the corporate form for tax-preferred investment. In theory, one could try to split the difference by making preferences slightly less generous across the board, without regard to whether they are being enjoyed through corporations, but in practice this "fair compromise" solution seems unlikely to be politically feasible, at least in the short run.

Cross-Border Issues

Corporate integration also potentially disrupts existing patterns of taxation when foreign shareholders own stock in U.S. companies, or U.S. shareholders own stock in foreign companies. With the United States not currently levying both levels of tax, other than through withholding taxes on foreign shareholders that often are reduced or eliminated through bilateral tax treaties, the questions of how and whether to integrate become more complicated.

In theory, if corporate integration is a good idea domestically, one would think it is also likely to be a good idea in the cross-border setting. Thus, it might be optimal for countries (assuming they agreed about the merits of integration) to cooperate with each other in ensuring that corporate income is not taxed twice, even if the corporation and a given shareholder are residents of different countries. If one assumes that source-based taxation will have priority, as typically it does in the cross-border setting, then this might imply that the United States (1) should not tax foreign shareholders on the receipt of dividends from U.S. companies and (2) should in some fashion take account of foreign corporate taxes paid by U.S. shareholders of foreign companies. However, even if these concessions are worth making on a bilateral basis, at least the second of them might not be in the United States' best interest when acting unilaterally,[5] and conceding either of them up front might be inferior to using both as leverage to demand reciprocity in treaty negotiations.

Leading Corporate Integration Methods

The Question of Where to Levy the Tax

Corporate integration can take a stupefying variety of forms. A key design question, however, if double taxation is being eliminated, is where to locate the single tax that remains. Ideally, it might go purely at the individual level, so that whether one invested through a corporation and/or held equity would make no difference to the measurement of income or to the applicable tax rate.

Once flow-through taxation of corporate investors is ruled out, however, the case for collecting the tax purely at the individual level becomes less clear. Corporate-level collection may be administratively more efficient, since it is more centralized than taxing all the investors individually and since corporate headquarters may be the best place to look for relevant transactional information. Further, waiting for corporate-level gain to be realized by investors, such as through stock sales or the receipt of dividends, is unfeasible within the broader setting of an income tax (as noted in chapter 2). Suppose I have an investment that earns 10 percent a year, whether from sitting in a bank account or being used in a noncorporate business. An income tax reaches the annual 10 percent return on a current basis even if the money stays in the bank account or the business rather than being withdrawn and used. If a purely individual-level, realization-based corporate income tax does not do the same by making corporate-level profits currently taxable even if they are not withdrawn from the entity, then essentially corporations have been converted into tax-free savings accounts for investors—an approach that makes little sense unless we do it generally, such as by having a consumption tax rather than an income tax, without regard to use of the corporate form.

For this reason, nearly all corporate integration methods make at least some use of the corporate level in collecting the tax on corporate income. They vary, however, in how extensively they confine tax collection to this level, and in exactly how they divide the tax base between the two levels or otherwise coordinate potentially overlapping tax collection in order to avoid or mitigate true double taxation.

Dividend Exemption

The leading approach to corporate integration, among policymakers if not academics, is to make dividends tax exempt (in addition to remaining nondeductible at the corporate level), while interest expenses remain includable and deductible. This is the corporate integration approach that the George W. Bush administration advocated in 2003. Other key features of the proposal included retention of shareholder-level capital gains taxes and rules limiting the dividend exclusion to distributions of previously taxed corporate income.[6]

While the proposal would largely have eliminated the double tax, in other respects its policy payoff would have been disappointing. In particular, given varying marginal tax rates, it would have preserved (even if somewhat mitigating) all four of the classical corporate tax distortions. The tax desirability of using corporate entities would still have depended on how the corporate rate compared to particular investors' rates. Debt-equity choices would have remained distorted, with tax-exempts preferring the former and anyone whose marginal rate exceeded that applying to corporations preferring the latter. Distributions of income that had not been taxed at the corporate level due to preferences would have remained tax discouraged, along with sales of appreciated stock. Finally, dividend distributions would still have been tax favored relative to share repurchases where the stock was appreciated. And such improvement as there was would have come at the cost of a significant increase in the long-term U.S. fiscal gap, given the Bush administration's unwillingness to finance the tax cuts it was proposing.

Integrated Two-Level Tax on Equity-Financed Income

While the unfeasibility of flow-through corporate taxation prevents applying investors' tax rates to their shares of corporate income on a current basis as it is earned, numerous countries around the world have tried to reconcile the applicable tax rate later on, when the investors receive corporate distributions or sell their shares. The main mechanism is called imputation.

Imputation Method

The basic idea behind imputation is to combine corporate-level taxation with taxing distributions to shareholders, but to treat corporate-level taxes paid as creditable against shareholder liability so that a true double tax does not apply. Thus, suppose the corporate rate is 35 percent and that I receive a dividend, deemed to have been paid out of after-tax corporate earnings, in the amount of $65. For tax purposes, I am treated as having received $100 (i.e., my inclusion is grossed up to include the corporate-level taxes that were paid on this income). However, the $35 of corporate-level tax is not just included, but also treated as a tax credit that I can claim against my own tax liability on the distribution or more generally.

Thus, if my tax rate, like that of the company, is 35 percent, the receipt of the dividend has no net tax consequences for me. By contrast, if my tax rate is 40 percent, I will owe $5 of tax on my deemed $100 receipt even after using the $35 credit. And if my tax rate is only 30 percent, then absent any limits (akin to foreign tax-credit limits) on use of the credit, I will actually get $5 from the government by reason of the dividend receipt. In effect, then, absent any limits on use of the credit, the corporate-level tax is merely a withholding tax, like that on employees' paychecks under the existing income tax on individuals.

The imputation method reduces tax-induced distortions in entity choice and between debt and equity, relative to dividend exclusion, by ultimately adjusting the taxes paid on equity-financed corporate income to reflect the investor's marginal rate. While this potentially makes it a much better corporate integration method than dividend exclusion, there has been worldwide movement away from it in recent years because of concern about its complexity in practice, such as in determining what corporate-level taxes relate to particular distributions (Ault and Arnold 2004, 327), along with cross-border coordination problems between countries. However, Canada, Australia, and New Zealand retain impu-tation systems, and the method has also prominently been proposed for the United States (American Law Institute 1993).

Dividend Deduction

A substantively similar approach to corporate integration would make div-idends deductible by corporations that pay them while requiring share-holders to include dividends received as fully taxable ordinary income. Superficially, this system may look quite different from imputation, since distributions yield a corporate-level refund rather than a shareholder-level credit. In substance, however, the two systems are quite similar, given that, in both, paying a dividend effectively converts the applicable tax rate from that at the corporate level to that at the shareholder level.

In illustration, consider again the above example in which the corporate rate is 35 percent while the individual rate is either 30 percent or 40 percent. If the company earns $100 and does not pay an immediate dividend, it owes $35 of tax, leaving $65 of after-tax income. By paying a $100 dividend, however, it gets a tax refund worth $35 and thus is able to pay $100 to its shareholders, on which they will pay either $30 or $40 of tax, depending on their marginal rates. In terms of overall cash flows, this is equivalent to the case where the corporation pays $35 of tax that is not refunded to it but that it gets to treat as a refundable tax credit against its own liabilities.[7]

Dividend deductibility has nonetheless tended to be less used than imputation for two main reasons. First, when corporations pay dividends during loss years, dividend deductions may fail to have value if losses are generally nonrefundable. Second, if one favors retaining the existing corporate-level tax's indirect levy on tax-exempts, this may be politically and administratively easier to accomplish by making imputation credits nonrefundable than by trying to collect dividend taxes from the otherwise tax exempt.

The Comprehensive Business Income Tax

Imputation, even if feasible despite recent complaints about its complexity, retains at least one pillar of sand in its foundations by relying on the debt-equity distinction. In 1992, the U.S. Treasury released a study of corporate integration that described how one could try to eliminate this distinction through the adoption of what the study called a comprehensive business income tax (CBIT). The CBIT would apply to all businesses, without regard to whether they were incorporated, subject to a small-business exception. As a first step, it would make dividends excludable to shareholders. In addition, however, the CBIT (unlike dividend exclusion) would extend the same basic regime to debt-financed corporate income by making interest payments, no less than dividends, both nondeductible at the corporate level and excludable by the recipient.

The CBIT thereby would eliminate all investor-level taxes on corporate (and other business) income, subject to one possible exception. Without taking a definite stand, the Treasury proposal describes arguments in support of the view that investors that hold financial interests in businesses, such as corporate stock, should pay capital gains tax when they sell these interests at a profit (as well as being allowed to deduct capital losses). It notes that while there is no reason to tax undistributed corporate earnings at the investor level, given that they already have been taxed at the business level, one could argue for an investor-level tax in other instances. Suppose, for example, that a shareholder sells her stock for a profit, even though all corporate earnings have been distributed as dividends, by reason of (1) income that was sheltered at the corporate level by tax preferences, (2) unrealized appreciation in the value of corporate assets, or (3) changes in the anticipated value of future corporate earnings. In each of these cases, an investor-level tax arguably is appropriate under a realization-based income tax, albeit potentially at the cost of creating lock-in.[8] However, the Treasury study leaves for another day the question of whether (and if so, how) to impose such a tax.

The CBIT potentially goes a lot further than dividend exemption or even imputation in mitigating the four basic corporate tax distortions. Entity choice ceases to be an issue if the business tax applies generally—although the small business exception, along with the choice to be in business rather than, say, being an employee, may matter due to marginal tax rate differences. Further, the tax treatment of debt and equity are conformed. The existence of lock-in and bias between dividends and share repurchases would depend on whether investor-level capital gains taxes were being retained.

The Business Enterprise Income Tax

In 2005, Edward Kleinbard, a distinguished tax practitioner who subsequently became Chief of Staff of the U.S. Congress's Joint Committee on Taxation, proposed the business enterprise income tax (BEIT), a corporate integration plan that resembles the CBIT not only in applying to businesses generally, but also in eliminating the debt-equity distinction (Kleinbard 2005, 2007b). However, the BEIT reverses the CBIT's methodology for eliminating the distinction. Whereas the CBIT, by denying business-level interest deductions, in effect would treat debt like current-law equity, the BEIT would treat equity like current-law debt by providing annual business-level deductions and investor-level inclusions even if no distributions are made.

Specifically, for all financial capital invested in a business enterprise, the BEIT would provide a business-level deduction, called the cost of capital allowance (COCA), computed at a suitable interest rate. Thus, suppose a company held $100 million of capital, defined as the tax basis of all its assets (Kleinbard 2005, 101), and that the applicable interest rate (which might be based on U.S. Treasury bond rates) was 5 percent. The company would deduct $5 million, without regard to what distributions it actually made. On the investor side, holders of debt and equity alike in the company would include a 5 percent return, computed on the tax basis of the instruments, even if they received no current distributions. In effect, then, debt and equity alike would be treated like OID bonds, which give rise to interest deductions and accruals even if no interest is currently paid.

In the above example, if the investors' "outside" tax basis for their financial positions equaled the company's "inside" tax basis for its assets, the end result would resemble that under the CBIT, except that $5 million (instead of zero) would be deducted at the company level and included at the investor level. This would have no net tax consequences if the investor and company tax rates were the same.

For two reasons, however, using the BEIT instead of the CBIT approach could make a difference. First, investors may have different marginal tax rates than the company. Use of the BEIT results in taxation of the normal rate of return (as embodied in the applicable interest rate) at investor rather than company rates. Second, the amount included by investors might differ from—and typically would exceed—the amount deducted by the company. Outside basis usually is higher than inside basis, because the latter may be reduced by tax depreciation for the company's assets whereas the former will increase whenever investors sell their financial instruments at a profit.

Shareholder-Level, Market Value–Based Tax

A final approach to corporate integration dispenses with entity-level taxation altogether, at least for publicly traded companies, but without turning corporate investment into an income tax-free zone. Joseph Bankman (1995), Joseph Dodge (1995), and Michael Knoll (1996) have each proposed entirely replacing the corporate-level tax on the income of publicly traded companies with a shareholder-level tax on unrealized as well as realized income, computed by measuring changes in the market value of financial instruments such as stock. Thus, if Microsoft in a given year paid $100 million in dividends and enjoyed a $200 million increase in the price of its outstanding shares, $300 million would be taxed to the shareholders—wholly without regard to any accounting-style measure of Microsoft's earnings for the year.

Among the issues raised by these proposals are how to coordinate taxation of the publicly traded and non-publicly traded sectors and how to value financial positions in public companies (such as specialized options or convertible debt) that are not themselves sufficiently traded to have readily observable market values. In addition, one would have to accept the idea of assigning current tax consequences to the at times large gyrations in stock market prices, which generally are a lot more volatile than annual earnings measures. Thus, consider the stock market boom of the late 1990s, during which a number of Internet startup companies had high and rapidly rising market capitalizations but eventually failed without generating any earnings. Had a shareholder-level, market value-based tax been in effect at the time, shareholders in these companies would have had to report huge income amounts, subsequently offset by major losses. This might have proven politically controversial, even before Internet stock prices collapsed, given liquidity arguments that the shareholders might have made to the effect that they did not have the cash to pay current tax on their unrealized gains.

What (if Anything) Should Be Done?

Despite the logical appeal of corporate integration, there is little reason for optimism that it will happen any time soon, or be done well if it happens. The problems start with limited public enthusiasm for the idea, given that the visible gulf between large public corporations and their shareholders gives intuitive appeal to the idea that each ought to pay tax. In addition, as noted in chapter 1, corporate managers tend to be decidedly unenthusiastic about it, whether because they want an excuse to avoid paying dividends or because they prefer to lobby for more targeted (such as industry-specific) tax benefits. Finally, increasing the long-term U.S. fiscal gap through its adoption without financing might be unwise, yet one could scarcely imagine Congress agreeing to pay for it (even if fiscal responsibility becomes more popular) when its political appeal is borderline to begin with.

The seemingly most popular, salient, and simple way of advancing corporate integration, through dividend exemption, is probably the worst method substantively, given its limited effect on the four main distortions. In addition, if corporate integration through dividend exemption is not generally accepted across the political spectrum, then Republicans' efforts to move toward it while Democrats continue to resist, assuming that the parties will take turns controlling the federal government, suggests a strong prospect of repeated up-and-down adjustments to the dividend rate.

Perhaps it would help to reframe advocacy of corporate integration as an effort to rationalize the taxation of financial instruments by conforming the tax treatment of debt and equity. This could involve either combining dividend exclusion with parallel treatment for interest expense, as in the CBIT, or adopting a COCA approach, as in the BEIT. The broader structural character of such reforms not only might make them better in a pure policy sense than simple dividend exclusion, but also might tend to insulate them from ongoing political fickleness. A separate dividend tax rate, be it 0 or 15 percent, almost invites ongoing adjustment in a way that conforming the tax treatment of dividends and interest arguably would not. In addition, both the CBIT and the BEIT avoid relying to the same degree as partial or varying dividend exemption on companies' discretionary decisions regarding when to pay dividends.

In the interim, however, it is wise to consider what less-fundamental changes to the structure of U.S. corporate taxation might be either desirable or likely (or better still, both). Chapter 11 examines several of the main possibilities.

11

Other Possible New Directions for the U.S. Corporate Tax

E ven if the basic structure of the U.S. corporate tax remains unchanged, much could happen to improve its functioning. This chapter addresses three possible directions of significant change that might be beneficial and easier to accomplish than corporate integration, and then briefly asks what is likely to happen.

Significantly Reducing the U.S. Corporate Tax Rate

The U.S. corporate tax rate of 35 percent, which applies not just to U.S. companies but to the U.S.-source income of foreign companies classified as C corporations, is on the high end among developed countries. This reflects that the United States, after precipitating worldwide corporate rate reductions when it lowered its corporate rate in 1986 from the previous level of 46 percent, has stayed on the sidelines while other countries have been further reducing their corporate rates in recent years.[1]

This observation has prompted widespread calls for reducing the U.S. corporate rate so that it is back in the worldwide mainstream. Thus, Senator John McCain's 2008 Republican presidential campaign featured a proposal to reduce the rate to 25 percent. Further, while Republicans typically favor lower business taxes than do Democrats, Congressman Charles Rangel, Chair of the House Ways and Means Committee and a prominent Democrat, likewise has proposed comprehensive tax reform that would include significantly reducing the corporate rate.

That other countries have lower corporate tax rates than the United States does not automatically mean that we ought to go along. After all, they might be making a mistake (perhaps reflecting domestic political forces), or their circumstances might differ from ours. For example, it is plausible that individual countries in the European Union (EU) face stronger tax-competitive pressures, from both their EU and non-EU neighbors, than does the United States, given its large size and relative paucity of affluent, comparably sized neighbors.

It is hard to deny, however, that lower corporate rates abroad have an important bearing on what the U.S. corporate tax rate ought to be. After all, the United States, in an era of high and rising worldwide capital mobility, clearly faces significant tax-competitive pressures even though the world's two largest oceans separate us from most potential alternative locations for capital investment.

This section argues that U.S. corporate rate reduction, such as to 25 percent, does indeed make sense, if properly coordinated with progressivity-maintaining elements of the individual income tax and if adequately financed so that its adoption does not increase the long-term U.S. fiscal gap.

Why Reduce the U.S. Corporate Rate?

The core argument that, as a matter of effective tax competition, the United States should lower its corporate rate by at least enough to place itself back in the worldwide mainstream among developed countries rests on two closely related points. The first is that actual business activity will tend to shift at the margin from higher-tax to lower-tax countries, reflecting investors' pursuit of the highest available risk-adjusted after-tax return. Lowering the U.S. rate could therefore increase the country's share both of available worldwide tax revenues and of any surplus captured by a country's residents by reason of investment there.

The second point concerns where taxable income is reported, even holding constant the actual location and level of all business activity. As noted in chapter 7, multinational companies have considerable flexibility, through such instruments as transfer pricing and how they structure their worldwide borrowing and internal cash flows, to determine where their taxable income (and consequent source-based income-tax liability) will be deemed to arise. The lower a given country's tax rate, the more multinationals are likely to tilt in favor of (or reduce their tilting against) locating taxable income there.

Of course, it is generally true that the lower the tax rate, the lower the disincentive to earn and report income of any and all kinds. What makes corporate taxation special? The answer is that the term "corporate" here is serving as a proxy for "business investment," which is the thing that can shift readily between competing tax jurisdictions. Individuals' place of residence remains considerably less tax responsive, as does the place where they work if it must be near where they reside. A standard tax efficiency norm holds that, all else equal, the tax rate should be lower for things with relatively elastic supply or demand (making them less tax responsive) than for those that are more elastic (see chapter 2).

The efficiency case for reducing the corporate tax rate, compared to individual rates that presumably would remain about where they are today absent distinct reasons for changing them, therefore rests on the adequacy of "corporate income" as a proxy for "income from potentially mobile business investment." This is a variable that we can actually affect through the rules for defining corporate-level taxable income. The relationship between these two concepts is also critical for maintaining desired levels of progressivity, notwithstanding reduction of the corporate tax rate below the top individual rate.

Maintaining Progressivity with a Lower Corporate Rate

Having a corporate rate that is significantly below the top individual rate raises two challenges with respect to progressivity. The first concerns the incidence of the corporate-level taxes that are being cut, while the second concerns the leakage of taxable income from the high-rate individual tax into the low-rate corporate tax.

If corporate taxes mainly were borne by investors, as posited by the "old Harberger" model (discussed in chapter 4), then cutting the corporate tax rate would directly reduce progressivity. Recent studies, indicating that with freer worldwide capital flows, corporate taxes may predominantly be borne by workers, may seem to dispose of this concern. In fact, however, these studies indicate that if the corporate tax, as a presumed levy on capital income, is being relied on to achieve the desired level of progressivity, it has not been having this effect even prior to (and independently of) the rate reduction. Hence, the use of other instruments to replace the missing progressivity would merit consideration, with or without adoption of this particular change. Possibilities through the individual-level income tax (or payroll taxes) might include increasing rate graduation, broadening the base so that existing high-end rates would be more effective, and taxing capital income in such a way that U.S. residents could not avoid it by shifting their investments abroad.

The tax-base leakage is potentially more critical because it undermines progressivity directly. So long as the second level of tax can be avoided, a 25 percent corporate rate (compared to, say, a 35 percent individual rate) makes use of the corporate form with equity financing an appealing tax shelter, potentially available to activities having little to do with the rationale for a lower corporate rate. Sole proprietors of local businesses, people rendering services to businesses or households whether as employees or independent contractors, and people holding investment portfolios would all have reason to incorporate so they could take advantage of the lower rate.

This is a familiar problem with the U.S. individual income tax, reflecting that for decades the corporate rate was often significantly lower than the top individual rate. There already are rules in the tax code that affect these problems. For example, personal service company rules address the case of the incorporating employee, while personal holding company rules and the accumulated earnings tax address the case of the incorporated investment portfolio.[2] These, however, are essentially just antiabuse rules addressing the most egregious cases and perhaps reflecting past eras when top individual rates were so high that actually imposing them more generally had more limited appeal than actually collecting, say, a 35 percent rate today.

More generally applicable measures might therefore be advisable, both to prevent leakage via express tax planning and to make the 35 percent rate more generally applicable to high-bracket individuals who make use of the corporate form. One approach would be to apply "reasonable compensation" rules requiring owner-employees of closely held businesses to pay themselves adequate salaries. To illustrate the underlying problem, suppose I run a wholly owned, incorporated business (such as dry cleaning, a restaurant, or a hedge fund), nearly all the earnings from which are attributable to my personal services. I may have no economic motivation to pay myself (as my own employee via the corporation) an arm's length salary such as I would demand from a third-party owner, since this merely transfers the money, in effect, from my left pocket to my right.

Under present law, since the top corporate and individual rates are both 35 percent, I would have no income tax motivation to underpay myself. Indeed, I might instead want to overpay myself (where some of the income is from capital rather than my services) so that I could extract cash from corporate solution without risking the imposition of a dividend tax. Given that issue, "reasonable compensation" rules in the existing income tax apply purely to overpayment, rather than underpayment, of salary by an employee-owner. In the brave new world of a 25 percent corporate rate, ostensible underpayment would be the main case worth addressing.[3]

A lower corporate rate would also give new life to the Miller equilibrium (discussed in chapter 6) by making corporate equity investment affirmatively tax favored by high-bracket investors relative to holding debt, assuming sufficient ability to avoid the second level of tax. This might add substantially to the appeal of using a cost of capital allowance (as discussed in chapter 10), under which both debt and equity would generate corporate-level deductions and individual-level inclusions based on relevant interest rates.

Financing a U.S. Corporate Rate Cut

If Congress enacts corporate rate cuts that (however meritorious as policy) reduce net revenue, it no doubt will be tempted to provide no financing for them, either through offsetting tax increases or through commensurate spending cuts. Why should these tax cuts be any different from the many trillions of dollars worth (over the infinite horizon) of unfunded tax cuts and spending increases that Congress has happily busied itself enacting on a regular basis since 2001? There is evidently little, if anything, to be gained politically by taking account of long-term budget constraints or the rising risk that the United States could be headed for a catastrophic fiscal meltdown.

However, failing to finance corporate rate cuts would not just be bad policy as a general budgetary matter. It also would directly undermine the creation of investor expectations that the rate reduction could be regarded as reasonably stable. Enacting revenue-losing rate cuts against the background of an unsustainable set of long-term fiscal policies practically invites the suspicion that they will prove only temporary. And there is no good policy argument for having lower corporate rates today in exchange for likely facing greater pressures to raise them in the future.

U.S. International Tax Simplification

As we saw in chapters 7 and 8, the U.S. international tax rules provide an almost canonically bad system for taxing outbound investment given how little revenue they raise relative to the tax-planning, compliance, and administrative costs that they generate. Many of these costs would be reduced by moving to either of the poles between which our international tax policy is suspended—that is, to full worldwide taxation (with foreign tax credits but without deferral) or to exemption.

One natural response might be to adopt in full one of the two polar approaches. Yet neither pole seems politically likely to emerge as an outright victor given the offsetting political and ideological forces that have helped to place the United States in the middle. What is more, each pole could be seriously questioned as an appropriate setting for U.S. international tax policy.

The pole of full worldwide taxation, without deferral but with foreign tax credits, could be criticized as at once too harsh and too generous. It is too harsh because preventing U.S. resident companies from achieving lower tax rates by investing abroad, when companies that are treated as residents of other countries can do so, leads to capital ownership distortions along with substantial skirting of the U.S. tax through clientele effects. At the same time, however, foreign tax credits are too generous, from a unilateral national standpoint, insofar as they condition reduction of the full U.S. tax on the payment of foreign taxes. Even if one favors exemption, conditioning the elimination of U.S. tax liability on outbound investment on the payment of sufficient creditable foreign taxes has bad incentive effects from a U.S. standpoint, both on U.S. companies and on foreign governments. As noted in chapter 7, a full credit eliminates U.S. companies' incentive to save the U.S. Treasury money by reducing the foreign taxes they pay. Likewise, it eliminates foreign governments' incentive to worry that higher taxes will reduce inbound investment from the United States, and thus invites them to try to use their tax systems as devices for extracting money from the U.S. Treasury. At these margins, therefore, foreign tax credits are inferior to allowing mere deductions for foreign taxes—leaving aside, for the moment, the analytically distinct set of concerns about the *higher* taxes that would result from turning the credits into deductions without compensating adjustments (such as to the tax rate).

Exemption is problematic as well, however. An initial question is whether, in practice, it would actually eliminate ownership distortions, or instead potentially create inefficient subsidies for outbound investment based on the creation of opportunities to treat what would otherwise be U.S.-source income as arising in lower-tax foreign jurisdictions. However, even assuming the achievement of capital-ownership neutrality, it is unclear why one should seek to eliminate ownership distortions altogether rather than to balance them against the other distortions that inevitably result from taxing economic production. As Henrik Kleven and Joel Slemrod (2008, 25) have noted, "in general, it is not optimal to eliminate distortions completely: it is better to have small distortions 'everywhere' than large distortions somewhere and none elsewhere." Hence, if one started with a given domestic rate and a zero outbound rate, it is highly plausible that efficiency would be enhanced by a revenue-neutral rate change that involved lowering the domestic rate slightly in exchange for adopting a low but positive outbound rate.

Perhaps, then, the real problem is not so much one of being "stuck in the middle with subpart F" (Engel 2001, 1525) as of using deferral and foreign tax credits to hold down the tax burden on outbound investment that would arise if they were eliminated and everything else remained the same. In this connection, it is worth noting a recent proposal to adopt a "burden-neutral" repeal of deferral—that is, its repeal accompanied by "a reduction in the U.S. tax rate on foreign income so as to leave the overall residual U.S. tax on foreign business income unchanged" (Grubert and Altshuler 2008, 320).[4]

Given the incentive problems associated with foreign tax credits, along with the tax-planning and compliance issues associated with foreign tax credit limitations, one could argue for modifying this proposal to embrace as well replacing the credits with mere deductions for foreign taxes on a burden-neutral basis. Or the full credits could be replaced with percentage credits—say, for 50 percent of the taxes paid, and without foreign tax-credit limitations—so that foreign taxes paid were treated more favorably than general business expenses, but without making the U.S. taxpayer or the foreign government wholly indifferent to the tax level at the margin.

Just to give a ballpark sense of where such a proposal might shake out, consider that the repatriation tax was recently estimated to raise $5 billion annually on a $100 billion repatriation tax base (Grubert and Mutti 2002, 21). This suggests, as a very rough back-of-the-envelope first approximation, that at least a 5 percent rate on U.S. multinationals' outbound business income, as measured without deferral and treating foreign taxes paid as deductible rather than creditable, might be revenue neutral. Given the very high tax-planning and compliance costs that U.S. multinationals currently incur relative to the taxes they pay, a burden-neutral rate presumably could be somewhat higher than this.

Whether or not the 5 percent (or higher) rate on foreign-source income as thus determined would be optimal, it seemingly would be a clear-cut improvement over present law. At a 5 percent rate (if that is the correct number), it would raise the same revenue as present law with less distortion, while at the higher, burden-neutral rate it would convert burdens from waste into burdens from actually paying tax.

This is not to deny possible problems or obstacles. For one, the change would violate current U.S. treaty obligations concerning the allowance of foreign tax credits when income in a treaty partner is taxed. It also would be bound to have winners and losers politically, if burden neutral overall, potentially complicating its enactment. Finally, it might raise political economy concerns about the possibility that Congress, once it had eliminated foreign tax credits via burden-neutral rate reduction, would turn around and start raising the outbound rate again.[5] While these problems are significant ones, the prospect of generating a straightforward and unambiguous improvement in the efficiency of U.S. international tax policy is too appealing to be readily dismissed. After all, where we are now is hardly cause for satisfaction.

Corporate Governance and Tax Sheltering

A final area in which corporate tax policy could be improved concerns corporate governance, and in particular managerial pursuit of self-interest at the expense of shareholder welfare. Our system of corporate taxation unavoidably interacts with corporate governance, given the entity-level tax that managers encounter directly, along with the investor-level tax's potentially strong influence on the form and timing of corporate distributions.

Interactions between Tax Policy and Corporate Governance

As we have seen, governance issues help make debt-equity distortions and the lock-in of corporate earnings especially regrettable from the standpoint of efficiency, but these are only two from among a larger set of interactions between the corporate tax and governance systems. Other important interactions include the following:

- Corporate governance, like the tax system, makes use of an income measure, via the requirement that publicly traded companies publish audited financial statements. Because of this overlap, tax auditing can actually improve shareholders' ability to monitor managerial behavior where governance is otherwise poor, and thus can actually raise share values even if the audited companies have to pay more taxes (Desai, Dyck, and Zingales forthcoming).

- Managers have opposite incentives under the two income measures, as they typically want to raise reported earnings while reducing taxable income (Shaviro 2007b). Differences between the two income measures for a given company can therefore be highly informative. Thus, the IRS has learned that its recently devised Schedule M-3, requiring companies to explain the sources of difference between taxable and financial accounting income, can play an important role in steering auditors to the likely soft spots on a given tax return (Shaviro 2008c, 230). Likewise, a large excess of reported earnings over taxable income may be of interest to investors, as it tends to be associated with subsequent negative abnormal returns (Desai and Dharmapala 2006).

- As a side effect, aggressive corporate tax planning can lead to increased diversion of corporate profits from shareholders to managers due to production complementarities between the two activities. For example, once complex internal financial arrangements and chains of special-purpose corporate entities have been created on the grounds that they serve tax-planning objectives, they can also be used to serve private managerial goals and defeat oversight (Desai 2005; Desai and Dharmapala forthcoming).

- Managerial agency costs provide an important reason corporations often surprisingly underutilize opportunities to lower their taxes (Desai and Dharmapala 2006). For example, rules that require transactions to have economic substance and business purpose if they are to be tax effective often deter tax sheltering because managers are reluctant to bear transaction risks that shareholders ought not to mind (Shaviro 2000a). Managers also may undervalue tax savings that remain too uncertain to be claimed currently for financial accounting purposes (Shaviro 2007b).

- As the price of being able to report higher earnings to shareholders, some companies actually pay more taxes than necessary (Erickson, Hanlon, and Maydew 2004). Even where managers seek to reduce taxes, they almost always try to do so without affecting reported earnings. Thus, corporate tax shelters typically cannot be marketed successfully by promoters unless they are earnings neutral. Managers also devote significant resources to such otherwise wasteful devices as creating "hybrid" financial instruments that are debt for tax but not financial accounting purposes, thus generating interest deductions solely with respect to taxable income (Shaviro 2007b).

Taking Advantage of the Interactions

Attempts to address corporate governance problems through the tax system do not always go well. A case in point is the rule establishing a $1 million annual limit on deductible salary paid by a publicly traded company to a top executive, which (as discussed in chapter 1) apparently did less to rein in excessive salaries than to encourage a mix of salary increases for those not yet in the million-dollar club and overuse of incentive compensation for the rest. However, even if one doubts Congress's ability to do a good job in fine-tuning managerial incentives via the tax code, it is only rational to keep in mind the pervasiveness of interactions between the two spheres.

One obvious step, in response to managers' incentives to inflate book income while reducing taxable income, would be to give investors greater access to tax-return information that can be compared to the content of financial statements. At a minimum, companies should be required more specifically to disclose their annually reported taxable income and tax liability. (Required financial statements for publicly traded companies do not directly disclose this.) Beyond this, disclosure of the information on Schedule M-3 that offers detailed reconciliation as between taxable and financial accounting income would aid investors while not (as companies have argued might result from publishing their entire tax returns) disclosing confidential business information to competitors (Canellos and Kleinbard 2006).

Beyond this, some have suggested requiring publicly traded companies to use the same income measure for financial accounting and tax-reporting purposes (Desai 2005). Thus, managers of these companies would be unable to inflate the one while using tax sheltering to reduce the other, and arguably the economic accuracy of both income reports would be enhanced by the offset between conflicting objectives. Given pervasive anecdotal information suggesting that the managers care a lot more about increasing reported earnings than about saving taxes (see Shaviro 2007b, 28), the end result might be to raise revenue while greatly reducing public companies' tax planning.

Perhaps the biggest problem with such a proposal is that it would politicize the process of devising rules for measuring financial accounting income.[6] At present, the Financial Accounting Standards Board (FASB), a quasi-private government agency that is largely run by the accounting profession but is affiliated with the Securities and Exchange Commission, determines the U.S. rules for defining the generally accepted accounting practices (GAAP) that are used in measuring financial accounting income. While not above criticism, FASB appears to be far less subject to invidious political influence, such as from narrow interest groups seeking to benefit themselves at the expense of diffuse general interests, than the U.S. Congress in setting the rules for measuring taxable income. However, making GAAP determinative for tax purposes would almost certainly result in Congress's taking over FASB's job. The experience of other "one-book" countries, such as Germany (until recently), suggests that such a change might do more to undermine companies' financial transparency to investors than to improve the tax system (Shaviro 2007b).

I have argued elsewhere that a different approach might succeed where the one-book method fails in keeping Congress out of the business of defining GAAP, while still limiting managers' ability to engage in opposite manipulations of financial reporting and taxable income. Under my suggested approach, taxable income (as otherwise determined) would generally be adjusted by a fixed percentage (such as 50 percent) toward book income. Congress, however, would be encouraged expressly to exempt special tax rules (such as preferences) from the adjustment so that it would not need to worsen financial accounting income in order to get the tax results it wanted (Shaviro 2007b).[7] While this proposal is not without downsides—for example, it would risk worsening disparities between the tax treatment of publicly traded companies and other businesses— it would at least make both tax sheltering and earnings manipulation more costly and less effective for corporate managers. Thus, tax shelters that reduce taxable income but not financial accounting income would lose half their payoff under the 50 percent proposal, and managers would have less to gain from wastefully creating complicated tax-accounting hybrid financial instruments.

A further point to keep in mind is that financial accounting standards are increasingly being internationalized. Many countries around the world accept a common set of international financial reporting standards (IFRS), devised by the multinational International Accounting Standards Board (IASB), in lieu of their own national equivalents of GAAP. The head of the FASB recently opined that the United States, which remains an outlier, ought to consider adopting IFRS on the grounds that "the world has changed and we are not the only big player anymore" (Block 2007). Adoption by the United States of the IFRS for financial accounting purposes arguably would reduce concern that Congress, so long as it could still insist on the full applicability of particular income tax rules, would respond to the 50 percent rule by intervening on the accounting side. The IASB would obviously be harder for it to reach than the FASB, and there might be domestic political pressures to keep U.S. financial reporting on a par with that applying elsewhere.

An alternative (or supplementary) approach would conform the tax rules to GAAP in particular areas where existing disparities appear particularly senseless. The rules for defining debt and equity, and perhaps for defining consolidated reporting groups among U.S. companies with common ownership, provide possible examples.

It remains early in the day to assess what Congress really should do, or likely will do, in response to growing understanding about the complex relationships between tax policy and corporate governance issues. One can predict with decent confidence, however, that these issues—including but not limited to the relationship between the tax code and GAAP—will continue to be prominent and important in the years ahead.

A Gloomy Scenario

As we have seen in this and the prior chapter, there are several potentially constructive directions in which U.S. corporate tax policy could go. These directions tend to be complementary, rather than mutually exclusive. Thus, one could easily combine lower corporate rates and international tax simplification with the adoption of a COCA. Even adjusting taxable income 50 percent of the way toward book income is readily combined with these changes if book income is modified, solely for purposes of the adjustment, to use the COCA.

Grounds for Pessimism?

For these changes to be feasible, however, it is not enough that they prove intellectually persuasive as people think more about them. Even with expert support from across the political spectrum, their enactment and stable retention might require a better-functioning political system than we currently have. Adopting them might be politically challenging because they combine (1) making conceptual leaps, such as by discarding the traditional debt-equity distinction and perhaps the use of foreign tax credits, with (2) having transition losers as well as winners, and (3) requiring good-faith ideological compromises or ceasefires in place between opposing forces. Examples include keeping tax burdens on outbound investment approximately constant and attempting to maintain, not change, preexisting progressivity.

The U.S. political system used to be able to handle this sort of challenge. The Tax Reform Act of 1986 offers a canonical example. In 1986, Republicans and Democrats collaborated to broaden the base and lower the rates on a revenue-neutral and distribution-neutral basis. They agreed to lay aside their continuing tax policy differences and to seek shared credit for legislative accomplishment rather than opportunities to cast blame for the repeal of some existing tax benefits. To be sure, one key element that helped mitigate the political awkwardness of creating losers as well as winners was an overall shift of tax burdens to the corporate level, permitting all income groups among individuals to look like net winners, given that the burden of the corporate tax was not being attributed to anyone. This is not an option today if one wants to lower corporate rates and/or use the COCA to shift a portion of current tax liabilities to the individual level. But the parties, during the 1980s, also collaborated on measures, such as deficit reduction and improving Social Security's long-term solvency, that unmistakably made current voters short-term net losers, and thus could all too easily have invited the sort of buck passing and demagoguery that we routinely witness today in lieu of problem solving.

While easy to blame on the failings of our recent political leaders, the political failings of recent years may be more structural. Fareed Zakaria (2008) argues:

> As it enters the twenty-first century, the United States is not fundamentally a weak economy or a decadent society. But it has developed a highly dysfunctional politics. What was an antiquated and overly rigid political system to begin with (now about 225 years old) has been captured by money, special interests, a sensationalist media, and ideological attack groups. The result is ceaseless, virulent debate about

trivia—politics as theater—and very little substance, compromise, or action. A can-do country is now saddled with a do-nothing political process, designed for partisan battle rather than problem solving. . . .

Progress on any major problem—health care, Social Security, tax reform—will require compromise from both sides. It requires a longer-term perspective. And that has become politically deadly. Those who advocate sensible solutions and compromise legislation find themselves being marginalized by their party's leadership, losing funds from special-interest groups, and being constantly attacked by their "side" on television and radio. The system provides greater incentives to stand firm and go back and tell your team that you refused to bow to the enemy. It is great for fundraising, but it is terrible for governing.

What Would Muddling Along Look Like?

Political inability to engage in meaningful and lasting reform would lead to a near-term future of, at best, simply muddling along. Tax rates at the corporate level and for dividends might go up and down while international tax policy lurched in limited degree between the worldwide and exemption poles, but the core problems in corporate tax policy would remain unaddressed.

Muddling along would not necessarily imply stasis, however, even leaving aside year-to-year instability. Long-term secular trends would likely imply diminishing tax revenues from corporate business activity relative to the size of the economy, from ongoing shifts both away from U.S. corporate tax residence and from needing to have publicly traded stock that would make one a C corporation. Ever more refined use of debt and equity (among other financial arrangements) to achieve the tax-planning vision of the Miller equilibrium might have growing revenue consequences as well. Meanwhile, the overhang of the long-term U.S. fiscal gap may keep growing harder to ignore. If our political system cannot muster the realism and maturity that it often has had in the past, we are headed for all-too-interesting times—interesting in the wrong way—in which a gratuitously inefficient corporate tax is just one among a larger set of festering problems.

A Hollywood Ending?

The scenario of muddling along with a shrinking and needlessly unstable corporate tax, while a looming fiscal crisis fails to be addressed before things turn ugly, certainly represents one of our possible futures. But I see no reason to end this volume on so depressing a note when the gloomy scenario remains so far from being inevitable. Grounds for optimism exist as well, pertaining in particular to the level of actual and potential intellectual consensus among responsible tax-policy experts ranging from the left to the right of the political spectrum.

For example, experts largely agree about the general desirability of taxing all income or all consumption as uniformly as possible.[8] Base broadening and eliminating distortions such as those in the existing corporate tax therefore have wide-ranging intellectual appeal. Even in cases where consensus does not exist, widely shared acceptance of rigorous empirical inquiry creates the possibility of its emerging. Thus, it may come to be widely accepted, as supported by some recent research, that (1) in an era of worldwide capital mobility, the burden of the corporate tax largely falls on labor through lower wages, and (2) the United States does not lose domestic investment or jobs by lowering the tax burden on its multinationals' outbound investment. General acceptance of these points (if they are indeed confirmed by further research) might do much to ease and encourage the adoption of revenue-neutral and distribution-neutral corporate and international tax reform.

The corporate tax reforms discussed in this chapter—a fully financed corporate rate cut with greater reporting of income at the individual level, burden-neutral international tax simplification, and addressing the interaction between tax sheltering and corporate governance problems—are fairly technical and interstitial in character. Thus, enlightened White House and congressional leadership—accompanied, if not by outright bipartisanship, then at least by a reduction in scorched-earth partisan warfare and interest-group domination—might suffice to give them a chance at enactment.

Addressing the fiscal gap so that the tax rules for corporate business activity could both be and seem reasonably stable is obviously a more daunting proposition. Even here, however, hope is not impossible to summon. The well-known basic model for addressing the fiscal gap is the 1983 agreement between President Reagan and House Speaker Tip O'Neill to extend Social Security's solvency by enacting tax increases and benefit cuts. These unpalatable measures were paired together so neither party's policy preferences would fare the worse. Further, the task of specifying the needed changes was handed to an independent commission so that neither party's leaders could be charged with having done the dirty work.

Could the same sort of process take place on a larger scale (given the more urgent fiscal problems we now face) sometime in the near future? With a greater public sense of urgency, and if the Republican Party repudiated the hyperpartisanship and budgetary recklessness of the George W. Bush years in favor of its prior and more honorable traditions (Shaviro 2007a), the answer is conceivably yes. On the spending side, what mainly needs to be done is curbing the growth rate of programs such as Medicare and Social Security, as opposed to cutting current expenditure levels. On the tax side, we still have unused arrows in the quiver that would be less distortionary than raising income tax rates, and possibly politically more realistic over the long haul than eliminating income-tax preferences. One such possibility is a value-added tax or VAT, which nearly every other economically advanced nation has. A second is a carbon tax, which could enhance global economic efficiency and, at least as part of a sufficiently broad multinational agreement, directly increase U.S. economic welfare in addition to raising substantial revenue (Posner and Sunstein 2008).

As the old saying goes, "if wishes were horses, beggars would ride." There is little direct evidence these days that U.S. tax and budgetary policy are headed in more fruitful directions than they have been over the last few years. But knowing what to wish for is a start.

Notes

Chapter 1. Why Have a Corporate Tax?

1. A legal entity such as a partnership is considered publicly traded if interests in it are either (1) traded on an established securities market or (2) readily tradable on a secondary market or the substantial equivalent thereof, according to the U.S. Internal Revenue Code, section 7704(b). There is an exception to corporate status for publicly traded entities that derive at least 90 percent of their gross incomes from "passive-type" sources such as interest, dividends, and real property rents, according to section 7704(c).

2. Certain corporations with relatively few shareholders and simple capital structures can elect to be taxed instead under subchapter S of the Internal Revenue Code, which contains a very different set of rules imposing tax directly on the shareholders rather than on the corporate entity.

3. The basis of a share of stock is the amount that the holder gets to count against the amount realized on a sale for purposes of computing gain or loss. Thus, suppose your basis for a share of stock is $10. If you sell the share for $12, you have gain of $2, whereas if you sell it for $9, you have a loss of $1.

4. The recently enacted 15 percent tax rate for dividends reduces the incentive to do this but does not eliminate it. If your wholly owned company deducts a $100 payment to you at a 35 percent rate and you include it at that rate, the net tax is zero. Your $35 tax liability is precisely offset by your company's $35 tax savings. By contrast, in the case of a dividend, you pay $15 of tax and the company enjoys no tax savings.

5. S corporations, however, are required to pay reasonable compensation to owner-employees with respect to the payroll tax that funds Social Security and Medicare.

6. "Corporations' Taxes Are Falling Even as Individuals' Burden Rises," *New York Times*, A-1, February 20, 2000.

7. Personal communication, Alan Auerbach.

8. Thus, consider private equity fund managers, who may look a lot like hedge fund managers in that they (try to) make huge capital gains from buying and selling corporate stock, but with a different methodology. The conceptual distinction—although often, in practice, the same people may do both—is that the private equity route involves intervening in companies' operations to make them more profitable. In theory, even if private equity fund managers were tax exempt on their compensation, the value that they create for their funds is fully reached by a well-functioning corporate-level tax, except in the case where the increased value comes from reducing corporate taxes.

9. In theory, this argument applies to dividend taxation as well as to shareholder capital gains. If one predicts in advance of the market that a given company is going to become more profitable and therefore start paying more dividends, the analysis is exactly the same. In practice, however, a lot of the activity devoted to "beating" the market appears to be in quest of more immediately realized rewards that require a stock sale.

10. However, I consider and mainly reject such arguments about transitional unfairness in Shaviro (2000).

11. Whether McDonald's really enjoys rents is debatable, given competitive pressures from its trade rivals along with the money it invested to create the trade name and must continue investing to sustain it.

Chapter 2. Efficiency Problems with the Corporate Tax

1. How you and the teenager split the deadweight loss depend on how the two of you would have split the surplus from making the deal. If the wage would have been $8, the deadweight loss is all yours. If it would have been $10, it is all his.

2. Many commentators support the replacement of the income tax by a consumption tax so that only work decisions, rather than both work and saving decisions, will be distorted by the tax system (see Shaviro 2008a). A key argument is that only work decisions need be distorted, not both work and saving decisions, in order to achieve desired distributional aims.

3. Effective electivity could, however, indirectly cause inefficiency in two respects. First, the need to arrange everything properly might increase businesses' transaction costs. Second, since effective electivity permits one to reduce taxes paid, it might create tax bias between forms of economic activity if some permit taking greater advantage of it than others.

4. As noted in chapter 1, the ability to avoid C corporation status by making an election under subchapter S of the Internal Revenue Code is limited to companies with relatively few shareholders and a simple capital structure.

5. *Gilbert v. Commissioner*, 248 F.2d 399, 402 (2nd Cir. 1957).

6. *United States v. Title Guarantee & Trust Co.*, 133 F.2d 990, 993 (9th Cir. 1943).

7. In particular, capital gains from share repurchases are more tax advantageous than dividends if the taxpayer otherwise has net capital losses. Under Internal Revenue Code section 1211, capital losses can only be deducted to the extent of capital gains (plus $3,000 per year for individuals).

Chapter 3. Pillars of Sand in the Structure of Corporate Taxation

1. Internal Revenue Code sections 61 and 482.

2. A consumption tax burdens work because earnings are spent on market consumption. (See, for example, Shaviro 2008a.)

3. Code section 385.

4. See Weisbach (1999, 1627), noting that "no one has touched the subject" of debt versus equity since Plumb, reflecting the difficulty of advancing past a purely doctrinal analysis.

5. A good example of this was the so-called Feline PRIDES transaction structure, in which a company, by purporting to sell a note plus a forward contract to buy its stock, effectively sold its stock on the transaction date but got to claim several years of interest deductions without actually making interest payments (see Sheppard 2005).

6. Under Internal Revenue Code section 1259, one may be treated as having sold the stock if the risk of gain or loss is too tightly collared. However, the IRS has held this provision inapplicable to an arrangement in which the putative shareholder was protected from any downside risk if the stock price declined, and retained only the prospect of gaining from a price increase of up to 25 percent (IRS Revenue Ruling 2003-7, 2003-1 C.B. 363).

7. IRS Notice 94-47, 1994-1 C.B. 357.

8. The existing check-the-box election results in taxpayers' incurring transaction costs by reason of (1) the need to evaluate what elections to make and (2) the incentive to engage in positive-cost activities, such as establishing new entities under some jurisdiction's law and managing paper transactions between commonly owned entities, to maximize the available tax benefits.

9. An example is Code section 1259, providing that certain financial transactions economically resembling sales will be taxed as sales.

Chapter 4. "Old Harberger" versus "New Harberger" and the Incidence of the Corporate Tax

1. The suggested theoretical explanation for saving's posited zero tax elasticity was that substitution effects (saving less because the return was being reduced) might be precisely offset by income effects (needing to save more to reach a preferred wealth level given that one's income was being taxed away) (Harberger 1962, 216). The paper also notes that the corporate tax might simply have no savings effects relative to those from whatever taxes were enacted in its place (216). At the end, it explores the consequences of relaxing the assumption that the corporate tax does not reduce savings levels, and concludes that this "leads to only a minor modification of my over-all conclusion that capital probably bears close to the full burden of the tax" (236).

2. If being a corporation is tax-favored, yet for some reason is unavailable to the agricultural and real estate sectors, the analysis in Harberger (1962) would presumably flip

around, suggesting that capital wins at the expense of labor from its being drawn into industries where the labor force is large and easily replaced by machines.

3. Examples of open economy models in which the burden of the corporate tax shifts mostly to labor include Melvin (1982), Harberger (2008), and Randolph (2006).

4. See Hassett and Mathur (2006), Arulampalam, Devereux, and Maffini (2007), Felix (2007), Gentry (2007), and Desai, Foley, and Hines (2007).

5. This is perhaps an overstatement. An example of an incidence question that one would need economic models to understand concerns the speed with which investment would adjust, affecting the ratio of stock price increases (primarily benefiting older people that own shares at the time of the shift) to increases in after-tax returns from corporate stock (benefiting younger people with longer time horizons for stock ownership) (see Auerbach 2005, 13).

Chapter 5. The Old View versus the New View of Dividend Taxation

1. To be sure, differences between corporate and shareholder-level marginal tax rates might influence distribution decisions in practice. This would not, however, be a function of the taxation of corporate distributions as such, but of the continuing tax biases pertaining to corporate versus noncorporate investment and debt versus equity financing. That is, while (all else being equal) one would want to keep one's dollars wherever the tax rate was lowest, this would be unrelated to the question of whether money flowing from corporations to shareholders was a distribution of earnings for tax purposes.

2. More generally, under the new view, if Tobin's q were otherwise 1.0, a uniform distributions tax at a rate of x percent would cause it to be $1/(1 - .x)$.

3. In Shaviro (2000b), I suggest one reason we might want to allow corporate shareholders a windfall gain from corporate integration: to reduce the discouraging effect of the double tax on new corporate equity even before integration is adopted. The downside, however, is that anticipating the possibility of a windfall gain may increase lock-in of corporate earnings by suggesting, contrary to the new view, that the distributions tax currently on the books is not permanent.

Chapter 6. Debt and Equity: Trade-Off Theory versus the Miller Equilibrium

1. This is an asymmetric information problem because, if managers could be perfectly observed by shareholders, they would be unable to get away with anything.

2. Highly risky debt, such as a junk bond with a high, fixed interest rate that has a good chance of not being paid, is already somewhat equity-like in the sense that the payoff strongly depends on company performance. Even so, there arguably is no reason, under pecking-order theory, to replace the nominally fixed return on a junk bond with the completely variable upside return that classic equity would have.

3. This element of electivity in the structure of the corporate tax was earlier noted, though without full elaboration of the Miller view, in Stiglitz (1973).

4. A taxpayer election might reduce resource waste, however, if the basis on which taxpayers choose is to minimize their further administrative and compliance costs, rather than to minimize tax liability. In practice, it may often be hard to tell which choice is driving taxpayer elections. In the case of debt versus equity, however, it is hard to see why administrative and compliance costs would be strongly implicated.

Chapter 7. U.S. International Tax Rules: The Basics

1. The one big exception to large multinationals' predominant use of subsidiaries pertains to banks, which commonly face legal and regulatory obstacles to operating through subsidiaries and thus commonly use foreign branches.

2. Formally speaking, subpart F gives rise to a deemed dividend from the foreign subsidiary to the U.S. parent, which is taxed as if it were an actual dividend. The imputed dividend payment is then deemed to have been reinvested in the foreign subsidiary, increasing the basis of its stock so that the U.S. parent will not be taxed again on the very same income.

3. See Internal Revenue Code section 954(d).

4. However, interest and dividend payments by foreign companies that mainly operate in the United States are treated as U.S.-source income under certain circumstances.

Chapter 8. International Tax Policy Dilemmas

1. Admittedly, there are special cases within the domestic corporate tax where neutrality might not be the best approach from an efficiency standpoint. An example is the argument that a nonuniform dividend tax enhances efficiency by aiding the use of "money-burning"—wasteful from the firm's standpoint, but not a social standpoint, if the government gets extra revenue—to signal firm quality.

2. Thus, CIN could in theory be achieved through a hypothetical system featuring duplicative source-based and residence-based taxes, but with unlimited credits offered by source countries to foreigners for taxes they had paid to their residence countries. Such a system appears politically unlikely, to say the least.

3. Even without impatience, however, people would save insofar as they wanted to "smooth" their lifetime consumption, such as by saving for retirement, or to make bequests to their heirs (see Shaviro 2008a).

4. I address later in this chapter the distinct but related argument that taxing U.S.-Co at 35 percent and Australia-Co at only 25 percent on the same investment would place U.S.-Co at a competitive disadvantage. As we will see, under specified assumptions this actually (and counterintuitively) is not the case.

5. Suppose further that this is a special class of stock, the return from which is particularly tied to the profitability of the investment at issue, rather than just depending on the overall fortunes of U.S.-Co or Australia-Co (as the case may be).

6. See U.S. Treasury Department 2000, 25–42; Staff of U.S. Joint Committee on Taxation 1991, 232–248; Warren 2001, 163.

7. The act of paying wages to U.S. workers or rent to U.S. resource owners is also merely a transfer from one pocket to another, from the U.S. national standpoint. However, these amounts are viewed as compensation for the cost of providing services or making resources available, thus making them indicative of actual social cost rather than mere transfers.

8. This view is consistent with the view that aggregate local investment responds to the level of source-based taxations and declines if the local tax rate goes up. The key point about a country's tax regime for outbound investment is that it affects the relationship between the domestic rate and foreign rates only for domestic firms—not for all firms.

9. This assumes a comprehensive income tax. With tax preferences, the story gets more complicated. The value of deductions or exclusions depends on one's marginal rate. Tax preferences are thus worth more to high-rate taxpayers than to those facing low rates. This leads, however, not to pervasive competitive advantages for one group or the other, but rather to what economists call clientele effects. High-rate taxpayers will tend to congregate in businesses that offer greater-than-average tax preferences, while low-rate taxpayers will tend to congregate in those that come closer to taxing economic income accurately.

10. This resembles the point made earlier that, under some scenarios, CEN can satisfy CON and avoid distortion of ownership patterns if one faces the same higher tax rate on all possible investments.

Chapter 9. The Emerging Brave New World

1. The earliest tax case on the debt-equity distinction, prominently quoted in the text of Plumb (1971, 404) and dating from 1935, cites several earlier tax cases on this issue, going back as far as 1927, along with nontax cases going as far back as 1883.

2. Gretchen Morgenson, "Arcane Market Is Next to Face Big Credit Test," *New York Times*, A-1, February 17, 2008. One difference between the value of all shares in the U.S. stock market and the value of all credit default swaps is that the former represents net wealth in the from of profit claims on the underlying companies, while the latter merely represents opposing bets by counterparties (i.e., the holders and the obligors on particular swaps). Thus, the nation as a whole did not grow $45 trillion wealthier when offsetting claims and obligations in this amount were created through the rise of credit default swaps.

3. As Gergen (1995) noted early on, financial innovation also potentially helps the government in some respects by making it easier to measure changes in asset value even without an observed sale or exchange. This is little help, however, on issues such as defining corporations for tax purposes or distinguishing between debt and equity.

4. Thus, during the 2004 presidential campaign, Democratic nominee Senator John Kerry proposed significantly curtailing deferral. A prominent tax-reform proposal released by House Ways and Means Chairman Charles Rangel in 2007 would also have moved significantly in the direction of imposing a true worldwide system.

Chapter 10. Corporate Integration

1. Presumably, under this view, there was a windfall gain when the 15 percent dividend rate was enacted in 2003, assuming it was unanticipated and expected (despite the sunset provision) to become permanent.

2. For an example of the former approach, see American Law Institute (1989) (proposal to achieve corporate integration via dividend deductions that would be limited to new equity). For an example of the latter, see Auerbach (1990, 115) (suggesting that the same policy could be achieved by allowing dividend deductions to all corporate equity but imposing a one-time tax on existing equity equal to their expected present value).

3. Geraldine Fabrikant, "Harvard's $34.9 Billion Endowment Makes Its Choice for New Chief," *New York Times,* C-1, March 28, 2008.

4. The zero marginal rate faced by tax-exempts might be considered different from other taxpayers' positive rates on the ground that it is meant to be a finite subsidy rather than an instrument for implementing the distributional aims of the income tax (such as basing tax liability on ability to pay).

5. Exempting foreign shareholders might make sense unilaterally on the grounds that they will not invest in the United States unless they can match the after-tax return available elsewhere in the world. For U.S. shareholders investing abroad, however, unilaterally crediting foreign corporate taxes violates the unilateral national self-interest idea embodied in national neutrality (discussed in chapter 9) in a setting where the objections to it as to corporate investment do not apply because U.S. resident individuals presumably have an overall budget constraint.

6. To limit the potential application of the capital gains tax where earnings were taxed at the corporate level but not distributed, companies would have been permitted to declare deemed dividends that, even though not actually paid, would have been treated as if they had been first distributed to shareholders and then reinvested, thereby increasing stock basis for purposes of any subsequent sale.

7. In the above example, whether one uses the imputation method or dividend deductibility, the overall results are as follows: (1) the corporation ends up with zero cash, (2) the government ends up with $30 in the case of a 30 percent shareholder or $40 in the case of a 40 percent shareholder, and (3) a 30 percent shareholder ends up with $70 after-tax while a 40 percent shareholder ends up with $60.

8. Absent a rule taxing investor-level capital gains, the CBIT might be vulnerable to tax-avoidance schemes that involved converting all corporate-level sales of appreciated assets into sales of stock in purported companies that held nothing of significance but the assets that were being sold.

Chapter 11. Other Possible New Directions for the U.S. Corporate Tax

1. On the relatively high U.S. corporate rate and the trend elsewhere toward lower rates, see, for example, Mitchell (2007).

2. See Internal Revenue Code sections 269A (personal service corporations), 541–547 (personal holding companies), and 531–537 (accumulated earnings tax).

3. Reasonable compensation rules addressing ostensible underpayment of a salary by/to an employee-owner already exist under the payroll tax that finances Social Security and Medicare benefits. However, these rules are not generally regarded as very effective. A recent study indicated that perhaps $100 billion a year of corporate income reflects salary underpayments that serve to avoid payroll tax liability (Bull and Burnham 2008). Absent more rigorous enforcement, one might expect this amount to rise substantially if enactment of a 10 percent spread between the top individual and corporate income-tax rates raised the stakes substantially.

4. Grubert and Altshuler's proposal for a burden-neutral repeal of deferral calls as well for repealing required allocations of certain expenses (such as interest) to foreign-source income (320)—an important detail that I ignore here (and in chapters 7–8) in the interest of expositional simplicity.

5. The first of these three problems would be eliminated, and the latter two potentially mitigated, if the burden-neutral change were limited, as Grubert and Altshuler suggest, to changes (such as eliminating deferral) other than turning foreign tax credits into deductions.

6. In addition, a number of differences between financial accounting income and taxable income clearly follow from the two measures' different purposes. For example, whereas exemption of foreign-source active business income is at least plausible from a tax standpoint, clearly investors who wanted a measure of particular U.S. companies' economic performance would want the income of foreign affiliates to be included. See Shaviro (2007b).

7. The proposed adjustment to taxable income would be based on the financial accounting income of the tax reporting group (the membership of which might differ from that of the financial group), as determined in accordance with Schedule M-3. In addition, given the possibility that companies that were unconcerned about their publicly reported income would use the adjustment to reduce taxable income, negative adjustments to income by reason of the proposal might be limited to the amount of prior positive adjustments (Shaviro 2007b).

8. Experts also increasingly prefer consumption taxation to income taxation, assuming constant progressivity (see Shaviro 2008a).

References

Altshuler, Rosanne, and Harry Grubert. 2001. "Repatriation Taxes, Repatriation Strategies, and Multinational Financial Policy." Working Paper 8144. Cambridge, MA: National Bureau of Economic Research.

American Law Institute. 1989. "Federal Income Tax Project, Reporter's Study Draft: Subchapter C (Supplemental Study) Distributions—William D. Andrews, Reporter." Philadelphia: American Law Institute.

———. 1993. "Federal Income Tax Project, Integration of the Individual and Corporate Income Taxes, Reporter's Study of Corporate Tax Integration—Alvin C. Warren, Jr., Reporter." Philadelphia: American Law Institute.

Andrews, William D. 2007. "Comment on Dividends and Taxes by Gordon and Dietz." In *Institutional Foundations of Public Finance: Economic and Legal Perspectives,* edited by Alan J. Auerbach and Daniel N. Shaviro. Boston, MA: Harvard University Press.

Arlen, Jennifer, and Deborah M. Weiss. 1995. "A Political Theory of Corporate Taxation." *Yale Law Journal* 105:325–90.

Arulampalam, Wiji, Michael P. Devereux, and Giorgia Maffini. 2007. "The Incidence of Corporate Income Tax on Wages." Mimeo, University of Warwick.

Auerbach, Alan J. 1979. "Wealth Maximization and the Cost of Capital." *Quarterly Journal of Economics* 93:433–46.

———. 1990. "Debt, Equity, and the Taxation of Corporate Cash Flows." In *Debt, Equity, and Corporate Restructuring,* edited by John B. Shoven and Joel Waldfogel. Washington, DC: Brookings Institution Press.

———. 2005. "Who Bears the Corporate Tax? A Review of What We Know." Working paper 11686. Cambridge, MA: National Bureau of Economic Research.

Auerbach, Alan J., and Kevin A. Hassett. 2005. "The 2003 Dividend Tax Cuts and the Value of the Firm: An Event Study." http://www.econ.berkeley.edu/~auerbach/03divtax.pdf.

Auerbach, Alan J., Jason Furman, and William G. Gale. 2007. "Still Crazy after All These Years: Understanding the Budget Outlook." *Tax Notes* 116:765–78.

Ault, Hugh J., and Brian J. Arnold. 2004. *Comparative Income Taxation: A Structural Analysis.* New York: Aspen Publishers.

Avi-Yonah, Reuven. 1996. "The Structure of International Taxation: A Proposal for Simplification." *Texas Law Review* 74:1301–59.

———. 2000. "Globalization, Tax Competition, and the Fiscal Crisis of the Welfare State." *Harvard Law Review* 113:1573–1676.

———. 2004. "Corporations, Society, and the State: A Defense of the Corporate Tax." *Virginia Law Review* 90:1193–1255.

Bank, Steven A. 2003. "Is Double Taxation a Scapegoat for Declining Dividends?" *Tax Law Review* 56:463–536.

———. 2005. "The Story of Double Taxation: A Clash Over the Control of Corporate Earnings." In *Business Tax Stories,* edited by Steven A. Bank and Kirk J. Stark. New York: Foundation Press.

———. 2006. "A Capital Lock-In Theory of the Corporate Income Tax." *Georgetown Law Journal* 94:889.

———. 2007. "Entity Theory as Myth in the U.S. Corporate Excise Tax of 1909." In *Studies in the History of Tax Law, Vol. II.,* edited by John Tiley. London: Hart Publishing.

Bankman, Joseph. 1995. "A Market-Value Based Corporate Income Tax." *Tax Notes* 68:1347–53.

Berle, Adolf A., and Gardiner C. Means. 1932. *The Modern Corporation and Private Property.* New York: Harcourt, Brace, & World.

Bernheim, B. Douglas. 1991. "Tax Policy and the Dividend Puzzle." *Rand Journal of Economics* 22:455–76.

Bernheim, B. Douglas, and Lee S. Redding. 2001. "Optimal Money-Burning: Theory and Application to Corporate Dividends." *Journal of Economics and Management Strategy* 10:463–507.

Bernheim, B. Douglas, and Adam Wantz. 1995. "A Tax-Based Test of the Dividend Signaling Hypothesis." *American Economic Review* 85:532–51.

Bird, Richard M. 1996. "Why Tax Corporations?" Working Paper 96-2. Toronto: International Centre for Tax Studies, University of Toronto.

Birnbaum, Jeffrey H., and Alan S. Murray. 1987. *Showdown at Gucci Gulch: Lawyers, Lobbyists, and the Unlikely Triumph of Tax Reform.* New York: Random House.

Bittker, Boris I., and James S. Eustice. 2006. *Federal Income Taxation of Corporations and Shareholders.* Valhalla, NY: Warren, Gorham, & Lamont.

Block, Donna. 2007. "FASB Chief Backs Shift from U.S. Accounting Standards." *The Daily Deal,* October 26.

Blumenthal, Marsha, and Joel B. Slemrod. 1996. "The Compliance Cost of Taxing Foreign-Source Income: Its Magnitude, Determinants, and Policy Implications." In *The Taxation of Multinational Corporations,* edited by Joel B. Slemrod. Boston, MA: Kluwer Academic Publishers.

Bradford, David F. 1981. "The Incidence and Allocation Effects of a Tax on Corporate Distributions." *Journal of Public Economics* 15:1–22.

Bull, Nicholas, and Paul Burnham. 2008. "Taxation of Capital and Labor: The Diverse Landscape by Entity Type." Presentation at the National Tax Association Annual Meeting, May 15.

Burman, Leonard. 2003. "Taxing Capital Income Once." *Tax Notes* 98:751–56.

Canellos, Peter C., and Edward D. Kleinbard. 2006. "IRS Should Release Schedules M-3, Not Entire Corporate Tax Returns." *Tax Notes* 110:1485.

Chetty, Raj, and Emmanuel Saez. 2007. "An Agency Theory of Dividend Taxation." Working Paper 13538. Cambridge, MA: National Bureau of Economic Research.

Coase, Ronald H. 1937. "The Nature of the Firm." *Economica* 4:386–405.

Desai, Mihir A. 2005. "The Degradation of Reported Corporate Profits." *Journal of Economic Perspectives* 19:171–92.

Desai, Mihir A., and Dhammika Dharmapala. 2006. "Corporate Tax Avoidance and High-Powered Incentives." *Journal of Financial Economics* 79:145–79.

———. Forthcoming. "Corporate Tax Avoidance and Firm Value." *Review of Economics and Statistics.*

Desai, Mihir A., and James R. Hines, Jr. 2003. "Evaluating International Tax Reform." *National Tax Journal* 56:487–502.

Desai, Mihir A., I. J. Alexander Dyck, and Luigi Zingales. Forthcoming. "Theft and Taxes." *Journal of Financial Economics.*

Desai, Mihir A., C. Fritz Foley, and James R. Hines, Jr. 2007. "Labor and Capital Shares of the Corporate Tax Burden: International Evidence." http://www.people.hbs.edu/mdesai/PDFs/Labor%20and%20Capital.pdf.

Dodge, Joseph M. 1995. "A Combined Mark-to-Market and Pass-Through Corporate-Shareholder Integration Proposal." *Tax Law Review* 50:265–372.

Downs, Anthony. 1957. *An Economic Theory of Democracy.* New York: Harper and Collins Publishers.

Easterbrook, Frank H. 1984. "Two Agency-Cost Explanations of Dividends." *American Economic Review* 74:650–59.

Engel, Keith. 2001. "Tax Neutrality to the Left, International Competitiveness to the Right, Stuck in the Middle with Subpart F." *Texas Law Review* 79:1525–1607.

Erickson, Merle, Michelle Hanlon, and Edward L. Maydew. 2004. "How Much Will Firms Pay for Earnings That Do Not Exist? Evidence of Taxes Paid on Allegedly Fraudulent Earnings." *Accounting Review* 79:387–408.

Feldstein, Martin. 1976. "Compensation in Tax Reform." *National Tax Journal* 29:123–29.

Felix, R. Alison. 2007. *Passing the Burden: Corporate Tax Incidence in Open Economies.* PhD diss., chapter 1, University of Michigan.

Fiorina, Morris P. 2006. "Parties as Problem Solvers." In *Promoting the General Welfare: New Perspectives on Government Performance,* edited by Alan S. Gerber and Eric M. Patashnik. Washington, DC: Brookings Institution Press.

Fleischer, Victor. 2008. "Taxing Blackstone." *Tax Law Review* 61:89–120.

Frank, Murray, and Vidhan Goyal. 2003. "Testing the Pecking Order Theory of Capital Structure." *Journal of Financial Economics* 67:217.

Fried, Jesse M. 2005. "Informed Trading and False Signaling with Open Market Repurchases." *California Law Review* 93:1323–86.

Fuchs, Victor, Alan Krueger, and James Poterba. 1997. "Why Do Economists Disagree about Policy? The Role of Beliefs about Parameters and Values." Working Paper 6151. Cambridge, MA: National Bureau of Economic Research.

Gentry, William M. 2007. *A Review of the Evidence on the Incidence of the Corporate Tax.* Washington, DC: Department of the Treasury, Office of Tax Analysis.

Gergen, Mark P. 1995. "Apocalypse Not?" *Tax Law Review* 50:833–59.

Gilman, Nils. 2004. "What the Rise of the Republicans as America's First Ideological Party Means for the Democrats." *The Forum* 2(1). http://www.bepress.com/cgi/viewcontent.cgi?article=1025&context=forum.

Gordon, Roger, and Martin Dietz. 2007. "Dividends and Taxes." In *Institutional Foundations of Public Finance: Economic and Legal Perspectives,* edited by Alan J. Auerbach and Daniel N. Shaviro. Boston, MA: Harvard University Press.

Graetz, Michael J., and Michael M. O'Hear. 1997. "The 'Original Intent' of U.S. International Taxation." *Duke Law Journal* 46:1021–1109.

Graetz, Michael J., and Alvin C. Warren. 1998. "Integration of Corporate and Individual Income Taxes: An Introduction to the Issues." In *Integration of the U.S. Corporate and Individual Income Taxes: The Treasury Department and American Law Institute Reports,* edited by Graetz and Warren. Arlington, VA: Tax Analysts.

Gravelle, Jane G., and Laurence J. Kotlikoff. 1989. "The Incidence and Efficiency Costs of Corporate Taxation when Corporate and Noncorporate Firms Produce the Same Good." *Journal of Political Economy* 97:749–80.

———. 1993. "Corporate Tax Incidence and Inefficiency When Corporate and Noncorporate Goods Are Close Substitutes." *Economic Inquiry* 31:501–16.

Gravelle, Jane G., and Kent Smetters. 2001. "Who Bears the Burden of the Corporate Tax in the Open Economy?" Working Paper 8280. Cambridge, MA: National Bureau of Economic Research.

———. 2006. "Does the Open Economy Assumption Really Mean that Labor Bears the Burden of a Capital Income Tax?" *The B.E. Journal of Economic Analysis & Policy* 6.

Gruber, Jonathan. 2007. *Public Finance and Public Policy.* New York: Worth Publishers.

Grubert, Harry, and Rosanne Altshuler. 2008. "Corporate Taxes in the World Economy: Reforming the Taxation of Cross-Border Income." In *Fundamental Tax Reform: Issues, Choices, and Implications,* edited by John W. Diamond and George R. Zodrow. Cambridge, MA: MIT Press.

Grubert, Harry, and John Mutti. 2001. *Taxing International Business Income: Dividend Exemption versus the Current System.* Washington, DC: AEI Press.

Harberger, Arnold C. 1962. "The Incidence of the Corporation Income Tax." *Journal of Political Economy* 70:215–40.

———. 1995. "The ABCs of Corporate Tax Incidence: Insights into the Open Economy Case." In *Tax Policy and Economic Growth.* Washington, DC: American Council for Capital Formation.

———. 2008. "Corporate Tax Incidence: Reflections on What Is Known, Unknown, and Unknowable." In *Fundamental Tax Reform: Issues, Choices, and Implications,* edited by John W. Diamond and George R. Zodrow. Cambridge, MA: MIT Press.

Hariton, David P. 1994. "Distinguishing between Equity and Debt in the New Financial Environment." *Tax Law Review* 49:499–524.

Harris, Milton, and Artur Raviv. 1991. "The Theory of Capital Structure." *Journal of Finance* 46:297–355.

Hassett, Kevin A., and Aparna Mathur. 2006. "Taxes and Wages." Public Policy Research Working Paper 128. Washington, DC: The American Enterprise Institute.

Hines, James R. 2007. *Reconsidering the Taxation of Foreign Income.* Paper prepared for panel discussion at NYU Law School, November 14.

Horst, Thomas. 1980. "A Note on the Optimal Taxation of International Investment Income." *Quarterly Journal of Economics* 94:793–98.

Jensen, Michael C., and William Meckling. 1976. "Theory of the Firm: Managerial Behavior, Agency Costs, and Capital Structure." *Journal of Financial Economics* 3:305–60.

Joos, Peter R., and George A. Plesko. 2004. "Costly Dividend Signaling: The Case of Loss Firms with Negative Cash Flows." Working Paper 4474-04. Cambridge, MA: MIT Sloan School of Management.

Keynes, John Maynard, ed. 1964. *The General Theory of Employment, Interest, and Money.* San Diego, CA: Harcourt Brace.

King, Mervyn. 1977. *Public Policy and the Corporation.* London: Chapman and Hall.

Kleinbard, Edward D. 2005. "The Business Enterprise Income Tax: A Prospectus." *Tax Notes* 106:97–107.

———. 2007a. "Throw Territorial Taxation from the Train." *Tax Notes* 114:547–64.

———. 2007b. *Rehabilitating the Business Income Tax.* Washington, DC: The Brookings Institution.

———. 2007c. "Designing an Income Tax on Capital." In *Taxing Capital Income,* edited by Henry J. Aaron, Leonard E. Burman, and C. Eugene Steuerle (165–210). Washington, DC: Urban Institute Press.

Kleven, Henrik Jacobson, and Joel Slemrod. 2008. "A Characteristics-Driven Approach to Optimal Taxation and Tax-Driven Product Innovation." Working paper. http://personal.lse.ac.uk/KLEVEN/Downloads/MyPapers/workingPapers/Characteristics%20May%202008.pdf.

Knoll, Michael. 1996. "An Accretion Corporate Income Tax." *Stanford Law Review* 49:1–43.

Kraus, Alan, and Robert H. Litzenberger. 1973. "A State-Preference Model of Optimal Financial Leverage." *Journal of Finance* 28:911–22.

Melnyk, Z. Lew. 1970. "Cost of Capital as a Function of Financial Leverage." *Decision Sciences* 1:327–56.

Melvin, James R. 1982. "The Corporate Income Tax in an Open Economy." *Journal of Public Economics* 17:393–403.

Miller, Merton H. 1977. "Debt and Taxes." *Journal of Finance* 32:261–75.

Mitchell, Daniel J. 2007. "Corporate Taxes: America Is Falling Behind." *Tax and Budget Bulletin* 48:1–2. http://www.cato.org/pubs/tbb/tbb_0707_48.pdf.

Modigliani, Franco, and Merton H. Miller. 1958. "The Cost of Capital, Corporation Finance, and the Theory of Investment." *American Economic Review* 48:261–97.

———. 1963. "Corporate Income Taxes and the Cost of Capital: A Correction." *American Economic Review* 53:433–43.

Myers, Stewart C., and Nicholas S. Majluf. 1984. "Corporate Financing and Investment Decisions when Firms Have Information That Investors Do Not Have." *Journal of Financial Economics* 13:187–221.

Plumb, William T. 1971. "The Federal Income Tax Significance of Corporate Debt: A Critical Analysis and a Proposal." *Tax Law Review* 26:369–640.

Posner, Eric A., and Cass R. Sunstein. 2008. "Climate Change Justice." *Georgetown Law Journal* 96:1565–1612.

Randolph, William C. 2006. "International Burdens of the Corporate Income Tax." Working Paper 2006-09. Washington, DC: Congressional Budget Office.

Richman, Peggy Brewer. 1963. *Taxation of Foreign Investment Income: An Economic Analysis.* Baltimore, MD: Johns Hopkins Press.

Ridley, Mark. 1993. *The Red Queen: Sex and the Evolution of Human Nature.* New York: Harper Perennial.

Russell, Bertrand. 1959. *The Problems of Philosophy.* Oxford: Oxford University Press.

Shaviro, Daniel N. 1995. "Risk-Based Rules and the Taxation of Capital Income." *Tax Law Review* 50:643–724.

———. 2000a. "Economic Substance, Corporate Tax Shelters, and the Compaq Case." *Tax Notes* 88:221–44.

———. 2000b. *When Rules Change: An Economic and Political Analysis of Transition Relief and Retroactivity.* Chicago: University of Chicago Press.

———. 2002. "Money on the Table? Responding to Cross-Border Tax Arbitrage." *Chicago Journal of International Law* 3:317–31.

———. 2007a. *Taxes, Spending, and the U.S. Government's March toward Bankruptcy.* New York: Cambridge University Press.

———. 2007b. "The Optimal Relationship between Taxable Income and Financial Accounting Income: Analysis and a Proposal." Forthcoming in *Georgetown Law Journal.*

———. 2007c. "Why Worldwide Welfare as a Normative Standard in U.S. Tax Policy?" *Tax Law Review* 60:155–78.

———. 2008a. "Beyond the Pro-Consumption Tax Consensus." *Stanford Law Review* 60:745–88.

———. 2008b. "Simplifying Assumptions: How Might the Politics of Consumption Tax Reform Affect (Impair) the End Product?" In *Fundamental Tax Reform: Issues, Choices, and Implications,* edited by John W. Diamond and George R. Zodrow. Cambridge, MA: MIT Press.

———. 2008c. "Disclosure and Civil Penalty Rules in the U.S. Legal Response to Corporate Tax Shelters." In *Tax and Corporate Governance,* edited by Wolfgang Schon. Munich: Springer.

Shefrin, Hersh M., and Meir Statman. 1984. "Explaining Investor Preference for Cash Dividends." *Journal of Financial Economics* 13:253–82.

Sheppard, Lee A. 2005. "Having It Both Ways on Feline PRIDES." *Tax Notes* 106:632–39.

Simons, Henry C. 1938. *Personal Income Taxation.* Chicago: University of Chicago Press.

Skinner, Douglas J. 2003. "What Do Dividends Tell Us about Earnings Quality?" Working paper. Chicago: University of Chicago Graduate School of Business.

Smith, Adam. 1976 ed. *An Inquiry into the Nature and Causes of the Wealth of Nations.* Chicago: University of Chicago Press.

Spence, A. Michael. 1974. *Market Signaling.* Cambridge, MA: Harvard University Press.

Staff of U.S. Joint Committee on Taxation. 1991. *Factors Affecting the International Competitiveness of the United States.* Washington, DC: Government Printing Office.

Stiglitz, Joseph E. 1973. "Taxation, Corporate Financial Policy, and the Cost of Capital." *Journal of Public Economics* 2:1–34.

Tobin, James. 1969. "A General Equilibrium Approach to Monetary Theory." *Journal of Money Credit and Banking* 1:15–29.

U.S. Treasury Department. 1992. *Integration of the Individual and Corporate Tax Systems: Taxing Business Income Once.* Washington, DC: Government Printing Office.

———. 2000. *The Deferral of Income Earned through U.S. Controlled Foreign Corporations: A Policy Study.* Washington, DC: Government Printing Office.

———. 2007. *Approaches to Improve the Competitiveness of the U.S. Business Tax System for the 21st Century.* Washington, DC: Government Printing Office.

Viswanathan, Manoj. 2007. "Sunset Provisions in the Tax Code: A Critical Evaluation and Prescriptions for the Future." *New York University Law Review* 82:656–88.

Warren Alvin C. 1993. "Financial Contract Innovation and Income Tax Policy." *Harvard Law Review* 107:460–92.

———. 2001. "Income Tax Discrimination against International Commerce." *Tax Law Review* 54:131–69.

Weiner, Joann M. 2007a. "Measuring the Effects of the Dividend Repatriation Holiday." *Tax Notes* 117:853–54.

———. 2007b. "Tax Breaks for Sale." *Tax Notes* 117:855.

Weisbach, David A. 1999. "Line-Drawing, Doctrine, and Efficiency in the Tax Law." *Cornell Law Review* 84:1627–81.

Young, Sam. 2007. "JCT Chief Discusses Thorny Issues on Hill Agenda." *Tax Notes* 117:1110–11.

Zakaria, Fareed. 2008. "The Future of American Power." *Foreign Affairs* 87(3). http://www.foreignaffairs.org/20080501facomment87303/fareed-zakaria/the-future-of-american-power.html.

About the Author

Daniel N. Shaviro is the Wayne Perry Professor of Taxation at New York University Law School. Before teaching law, he spent three years in private practice at Caplin & Drysdale, a leading tax specialty firm, and three years as a legislation attorney at the Joint Congressional Committee on Taxation, where he worked extensively on the Tax Reform Act of 1986. In 1987, Shaviro began his teaching career at the University of Chicago Law School, and he moved to New York University in 1995. Shaviro's scholarly work examines tax policy, budget policy, and entitlements issues. His previous books include *Taxes, Spending, and the U.S. Government's March toward Bankruptcy* (2006), *Who Should Pay for Medicare?* (2004), *Making Sense of Social Security Reform* (2000), *When Rules Change: An Economic and Political Analysis of Transition Relief and Retroactivity* (2000), and *Do Deficits Matter?* (1997).

Index